D1633231

# Being in Time

*Being in Time* examines philosophical treatments of time and self-consciousness in relation to concepts of narrative, focusing on the literary aspects of philosophical writing. Genevieve Lloyd shows how philosophy bears on the human and emotional aspects of the experience of time which are often neglected by the history of philosophy. Starting with Augustine's treatment of the ways in which time makes him a 'problem to himself', the book traces the themes of unity and the experience of fragmentation and loss as expressed by Descartes, Hume and Kant. The idea of the past as 'lost' is explored through Bergson's philosophy of time and Nietzsche's doctrine of eternal return. The book concludes with a discussion of philosophical aspects of themes of self-consciousness, memory and writing in Proust's *Remembrance of Things Past* and the novels of Virginia Woolf. While offering a new perspective on historical texts, which will be of interest to professional scholars, this book will also be of interest to students interested in the relationship between philosophy and literature as well as to a more general audience of readers who share Augustine's experience of the problem of transience.

**Genevieve Lloyd** is Professor of Philosophy at the University of New South Wales in Sydney, and author of *The Man of Reason: 'Male' and 'Female' in Western Philosophy* (London, Routledge, 1984). She has published papers on the metaphysics of time, on the history of philosophy, philosophy and literature, and philosophical aspects of gender.

IDEAS
Series Editor: Jonathan Rée,
*Middlesex University*

Original philosophy today is written mainly for advanced academic specialists. Students and the general public make contact with it only through introductions and general guides.

The philosophers are drifting away from their public, and the public has no access to its philosophers.

The IDEAS series is dedicated to changing this situation. It is committed to the idea of philosophy as a constant challenge to intellectual conformism. It aims to link primary philosophy to non-specialist concerns. And it encourages writing which is both simple and adventurous, scrupulous and popular. In these ways it hopes to put contemporary philosophers back in touch with ordinary readers.

Books in the series include:

**Social Philosophy**
*Hans Fink*

**Philosophy and the New Physics**
*Jonathan Powers*

**The Man of Reason**
*Genevieve Lloyd*

**Philosophical Tales**
*Jonathan Rée*

**Morality and Modernity**
*Ross Poole*

*Forthcoming*

**Freedom, Truth and History**
*Stephen Houlgate*

**Children: Rights and Childhood**
*David Archard*

# Being in Time

## Selves and narrators in philosophy and literature

Genevieve Lloyd

London and New York

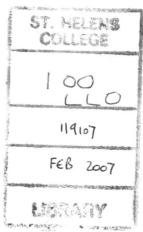
First published 1993
by Routledge
11 New Fetter Lane, London EC4P 4EE

Transferred to Digital Printing 2004

Simultaneously published in the USA and Canada
by Routledge
29 West 35th Street, New York, NY 10001

Typeset in 10 on 12 point Palatino by
Computerset, Harmondsworth, Middlesex

*British Library Cataloguing in Publication Data*
Lloyd, Genevieve
  Being in Time:Selves and Narrators in
  Philosophy and Literature
  I. Title
  126

*Library of Congress Cataloging in Publication Data*
Lloyd, Genevieve.
  Being in time: selves and narrators in philosophy and
  literature/Genevieve Lloyd.
      p. cm.
  Includes bibliographical references and index.
  1. Time. 2. Self-knowledge, Theory of. 3. Consciousness.
4. Literature–Philosophy. I. Title.
BD638.L56   1993
115–dc20   92–44132

ISBN 0–415–07195–X
      0–415–07196–8 (pbk)

. . . the things, which though they must have happened, yet, incredible though it seems, never did happen, death making an end of all these exquisite preparations.

Virginia Woolf, Reminiscences

For Rachel
with thanks for all that she was

# Contents

# Acknowledgements

For their assistance in the completion of this book – through comments on earlier drafts or through their interest, suggestions and encouragement – I am grateful especially to Lorraine Code, Paul Crittenden, Penelope Deutscher, Lisabeth During, Robyn Ferrell, Ann Game, John O'Leary-Hawthorne, Kimon Lycos, Catriona Mackenzie, John Mepham, Michaelis Michael, Paul Patton, Ross Poole and Amélie Rorty.

I wish to acknowledge the practical and financial assistance provided by the School of Philosophy and the Faculty of Arts and Social Sciences at the University of New South Wales; the research assistance of Sarah Redshaw; and the hospitality of the Philosophy Department at the University of Melbourne, where a visiting fellowship in the first semester of 1991 allowed me to begin the project.

Special thanks are due, once more, to Jonathan Rée for his generous encouragement and helpful editorial suggestions; and to my son Jerome for his interest, his healthy scepticism about philosophy, and his understanding of the emotions that made me want to write this book.

# Introduction

Consciousness and time have an ambiguous relationship. My individual consciousness had a beginning, though its starting point – if there was such a thing – may elude me. And it will have an end. Even if I believe that some form of consciousness as yet unknown will replace the centre of thought, desire and feeling I now call 'I', my imagination must falter at placing myself in it as in 'my' future. My future, like my past, reaches no further than what I can relate to as my individual consciousness. I may believe that the glimpses I have of a reality beyond my death are fore-shadowings of a mysterious transformation. I may believe that they are nothing more profound than intimations of my own mortality – unthinkable only because in the nature of things I cannot think beyond it. Either way, it seems, my consciousness – in any form in which I can identify it with myself – is circumscribed by time. Whether I think of death as end or as transformation, I know that both the time of the cosmos and the human time of pleasures anticipated and losses mourned will certainly continue when I am gone.

Time envelops my consciousness. Within it I come to know that and who I am; and my sense of its continued onward movement frames my anticipation of death. Time, beyond doubt, is independent of me. And yet this all-enveloping time, within which I come to exist, and which will assuredly continue without me, becomes elusive if I try to conceive it without any reference to consciousness. Does it not depend, if not on me, at least on the presence of some thought? It seems no less true that time is 'in' consciousness than that consciousness is 'in' it. Most certainly time does not depend on me. And yet it is something in which I, as consciousness, surely have some stake.

What then is this 'consciousness' on which time depends? What kind of dependence is it and what does it have to do with the individual consciousnesses which is me? We think of time as enveloping not only our individual consciousnesses but also human consciousness in its entirety. Whether human life emerged by cosmic coincidence or by divine plan, it was certainly a long time getting here. Nor can we expect that human consciousness will continue into an indefinite future. But when Immanuel Kant claimed in the eighteenth century that it is no more true to claim that consciousness is in time than that time is in it, and that indeed it comes to the same thing,[1] he was not denying the age of the universe, even if he thought it a little younger than we do. He was claiming that we cannot think consciousness without thinking time, or time without thinking consciousness – that if we take away the thought of consciousness, time also vanishes. That is to make a strong, but by no means counter-intuitive, claim about the relations between time and consciousness – a claim which has been made in varying forms throughout the history of western philosophy. But what does this dependence on consciousness amount to? The connections between time and consciousness are deeper than the relatively trivial ones which can make it seem impossible to think of any thing at all as independent of thought. Not only can I not think time without thinking; I cannot think it without also thinking thought. That need not mean that in thinking of time as preceding the emergence of human consciousness I must project an invisible observer into that otherwise mindless landscape. But it does seem to involve at least placing that unfolding reality in a past governed by the present of our consciousness. And this already gives us a connection between the ideas of time, consciousness and narrative. In thinking time we think the presence of consciousness; and in thinking that we set up even the reality of time before consciousness as a story we tell of the past.

If the consciousness on which time depends is not you, I, or even the entirety of human thought, what can it possibly be? Is it some 'world-soul' of the kind talked of by ancient philosophers as encompassing individual minds? Such talk seems to hard-headed moderns to issue from a mythology we should by now have shed, from mysticism or from sheer fantasy. Yet we still talk of 'consciousness' as something more than ourselves. We may 'know' that there is no world-soul. Yet talk of a general 'mind', 'consciousness' or 'spirit' recurs throughout the philosophical tradition. Sometimes – as with Hegel's 'spirit' – this can be understood in terms of collective norms embodied in a culture. Sometimes it is a relatively unpuzzling third-person equivalent of the 'I' used by philosophers to talk of minds in abstraction from their particularity – the 'I' of Descartes's 'I think therefore I am' or Hume's 'when I look into myself. . . '. That 'I' is a literary device for focusing on what is universal about self-consciousness – a way of adopting a first-person perspective without the trappings of individual subjectivity which accompany the more usual appearances of 'I'. But not all Hegel's utterances about spirit can be translated into something so straightforward. And there is often more involved in the philosopher's 'I' than a literary device allowing us to talk of ourselves without intruding our personal idiosyncrasies. Otherwise it would be difficult to see what point there could possibly be in contemporary preoccupations with decentring, dispersing, deconstructing, destabilizing and generally engineering the demise of the 'knowing subject'.

What is this 'subject' which is being demolished with such fervour? It seems to have as much and as little to do with our individual consciousnesses as does the dependence of time on consciousness. Indeed, it belongs in the same philosophical stories. Of course not all the philosophers who talk of it mean seriously to suggest that it is my own individual consciousness that I, with what unity of thought I can muster, am to think of as disconcertingly dispersed. But Eco's satirical bemusement, in his essay 'On the Crisis of the Crisis of Reason', about which 'subject' is having the crisis, and whether we can clear it up, does have a point.[2] What exactly is the 'unified knowing subject' which is currently undergoing such radical deconstructive surgery? Who or what is supposed to benefit? And how does it all relate to the individual selves that we are? One of the aims of this book is to get clearer about this question by focusing on the connections that have been drawn in the history of western philosophy between themes of self-consciousness and time. For the picture of self-consciousness which is under attack in these contemporary repudiations of the unity of the knowing subject has as much to do with time as with consciousness.

## TIME AND THE DISAPPEARANCE OF 'THE SUBJECT'

Reflection on time and consciousness has been central in some
major texts of twentieth-century philosophy – in the work of
Husserl, of Heidegger, of Sartre. But the influence of Jacques
Derrida's work has made more visible the connections between
the instabilities of temporal experience and the tenuousness of
the unity of the 'knowing subject'.[3] His version of the deconstruction of the subject highlights the connections between
the ideal of self-presence – of a consciousness translucently
present to itself – and ideas of temporal presentness. Derrida's
critique is directed at the model of a unitary consciousness,
which functions as the supposed originating source and foundation of meaning. It is the consciousness of no-one in particular.
Although Derrida's main concern with this idea of a unitary
consciousness is with its supposed role as originator of meanings, he presents it as also supporting a way of thinking of self-
consciousness in relation to time. The ideal of self-presence
evokes a sense of stability in the flux of time. The self is, if not
outside time, at least in a position of origin – a source of control
over the spreading out of moments and states. In its older and
perhaps purer forms this way of thinking of self and time had a
theological context. The ideal of a self stabilized in relation to
time has functioned as a human approximation to an idealized
divine consciousness, free of the fragmentation that ensues from
being in time, fully present to itself. It is an ideal we will see in
Augustine's *Confessions* – something glimpsed in the midst of his
wretchedness at being in time, given content in the idea of God's
self-presence in the 'eternal now', and articulated through metaphors drawn from experience of spoken language.

Augustine's treatment of time and self-consciousness brings
together in a striking way two ideas at stake in Derrida's critique
of western metaphysics – preoccupation with the spoken word,
and the idea of 'self-presence'. Derrida's rejection, following
Heidegger, of the 'metaphysics of presence' centres on a way of
thinking of meaning modelled on the familiar experience of
hearing ourselves speak – a phenomenon which fascinated Augustine and became for him a source of analogies for
understanding the relations between consciousness and time.
Augustine's fascination with the self-presence manifested in the
spoken word can be seen as a version of the model of thought's
relation to meaning which Derrida attempts to make visible and

question – the word as the 'calm, present and self-referential unity of concept and phonic material'.

Derrida tries to break the grip of such metaphors drawn from the spoken word, thus undermining the model of meaning as grounded in an originating consciousness – a self which stands behind language. But his critique of that view of meaning has implications also for the relations between consciousness and time; and it throws into relief the theological assumptions which frame philosophical conceptions of the self. Discussing his central notion of *différance*, Derrida comments on the similarities between the detours to which he has to recourse in articulating it and the strategies involved in negative theology. Talk of *différance* is talk of what is not, of what is never present, of what is always deferred. Hence the parallels with attempts to talk of the concept of God, which likewise can never be pinned down by determinate concepts. But whereas negative theology presents itself as a way of approaching a transcendent reality through saying what it is not, in the delineating of *différance* everything is 'strategic' and 'adventurous'. No transcendent truth outside the field of discourse governs the totality of the field. Here we have 'strategy without finality', 'blind tactics', 'wandering', 'play'. This 'unnameable' is not an 'ineffable Being which no name could approach'. Here there will be no unique name, not even if it were the name of 'Being' and we must accept this, Derrida insists, 'without nostalgia' for a 'lost native country of thought'. Derridean *différance* is inevitably and intentionally elusive. It is supposed to be conceivable neither as an action nor as a passion of a subject. It moves between the act of differentiating and the static state of difference. It is supposed to break the grip of the idea of meaning as originating in a unitary consciousness, showing its instability in the lack of the complementary theological ideal of divine self-presence.

What does all this have to do with time? In challenging the 'metaphysics of presence', the strategy implicit in Derrida's *différance* addresses the issue of 'the present' in both senses – what is psychologically presented to the mind and what is temporally present. Self-consciousness is associated in the philosophical tradition with present perception. But, as Heidegger argued in *Being and Time*, ancient Greek philosophy suppressed the temporality this introduced into the understanding of

'Being'; and modern philosophy has continued the misunderstanding, making time function as a criterion for distinguishing realms of being – the temporal and the eternal. The ordinary connotations of the phrase 'being in time', which provides the title for this book, are for Heidegger 'naïvely ontological' – as if time could of itself function as a criterion for distinguishing the 'non-temporal', the 'temporal', the 'supra-temporal', rather than being 'the horizon for all understanding of Being and for any way of interpreting it'.[4]

According to Heidegger, Descartes, despite his claims to put philosophy on a new and firm footing, altogether neglected the issue of the relations between time and the existence whose certainty he thought he had established. His supposedly new beginning in fact carried over from medieval scholasticism a 'baleful prejudice' which has made it difficult for posterity to discern the unacknowledged temporality of ancient ontology. 'Being' – supposedly timeless – in fact understands entities with regard to a definite mode of time, the 'Present'. The Greeks then took time itself as just one entity among others, trying to grasp its nature, failing to see that their very understanding of Being is itself 'naïvely and inexplicably oriented towards time'.[5] It is a limitation, Heidegger suggests, which runs through the entire tradition of philosophical conceptions of time – from Aristotle to Bergson and even later. It has meant that the ordinary understanding of 'being in time' is an inauthentic understanding of temporality as a levelled off, innocuous, infinite sequence of 'now's with no integral connection with consciousness.

The connections between 'presence' and a historic misunderstanding of being, scrutinized by Heidegger, are further unsettled in the strategies associated with Derrida's notion of différance. Through différance, Derrida challenges the alleged primacy and authority of 'presence'. In so far as différance can be thought of at all as giving an alternative view of the 'origin' of meaning, it has to be thought of as something very different from older ideas of unitary originating consciousness – as 'the non-full, non-simple, structured and differentiating origin of differences'.[6] Différance does not determine meanings from a position of 'presence'. It is supposed to replace the idea of the originating self-presence from which differences originate. But it is not to be thought of as an alternative kind of 'origin'. That it produces differences does not mean that it is somehow before

them, in a simple, unmodified presence. There is here no originating being that eludes the play of *différance*, no subject
somehow preceding speech in a 'silent and intuitive consciousness'. The privilege traditionally granted to consciousness
signifies the privilege granted to the present. The deconstruction
of the primacy of the present is at the same time the deconstruction of the self-presence of consciousness.

For Derrida, signification is possible only if each so-called
element appearing on the 'scene of presence' is related to something other than itself, thereby keeping within itself the mark of
the past and already letting itself be vitiated by its relation to the
future. What is called the present is constituted by its relation to
what is not – 'what it absolutely is not, not even a past or future as
a modified present'. But this lack of a real present affects also the
thinking subject which is thought on the basis of it. Rather than
being able to think of a subject outside and observing the
passage of time, what we have is a dynamic 'spacing' or 'tempor-
ization' – something that is exclusively neither time nor space
but which 'takes time into account' – 'the becoming space of time
or the becoming time of space'. *Différance* cannot be thought on
the basis of the present or of the presence of the present. It
involves a 'past that has never been present, and never will be' – a
past that cannot be thought as the production or reproduction of
presence. *Différance* 'is not'. It is not a 'present being', however
'excellent, unique, principal, or transcendent'.[7] The present, becoming just a function in a structure, ceases to be that to which
every reference in the last analysis refers.

Time, then, is crucial to understanding Derrida's rejection of
the idea of consciousness as 'self-presence' modelled on the
spoken word, and the connected view of the self as standing
behind language. But, as Derrida himself is aware, even if some
of his followers are not, the understanding of *différance* is not a
matter of exposing and definitively leaving behind ideas of the
unity of consciousness which were asserted with absolute confidence in the history of philosophy. Rather than confident
articulations of an established philosophical position, what we
have is a recurring fixing and unfixing of self-consciousness in
relation to time. In the history of western philosophy we see a
succession of attempts to respond to what is problematic and
unsettling in the human experience of being in time – to overcome the sense of time's encroachment on the stability of

selfhood and find a permanence for self-consciousness in the flux of time. Derrida's *différance* and the deconstructive strategies associated with it are often seen as replacing classical ideas of self-consciousness. They are perhaps better seen as aids to recognizing an instability that has already inhabited those traditional theories.

This book will address the ways in which philosophical treatments of self-consciousness have engaged with the lived experience of time – with transience, with the sense of the self as fragmented, and of the past as lost. It will focus also on ways in which the literary aspects of philosophical writing have interacted with the philosophical content of these treatments of time and self-consciousness – on philosophers' use of metaphors drawn from speech and writing, and on the centrality of the idea of narrative in their articulations of what is involved in being in time. It is a matter of some interest here that early twentieth-century fiction directly addressed issues of time and self-consciousness; and that the two novelists I have singled out for special attention – Proust and Virginia Woolf – have explicitly linked these issues with reflection on the process and nature of writing.

## TIME-CONSCIOUSNESS AND THE MODERN NOVEL

The novels of Proust and Woolf reflect the interest in questions of time consciousness evoked by the changed conditions of modern urban life. Many classical writings on the idea of modernity discuss the impact on self-consciousness of the constant bombardment of stimuli in city life. It is a central theme in Baudelaire's essay 'The Painter of Modern Life'[8] and Simmel's 'The Metropolis and Mental Life'[9] as well as in Marx's *Communist Manifesto*. There is a certain nostalgia in much of this concern with the changed time consciousness of modernity. In 'The Metropolis and Mental Life', Simmel suggests that city life exacts from consciousness a much higher degree of discrimination, changing the sensory foundations of psychic life. For the more conservative rural self-consciousness, the rhythm of life – resting on deeply felt emotional relationships – flows more slowly, habitually and evenly. The power of the metropolis throws such a consciousness into shock and upheaval. Coping with it demands a shift to intellect, able to adapt to the 'rapid crowding of changing images', the sharp discontinuities, the unexpectedness of onrushing impressions, without being 'completely atomised' internally. Simmel says, in an essay on Rodin, that the essence of modernity resides in experiencing and interpreting the world in terms of the reactions of our inner life, and indeed as an inner world. Fixed contents dissolve in the 'fluid elements of the soul, from which all that is substantive is filtered and whose forms are merely forms of motion'.[10] In the lack of a natural rhythm of consciousness to secure a firm distinction between self and world, the boundaries of inner and outer are unsettled. Change in temporal consciousness transforms self-consciousness itself.

Baudelaire, in 'The Painter of Modern Life', presents a more positive picture of the consciousness appropriate to the metropolis. His 'painter of modern life' revels in the constant bombardment of stimuli, leaping headlong into the crowd in a passionate search for the fleeting, the transient. The crowded city is the arena for the free play of impressions; and the shocks it produces in consciousness are the impulse to artistic inspiration and delight. Traditional philosophical ways of thinking, Baudelaire suggests, are at odds with the experience of city life with its changing kaleidoscope of impressions. Whereas the philosopher loves eternal forms, the painter of modern life is 'a kaleidoscope gifted with consciousness', loving visible, tangible things. The point of the metaphor is that consciousness does not merely mirror change but is itself fragmented by it. There is not a stable self perceiving a changing world, but a self which is itself shifting and unstable. However, its capacity for reflection saves it from complete disintegration into the fragments out of which its patterns are formed. Baudelaire's kaleidoscopic self of modernity is made up of temporally discontinuous impressions, but it is not a consciousness in chaos.

Such reflections on the time-consciousness of modernity see older ideals of the unity of the self as vulnerable to shock and the breakdown of habit.[11] Their themes of fragmentation and fragile unity – of the threats and the exhilarations of the life of the city – are echoed, as we shall see, in the novels of Proust and Woolf. But the issues of time and self-consciousness which the novels address also intersect with the concerns of older philosophical treatments of the self in relation to time. Themes of unity and fragmentation of consciousness are played out in the philosophies of Descartes, Hume and Kant, as well as in more recent misgivings about traditional ideals of selfhood expressed in theories of the de-centred subject. To bring the novels into relation with these older philosophical treatments of self-consciousness can enrich our understanding of what is involved in the supposed fragmentation of the 'new' self of modernity and the decentred subject of post-modernity. Bringing these threads together may help us see more clearly what is at stake in both traditional and more recent treatments of the unity of consciousness, as well as enriching our understanding of some of the concerns of the modern novel.

This book, then, will explore the ways in which ideas of the spoken word, of writing and narrative, have figured in philosophical reflections on self-consciousness. By juxtaposing philosophical and literary ways of dealing with the relations between time and consciousness, it highlights both the significance of the literary aspects of philosophical writing and the importance of the philosophical dimensions of the novelists' subtle use of narrative techniques to engage with issues of time and selfhood.

## TIME AND NARRATIVE

How should we think of the limits of the 'philosophical' and the 'literary' – of their relations and their differences? Paul Ricoeur has argued that narrative responds to problems of time which philosophy of itself cannot resolve – that it offers a different, and in some respects more fruitful, response to the experienced instabilities of self-consciousness in relation to time from that offered by theoretical speculation.[12] This book will attempt to clarify what these 'problems' of time might be, and in what way narrative constitutes a 'response' to them. The idea of narrative is of course in some ways at odds with contemporary treatments of the dispersion of the knowing subject, which resist assumptions of the continuity of consciousness implicit in the aspiration to unified stories of the past. But the idea of narrative has also figured more positively in contemporary reflection on issues of time and consciousness. There are resources in narrative which go beyond the tightly structured telling of a unified story, with a beginning, a middle and an end. And the limitations of continuous narratorial perspective or voice were confronted by modern novelists even before they were addressed in post-modern theory. The novels of Virginia Woolf especially, as we shall see, challenge the possibility of articulating a life as a coherent whole. What role is there for the idea of narrative in understanding the relations between time and self-consciousness? The concept has taken on in recent philosophy a significance that reaches beyond its role in theory of literature. It comes up in philosophy of action, in philosophy of history, in ethics. Alasdair MacIntyre, for example, used it in *After Virtue* to link ethical concepts to the idea of the unity of a life. The most important articulation of its philosophical importance, however, is Ricoeur's *Time and Narrative*. Let me now try briefly to position the concerns of this book in relation to that foundational study of the philosophical dimensions of the relations between time and narrative. Ricoeur frames his book with juxtaposed readings of Augustine's treatment of time in the *Confessions* and Aristotle's treatment of plot in the *Poetics*. The philosophical understanding of time, he argues, collapses into *aporias* which cannot be resolved within the limits of the dichotomy between treatments of time centred on 'the time of the cosmos' and those centred on 'the time of the soul'. The two approaches are complementary and irreducible. Neither can accommodate or absorb the other into a unified account of the nature of time. From within a definition which emphasizes physical motion, we cannot understand human time; but nor can we coherently think the time of the soul as constituting the reality of time. Cosmological and phenomenological approaches to time cannot be reconciled. There is an 'intractable reality' to time which resists all attempts to reduce or internalize it to consciousness. Nor can we offer a coherent account of time without consciousness. But these *aporias* find a kind of poetic resolution in narrative. Time and narrative thus draw together. Narrative in general is seen as an active response to the 'discordance' of time – to the experience of contingency, randomness, fragmentation. Time becomes human in being organized after the manner of a narrative; and narrative in turn is meaningful to the extent that it portrays features of temporal experience. Narrative articulates our experience of time; and time is brought to language by narrative. This reciprocity between time and narrative is Ricoeur's central thesis. Narrative activity responds to the necessarily inconclusive ruminations of theoretical speculation on time.

There is, however, much that remains obscure in Ricoeur's treatment of exactly how narrative 'resolves' or even 'responds to' the dilemmas of time which remain impenetrable to philosophy, especially in his treatment of fictional narrative. There are different strands in Ricoeur's answer, which seem less illuminating and interesting when unravelled. We have, on the one hand, a structural aspect of narrative. In virtue of its form, narrative brings together fragments of temporal experience, allowing them to be grasped in a unity. Narrative gets it all together, as it were, transforming the inchoate sense of form in our experience of temporal fragments into poetic universals through which we come to understand our experience of the particular. Developing Aristotle's treatment of tragedy, Ricoeur presents fictional narrative as true not to what actually happened, but to what might have happened. Free from the restraint of the actual, it can reach to 'the most hidden and remote layers of our temporal experience'. But the content of narrative is also important to Ricoeur's treatment of its role in responding to the *aporias* of time. Narrative concerns action. It is through its power to 'refigure' past and future action that it allows us to reshape our worlds, to carry the past into the future. And there are other more specific ways, too, in which the content of narrative plays a part in Ricoeur's analysis. Fictional narrative, unlike philosophy, he suggests, can combine cosmological and phenomenological aspects of temporality. It can act as a kind of laboratory of thought experiments where the imagination tries out plausible solutions to the quandaries of temporality. But this aspect of fiction's relations to time is specific to particular fiction. All novels have action, the human world, as a subject matter and hence have an indirect concern with time. Time has to be dealt with in the construction of plot. But not all novels are 'tales of time'. Ricoeur shows us Proust's *Remembrance of Things Past*, Mann's *The Magic Mountain* and Virginia Woolf's *Mrs Dalloway* grappling with complex issues of time which elude philosophical writing. But at the end of the book we are left with a picture of them too as doing little more than gesturing at the wonders and mysteries of time, leaving the reader in a state of awe-struck contemplation. It may be a realistic assessment of the limited resources which both philosophy and literature bring to understanding of the major issues of human experience. But it may also leave us wondering what has become of Ricoeur's central thesis about the contrasts between philosophy and literature, and whether they can be separated as clearly as he seems to think.

Perhaps the conclusion should be not so much that fiction achieves a kind of resolution of problems of time which philosophy cannot solve, as that philosophy too offers 'fictions' through which we can articulate our anxiety and our wonder at the mysterious experience of being in time. The unified self, lying behind language as the originator of meanings, is perhaps itself just such a fiction, taking different forms throughout the history of western philosophy. In later chapters we will see some of the metaphors through which that fiction has been maintained – of the soul as stretching out in time, or as enduring substance. And we will also see metaphors which pull against thinking of the unity of consciousness as the unity of substance – metaphors of speech, of writing and narrative.

By attending to literary dimensions of philosophical writing, this book brings into focus some of the emotional aspects of being in time which are relegated to the margins of more conventional readings. Our separation from things in space can have deep emotional effects. But it does not have the unthinkability of the lost past or the indeterminate future, the strangeness of the presence of what did not exist, the mind-stopping absence of what did exist, which we try ineffectually to map onto the more comfortable and comforting images of spatial presence and absence. Although it addresses some central aspects of the human experience of time, this book does not offer a phenomenology of time consciousness. Nor is it primarily concerned with finding the correct answers to issues of metaphysics of time, although it examines ways in which philosophers, ancient and modern, have attempted to resolve dilemmas of time and selfhood, and ways in which ideas of narrative have implicitly or explicitly figured in those philosophies. It pursues Ricoeur's fruitful suggestion that narrative can be seen as a point of connection between the metaphysical and the human dimensions of the problem of time, although it traces a different route through the separate but sometimes converging paths of philosophy and literature.

# Chapter 1

# Augustine and the 'problem' of time

The connections between the idea of narrative and philosophical reflection on time and consciousness go back as far as Augustine's *Confessions* – that remarkable venture into autobiography, written by the Bishop of Hippo around AD 396. What philosophers most often quote from Augustine's discussion of time in Book XI of the *Confessions*[1] is his famous remark that he knows well enough what time is, as long as no-one asks him, but is reduced to bewilderment if asked to define it. His positive account of time is usually regarded as something of an oddity – a curiously implausible reduction of the reality of time to the workings of the human psyche. Time, he argues, rather than being an 'objective' feature of the world, is a 'distension' of the soul. The mind stretches itself out, as it were, embracing past and future in a mental act of attention and regulating the flow of future into past. Taken in isolation from the autobiographical reflections which frame it in the *Confessions*, such claims about time do seem implausible. As a theory of the nature of time, such a radical psychologizing of its reality must seem counter-intuitive.

Although Augustine presents his view as a theory of time's nature, his interest in that question is framed by reflection on the experiential and emotional dimensions of being in time. Such concerns are, perhaps all too readily, now commonly regarded as extraneous to philosophical enquiry; but they are integral to Augustine's treatment of time. In the *Confessions* he attempts to take account of time as it bears on human existence – to engage with the ways in which time makes him 'a problem to himself'. The work tells the story of his gradual coming to understand what it is to be a consciousness in time. If we are to understand

fully what he has to say about time, we must take seriously the
fact that it occurs in the context of an autobiography. The philosophical content of the work is interwoven with its narrative
form.

The relations between God's eternity and the temporality of
the individual soul, for example, can seem extraneous to Augustine's treatment of the nature of time – a theological excursion
which is irrelevant to philosophical content. But to ignore the
theological context is also to set aside the literary structure of the
work. The central significance of his religious belief is enacted in
the narrative form of the work as a whole. Augustine, in the role
of the narrator, is able to see each event in relation to a recounted
past. Everything finds its place in relation to the crucial event –
his conversion to Christianity. The narrator's complete vision
here represents the human approximation to the complete
knowledge of a changing reality which Augustine attributes to
God. In the position of the protagonist in the narrative, Augustine sees his life only in a confused way. His past is
continually re-shaped by the addition of new experience and by
expectations of the future which are continually revised in the
light of that experience. In the position of the narrator, in contrast, he presents himself as seeing each event in a fixed relation
to a past which has achieved its final form. From this god-like
perspective, the self has a completeness and stability which the
protagonist cannot attain. Through the act of retrospective narration, Augustine is able to achieve a view of himself as object
which eludes him in the midst of the life he now narrates. His
narrated life takes on a unity, a wholeness.

The narrator has knowledge denied to the protagonist of how
the story goes on. He is able to bestow unity and meaning on the
events of a life directly experienced as fragmentation. The autobiographical form of the work can in this way be seen as the
vehicle of an attempt to achieve an elusive goal which being in
time puts out of reach. God is envisaged as having a completeness of self-knowledge in which no aspect or element of his being
remains absent or opaque. The human mind, in contrast, cannot
have it all at once. But the distension of the soul – epitomized for
Augustine in memory and enacted in narrative – functions as a
semblance in the midst of time of the standing present of eternity. Past, present and future, in Augustine's theory of time, are
held together in a unifying act of attention; and this extended

present of the act of attention – modelled on God's eternal self-presence – finds expression in the autobiographical form of the work as a whole.

To properly understand what Augustine has to say about time then it is crucial to see the interconnections between philosophical content and literary form. But the content of earlier sections of the work is also important to understanding what he is about in internalizing time to the mind. The philosophical discussion in Book XI is not an answer to a timeless philosophical question as to the nature of time. It is rather an attempt to resolve a problem posed to consciousness by the human experience of time. What exactly is Augustine's 'problem', and how does it relate to the nature of time? To answer these questions we must examine both his account in earlier sections of the *Confessions* of the ways in which he has become a 'problem to himself', and the philosophical picture to which he responds with his daring assertion that time is nothing more than the distension of the soul.

## LIVING WITH 'HALF A SOUL': AUGUSTINE ON GRIEF

Augustine describes two major episodes of grief in the *Confessions*. First, in Book IV, he recounts his youthful response to the death of a friend. The description of grief is here interwoven with reflections on friendship which echo themes from the concluding books of Aristotle's *Nicomachaean Ethics*, especially the idea of the friend as 'another self'. Because he lives outside himself, pouring out his soul 'like water upon sand' (IV, 8; 79), the young Augustine experiences grief as a disorienting loss of self. He becomes a puzzle to himself – a stranger, tormented in his own country and finding even his own home 'a grotesque abode of misery'. Familiar places become unbearable in the experience of this new, strange absence for they no longer whisper 'Here he comes!' as they would have, had he only been absent a while (IV, 4; 76).

In the immediate experience of grief, Augustine cannot understand what is happening in his own soul. Reflecting on it now in memory, he comes to an understanding of what was lacking in his apparent possession of selfhood before his friend's death. His misery, it now seems to him, came from his soul's being directed outside himself – from its being 'tethered by the love of things that cannot last', so that it is then agonized to lose them (IV, 6; 77).

Reflection on this past loss makes visible flaws in his early loves. He had loved something mortal as though it could never die, as something more than human. This defect of love has rendered his soul 'a burden, bruised and bleeding', which he cannot set down. The loss of a friend loved as another self makes the soul a burden to itself. But this loss only makes visible a wretched state of separation from himself which was already there, fuelled by the attachment to something external. 'Neither the charm of the countryside nor the sweet scents of a garden could soothe it. . . . Everything that was not what he had been was dull and distasteful. Where could I go, yet leave myself behind? Was there any place where I should not be a prey to myself?' (IV, 7; 78).

With self bound up with what is external, grief becomes intermingled with the fear of death. Augustine is obsessed by a 'strange feeling', quite the opposite of the altruistic desire of friends ready to die for each other's sake. Sick and tired of living, he is yet afraid to die. Death, which has snatched away his friend, seems the most terrible of enemies, likely to seize all others too without warning. He wonders that other men should live when his friend is dead, having loved him as though he would never die. And still more he wonders that he himself, having been his 'second self', the 'half of his soul' should remain alive. 'I felt that our two souls had been as one, living in two bodies, and life to me was fearful because I did not want to live with only half a soul. Perhaps this, too, is why I shrank from death, for fear that one whom I had loved so well might then be wholly dead' (IV, 6; 78).

Augustine is delivered from this early grief by the passage of time and the possibilities it brings of new friendship. Time, which never stands still nor passes idly without effects upon the feelings, works its wonders on the mind. As it passes, it fills him with fresh hope and new thoughts to remember. Little by little it pieces him together again by means of the old pleasures he had once enjoyed. But time, by bringing new attachments, brings also new vulnerability – new captivations of the heart by the 'huge fable' of friendship – 'the long-drawn lie which does not die with the death of any one friend' (IV, 8; 79).

Augustine's powerful evocation of the pleasures of friendship in Book IV, section 8, is double-edged. The mutual learning and teaching, the laughter and kindness, the shared pleasures of books, the regrets at absence, the glad welcomes of return are tokens of affection between friends. Signs read on the face and in the eyes, spoken by the tongue and displayed in countless acts of kindness, all 'kindle a blaze to melt our hearts and weld them into one'. But they hold the 'germ of sorrow still to come'. The delights of friendship, especially those centring on the spoken word, are woven into a fable – a long-drawn lie which our minds are 'always itching to hear, only to be defiled by its adulterous caress' (IV, 8; 79). He loved this fable instead of God. The passage of time, though it may heal a specific grief, is itself now seen as a source of anguish – of separation and internal fragmentation of the self.

What the passage of time cannot deliver, however, Augustine finds in his own activity of narration. Reflection on memory – foreshadowing the later, more extended philosophical discussion of time – yields the kind of self-knowledge in which he sees his deliverance from the anguish of temporal experience. Memory, a 'sort of stomach for the mind' in which grief can be reflected on without grief, allows him to recover himself (X, 14; 220). Through self-reflection he turns away from the love of changeable things – from friends conceived as other selves – to his own self. His reflections on past grief, and on the memory through which he is able to reflect thus, here prepare the way for the discovery of the distension of the soul, through which he will both understand and escape from the distress of the temporal. Time's destructive flight into non-existence is countered by the act of memory. Having found in his own soul the act of attention which approximates in its all-encompassing presence the 'standing present' of eternity, he will now be free to love changeable and mortal things in God, who is never lost. No longer clinging to the external and thus clasping sorrow to itself, his soul is freed to a new joy.

The second major episode of grief recounted in Augustine's narrative concerns the death of Monica, his mother. It is separated from the earlier grief by the crucial event which forms the pivotal point in the *Confessions* – his conversion to Christianity. He now knows of the 'eternal wisdom' which creates 'all things that ever have been and all that are yet to be', while yet it itself 'simply is', subject to neither pastness nor futurity. Monica's death is preceded by a conversation in which she speaks with Augustine of this eternal wisdom. They felt their minds touch it, he tells us, for one fleeting instant, before returning to the sound of their own speech, in which each word has a beginning and an end (IX, 10; 197–8).

Enlightened by this moment of contact with eternity, Augustine, as we might expect, presents his second grief as in marked contrast with the earlier one, although his immediate emotional response to it is, to his chagrin, not fully in accord with what he now knows of time and eternity. The 'great wave of sorrow' which surges in his heart is, he thinks, at odds with his religious beliefs; and his misery at finding himself so weak a victim of these human emotions becomes an added source of sorrow. Grieved by his own feelings, he is tormented by a 'two-fold agony'. He is plunged again into the restlessness and oppressiveness of grief. But little by little memory returns, bringing back to him his old feelings about his mother accompanied by the comfort of tears.

In his earlier discussion of grief, Augustine reflected on why it should be that tears are sweet to those grieving and found no clear answer. Weeping now becomes the expression of a hope which eluded him at the death of his friend. 'I had no hope that he would come to life again, nor was this what I begged for through my tears. I simply grieved and wept, for I was heartbroken and had lost my joy' (IV, 5; 77). In that context tears are sweet only because in his heart's desire they take the place of his friend (IV, 4; 76). His new grief, in contrast, is integrated into his own confession and transformed into prayer for his mother's soul. Memory is gathered up in a move forward in the hope of eternal life.

Augustine's new-found religious faith makes of this grief a different experience from his earlier hopelessness in the face of loss, even if his emotions lag behind his intellect. The two griefs express different responses to time. In the second episode, the destructive passage of time is framed by the soul's journey towards eternity. Memory of what he has lost is no longer a source of misery, but a delight in the life which held the seeds of transformation into contact with the eternal. Eternity is here not an empty abstract contrast with the reality of time, but a fullness of presence to be attained after death – a fullness towards which the soul strains during life and of which it gets occasional glimpses. This shift in the emotional resonances of grief foreshadows the later discussion of time. The soul's stretching out in memory, though itself a source of distress at the lack of self-presence, becomes – through the narrative act, centred on the significance of his conversion – the basis for a reaching-out of a different kind, from time into eternity. The reflections on grief foreshadow Augustine's discovering in the distension of the soul an image of eternity. The 'problem' of time is resolved through finding unity amidst fragmentation. This unifying of the fragments of experience is epitomized in memory, articulated through metaphors drawn from the unity of speech, and acted out in autobiographical narration.

Memory represents for Augustine the soul's inward turning, away from the delights of the world grasped through the senses, to search for the good and the eternal within itself. The search echoes the famous passages in Plato's *Symposium* describing the soul's ascent from things of sense towards the intelligible forms known through the higher faculties of the soul. In Augustine's version of this journey, memory represents a higher stage than sense, marking the crucial inward turning which will yield the desired contact with the eternal. To reach God, he thinks, he must carry self-reflection from sense, which he shares with the animals, on to the extraordinary human power of memory. He compares memory to a 'great field or a spacious palace', a 'storehouse for countless images of all kinds which are conveyed to it by the senses' (X, 8; 214). In its 'vast cloisters' are the sky, the earth, the sun, ready at his summons. But memory, as well as bringing the world into the self, also contains the self. He finds himself, along with other things, within this 'vast, immeasurable sanctuary'; and yet it is a faculty of his soul (X, 8; 215–16).

Reflection on memory makes the self an object of wonder – an astonishment previously reserved for the contemplation of the world with its 'high mountains, the huge waves of the sea, the broad reaches of rivers, the ocean that encircles the world, or the stars in their courses' (X, 8; 216). Although the soul's search takes it beyond memory to intellect, it is in some ways memory that best represents the crucial shift to the self, encompassing in its cloisters even the supposedly higher faculty of intellect. For Augustine, memory retains a certain primacy in understanding the nature of the mind. Mind and memory, he says, are one and the same (X, 14; 220). To understand memory is to understand the self: 'I am working hard in this field, and the field of my labours is my own self' (X, 16; 222–3). He has become a problem to himself – a problem which is to be resolved through the investigation of his self, his memory, his mind. Awe-inspiring though the profound power of memory is, it is identified with his mind, with himself.

> What, then, am I, my God? What is my nature? A life that is ever varying, full of change, and of immense power. The wide plains of my memory and its innumerable caverns and hollows are full beyond compute of countless things of all kinds. . . . My mind has the freedom of them all. I can glide from one to the other. I can probe deep into them and never find the end of them. This is the power of memory! This is the great force of life in living man, mortal though he is.
>
> (X, 17; 224)

Intellect may transcend that form of memory which retains sensory images, grasping rather 'the facts themselves' (X, 10; 217). But even this achievement of intellect is framed by memory. The power of intellect resides just in its capacity to gather things which, although they are muddled and confused, are already contained in memory: '. . . once they have been dispersed, I have to collect them again, and this is the derivation of the word *cogitare* which means *to think* or to *collect one's thoughts*' (X, 11; 218). It is memory, with its capacity to make all things present, that yields the clue to the idea of eternity. It is like a mental replica of the world, but it contains more – intellect, and even God himself. It thus offers possibilities of understanding and dealing with time of a kind which eludes the soul in its thought about the physical world as object. Even the immutable God has deigned to be present in memory, and forms there a 'safe haven' for the mind. Memory provides the material for reflection which allows Augustine to find in God the 'gathering-place' for his 'scattered parts'; and as a 'sort of stomach for the mind' (X, 40; 249), retaining experience without its original 'taste', it allows the reflection which is impeded by the immediacy of emotion. Memory and self-knowledge thus belong together. The turning away from world to self which it epitomizes yields a self-knowledge in which Augustine will find the divine. The self becomes visible through a kind of detachment – it draws back from the mindless world to turn its gaze on consciousness. It is the incapacity of that mindless world of physical motion to reveal what is involved in being a mind, capable of understanding time and eternity, that Augustine stresses in his discussion in Book XI of the nature of time. Let us now look at his own account of what it is to be in time in relation to what he sees as the inadequacies of the Aristotelian treatment of the relations between time and consciousness.

## THE 'MEASURE OF MOTION': AUGUSTINE AND ARISTOTLE

Augustine's psychologizing of time aims both to secure the reality of time and to resolve puzzles about its measurement. On either side of the present, he reasons, lies an abyss of non-existence. And even the present, in abstraction from the mind's attention, collapses internally into a non-existent future and an equally non-existent past, on either side of a durationless instant in which nothing can happen. His arguments for internalizing the reality of time to the mind centre on puzzles about measurement. What, he asks, do we measure when we measure time? Not the future; for it does not yet exist. Nor do we measure the past, for it no longer exists. Do we then measure time 'as it is passing'? But, if so, while we are measuring it, where is it coming from, what is it passing through, and where is it going? It can, it seems, only be coming from the future, passing through the present, and going into the past. 'In other words, it is coming out of what does not yet exist, passing through what has no duration, and moving into what no longer exists' (XI, 21; 269).

We are left then with a paradoxical passage from non-existence, through a fleeting, existence-bestowing 'present' into non-existence again. The fragile hold of the present on reality, moreover, is itself encroached upon by the surrounding, voracious non-existence of future and past. The measurement of time in the fleeting present, as it passes, cannot be insulated from the puzzles that beset the measurement of non-existent past and future. The only time that can be called present is an instant – if we can conceive of such a thing – that cannot be divided even into the most minute fractions. However a point of time as small as this passes so rapidly from the future to the past that its duration is without length; for, if its duration were prolonged, it could be divided into past and future. When it is present, then, it has no duration. But such a present can hardly be thought of as bestowing reality on that strange being or non-being which comes out of, and vanishes into, nowhere. There is for Augustine another dimension too to the implication of the present in the non-existence of past and future. The present itself participates in non-being; for if it were always present and never moved on to become past, Augustine reasons, it would be not time but eternity. If, therefore, the present is time only by reason of the fact that it moves on to become the past, how can we say that even the present 'is', when the reason why it is, is that it is not to be? In other words, we cannot rightly say that time is, except by reason of its impending state of non-being.

From all this we might expect Augustine to adopt a sceptical attitude towards the reality of time. These puzzles do indeed echo the temporal paradoxes which Aristotle discussed in the *Physics*. But Augustine's conclusion is that it must be in his own mind that he measures time. Everything that happens leaves an impression which remains after the thing itself has ceased to be. It is the impression that he measures, since it is still present when the thing itself, which makes the impression as it passes, has moved into the past. From this he moves – in a step which may well seem, from our own perspective, all too swift – to the conclusion that time itself must be something mental. 'Either, then, this is what time is, or else I do not measure time at all' (XI, 27; 276).

From the consideration of time's measurement then Augustine derives a shift in the understanding of its nature. From seeing past and future as non-existent times, he moves to the claim that what we call past, present and future are not really three different 'times'. Rather, there are three kinds of present: a present of past things – memory; a present of present things – direct perception; and a present of future things – expectation. But this distinction between three 'presents' gives way to a transformed sense of the present, which accommodates the present of memory and expectation in an all-embracing act of attention. The mind's attention persists, and through it that which is to be passes towards the state in which it is to be no more.

Taken as an analysis of the nature of time, all this may well seem counter-intuitive. Augustine presents his problem as understanding the fundamental nature of time and what power it has. But his description of the passage from expectation through perception into memory seems to demand an objective temporal sequence, in which the states can be said to precede or succeed one another. However, there is more going on here than a misguided attempt to totally absorb the reality of time into his own mind. The force of Augustine's remark, 'Either, then, this is what time is, or else I do not measure time at all', is that if time is not integral to consciousness, then it is as nothing to him. What may seem a non sequitur deriving the nature of time from consideration of its measurement takes on a different aspect when seen in the context of the view of the relationship between time and measurement which Augustine is rejecting – the Aristotelian definition of time as the measure of motion. From that, Augustine is suggesting, it is impossible to derive an adequate understanding of what it is for consciousness to be in time. A brief look at the discussion of time in Aristotle's *Physics*[2] will clarify what kind of 'problem' it is to which Augustine's talk of time as a distension of the mind is meant to offer a 'solution', and why that problem cannot be adequately addressed within the confines of the Aristotelian definition.

In Book IV of the *Physics* Aristotle presents some considerations about time which could, he suggests, make one suspect that time does not exist at all, or 'barely and in an obscure way'. His formulation of the dilemma is similar to Augustine's. One part of time 'has been and is not', while the other 'is going to be and is not yet'. Yet time is made up of these apparently non-existent parts; and one would naturally suppose that 'what is made up of things which do not exist could have no share in reality'. Further, if a divisible thing is to exist, it is necessary that all or some of its parts exist. 'But of time, some parts have been, while others have to be, and no part of it *is*, though it is divisible' (IV. 10. 218a).

From Aristotle's presentation of the paradoxes, it is clear that he does not intend them to be accepted as showing the unreality of time, although he does not offer any explicit solutions to them. His own treatment of time ties its reality securely to that of motion. Time is not movement, but nor is it independent of movement. Aristotle defines it somewhat cryptically as 'number of motion in respect of "before" and "after"' (IV. 11. 219b2). Time is 'movement in so far as it admits of enumeration' – what is countable in movement. Time then is a kind of number, provided we understand this, he insists, not in the sense of that with which we count, but rather in the sense of what is counted. The 'nows' involved in this enumeration are to be understood not as parts of time, but rather as boundaries of temporal intervals. Time is both made continuous by the 'now' and divided at it, just as a point both connects and terminates length – the beginning of one and the end of another.

Any idea of time as made up of a succession of 'nows' is foreign to Aristotle's way of thinking of time. The 'now' can be thought of either as a boundary of intervals of time, similar to the point's role as spatial border, or as the number which measures motion. But the identification with number is only partial. Being a boundary, it cannot be detached from what it numbers in the way that the number ten can be detached from the horses it numbers when we refer to ten horses. Since the instants picked out as 'now' are for Aristotle not parts of time, he is able to side-step the sceptical paradoxes about time's existence: '. . . what is bounded by the "now" is thought to be time – we may assume this' (IV. 11. 219a29).

Having defined time in terms of movement and measurement, Aristotle goes on to offer a definition of being in time. To be in time means that movement – both it and its essence – is measured by time; and he thinks it is clear that 'to be in time' has the same meaning for other things also: namely, that their being should be measured by time. To 'be in time' means either 'to exist when time exists' or to be 'contained by time as things in place are contained by place' (IV. 12. 221a10–20). That which is in time necessarily implies that there is time when it is; and it is necessary that all things in time should be 'contained by time'. Augustine's treatment of time can be read as expressing dissatis-faction with the implications of Aristotle's picture of time for the understanding of time's relations with mind or consciousness. He sees the Aristotelian definition of 'being in time' as inade-quate for understanding what it is to be a self in time.

Aristotle himself touches on the issue of time's relations with consciousness when he raises the possibility that if there were no consciousness there would be no time: '. . . if nothing but soul, or in soul reason, is qualified to count, there would not be time unless there were soul, but only that of which time is an at-tribute . . .' (IV. 14. 223a25). On Aristotle's model, mind is outside change, located as an external observer – a measurer of motion. Minds can, it is true, be said to change and hence to be in time; but there is no privileged position for soul in the definition of time, other than that of the observer and measurer of change. With this model, to say that there would be no time without mind is just to say that without the possibility of measurement there would be not time, but only the substratum of time – only whatever it is about motion which makes it measurable.

For Augustine there are dimensions of the relations between mind and time which cannot be captured in this Aristotelian picture. We will never understand the problem of time, he thinks, until we learn to examine our own consciousness, rather than treating it as the transparent performer of measurement of external change. What is problematic about our being in time is not resolvable through consideration of change in the physical world. But Augustine wants to go further – to account for the reality of time itself in terms of the capacity of consciousness to stretch itself out. It may seem, on the face of it, an extraordinary non sequitur. But it reflects a way of thinking of the relations between time and consciousness very different from that of Aristotle – a way which has some things in common with the neo-Platonism of Plotinus.

## PLOTINUS: THE 'STRETCHING OUT OF THE SOUL'

In the *Enneads*,[3] the third-century Greek Platonist Plotinus is strongly critical of the Aristotelian definition of time in terms of the measurement of motion. Such approaches, he says, do not really get us to the nature of time. 'It comes to this: we ask "What is time?" and we are answered "Time is the extension of Movement in Time"' (III. 7. 8; 231). There are great difficulties, he thinks, even in making the identification of time with any kind of measure. Does such a measure itself have magnitude, like a foot-rule? Time would then be understood as a line traversing the path of movement. But, if it thus shares in movement, how can it be the measure of movement? Why should the traversing line be the measure rather than the movement itself? And why should the mere presence of a number give us time if it is not given by the fact of movement? Time must be something more than the mere number of movement.

Some of Plotinus's criticisms seem to depend on the interpretation of the idea of time as measure which Aristotle himself explicitly set aside – the identification of time with number in the sense of 'what we measure with', rather than what is measurable in motion, the measurable aspect of change. Plotinus's insistence that to understand time we must think of 'a combined thing', a 'measured movement', seems to come close to Aristotle's own observation that time, unlike number, is not detachable from what it measures. But the more substantive aspect of Plotinus's rejection of the identification of time with measurement concerns the relationship between time and the soul. For him, it is not as measurer that soul is essential to the reality of time. 'It is we that must create Time out of the concept and nature of progressive derivation, which remained latent in the Divine Beings' (III. 7. 11; 233–4). But the 'we' here does not refer to calculating, measuring intellects. Time for Plotinus depends on soul in a deeper, more metaphysical way, which makes movement itself imbued with soul. Soul is manifested in movement, not just present to it as external measurer of a soulless substratum of time.

Plotinus's way of thinking of soul has its background in cosmological ideas developed in Plato's *Timaeus* and rejected by Aristotle in the *De Anima*. But Plotinus develops the Platonic 'world soul' in ways that Plato did not, giving it explicit connections with the nature of time and change. In the *Timaeus* time, though subject to change, is created to a pattern of the changeless. Soul interfuses and envelops the world; and this presence of soul is prior to the creation of time. The creator, the story goes, rejoicing in the moving, living world creature he has made in the image of the eternal gods, determines to make the copy still more like the original – the eternal, living being. So he seeks to make the universe eternal, so far as this is possible. The everlasting nature of the ideal being cannot be bestowed in its fullness on something created. So he resolves to make a 'moving image of eternity'. When he sets the heavens in order, he makes an eternal image, but one 'moving according to number', while eternity itself rests in unity. And this image we call time.

The philosophical implications of the *Timaeus* story of time as the moving image of eternity are not entirely clear. It suggests that there is some movement and change in the world independently of time – that what time adds is ordered movement. Time and the heavens begin together – framed after the pattern of the eternal nature. The creation of time is the creation of orderly motion – predictable, law-governed, and hence fit to convey something of the nature of the eternal. In this picture, the presence of soul in the world is not particularly tied to the nature of time. The idea of time as the moving image of eternity is not specifically connected with that of the movement of the world soul which diffuses the whole of creation.

In Plotinus's version, time and soul are much more closely connected. In the first *Ennead*, he describes as 'apt' the reference to time as a 'mimic' of eternity (I. 5. 7; 54). But his version of time as a representation of eternity suggests an active *mimesis*, rather than a passive image made by an external creator. And what makes the idea 'apt' for Plotinus is in some respects the opposite of its Platonic role. For Plato the associations of time as image of eternity are with order, predictability, permanence. Time, as the image of eternity, bestows something of its permanence on the disorderly change of a world lacking true temporal order. For Plotinus, there is a darker side to the idea of mimicry. The emphasis is on the introduction of transience where before there was permanence. Time is aptly described as the mimic of eternity in that it 'seeks to break up in its fragmentary flight the permanence of its exemplar'. Whatever time 'seizes and steals to itself' of the permanent in eternity is annihilated – 'saved only in so far as in some degree it still belong to eternity, but wholly destroyed if it be unreservedly absorbed into time'. Time as mimic is time the destroyer. This twist to the Platonic idea becomes clearer in Plotinus's fuller discussion of time in the third *Ennead*. Time as the 'representation in image' of eternity, he says there, can be clearly apprehended through understanding its exemplar, though we could also proceed in the other direction – from an understanding of time 'upwards' to the awareness of eternity, the 'Kind' which time images (III. 7. 1; 222–3). Our awareness of eternity is crucial in Plotinus's account of time. Time, rather than being the measure of change, or even a feature of change as measurable, is a product of soul. It is a mimesis performed by soul in response, not to the perception of change but rather to the eternal.

Soul, in the form in which it figures here, is not 'we', who might – in the Aristotelian account – be said to measure change, but something closer to Plato's 'world soul'. But the participation of individual minds in that soul is manifested by our awareness of eternity. We participate in the Soul whose mimicry of eternity produces time. Eternity is for Plotinus thus not 'alien' to time. 'What understanding can there be failing some point of contact? And what contact could there be with the utterly alien?' (III. 7. 7; 228). But if we do have some understanding of eternity, we must, he reasons, then have some part or share in it. And how is this possible to us who exist in time? The whole question, he thinks, turns on the distinction between 'being in time' and 'being in eternity'; and this is best understood by probing the nature of time. To explore the nature of time Plotinus proceeds to devise a fiction, to tell a story of the origin of time. Something thus, he says, the story must run: time lay, though not yet as time, in the 'All-Soul', the active principle which aimed at something more than its present. It stirred from its rest and the cosmos stirred with it.

> 'And we (the active principle and the Cosmos), stirring to a ceaseless succession, to a next, to the discrimination of identity and the establishment of ever new difference, traversed a portion of the outgoing path and produced an image of Eternity, produced Time.'
> For the Soul contained an unquiet faculty, always desirous of translating elsewhere what it saw in the Authentic Realm, and it could not bear to retain within itself all the dense fullness of its possession.
>
> (III. 7. 11; 234)

Time is seen as originating in the unfolding of Soul – the unwinding of 'unity self-gathered'. Soul in 'going forth from itself' fritters its unity away, advancing into a 'weaker greatness'. Soul lays aside its eternity and clothes itself with time.

> For the Cosmos moves only in Soul – the only Space within the range of the All open to it to move in – and therefore its movement has always been in the Time which inheres in Soul. . . .
> Time, then, is contained in differentiation of Life; the ceaseless forward movement of Life brings with it unending Time; and Life as it achieves its stages constitutes past Time.
>
> (III. 7. 11; 234)

Time, Plotinus concludes, can be defined as 'the life of the Soul in movement as it passes from one stage of act or experience to another'. Eternity is Life in repose, unchanging and self-identical, always endlessly complete. And time is the image of this Eternity. On this version of the Platonic idea of time as the image of eternity, the 'mimicry' is something acted out by Soul – an unfolding, a stretching out. Time is not conceived as outside of Soul; nor is it a 'sequence or succession' to Soul. It is 'a thing seen upon Soul, inherent, co-eval to it.' But, although time is

not independent of Soul, this does not mean that Plotinus regards it as merely subjective. It is a 'certain expanse', a
quantitative, 'outgoing phase' of the life of the Soul. If Life could
conceivably revert, he says, to the 'perfect unity', time and the
Heavens would end at once. If Soul were to cease its outgoing, if
it became once more turned to the 'tranquilly stable', nothing
would then exist but Eternity. If the Soul withdrew, sinking into
itself again – into its primal unity – time would disappear (III. 7.
12; 235–6).

Movement as a feature of Soul here takes precedence over
physical motion in understanding the nature of time. It cannot be
reasonable, Plotinus argues, to recognize succession in the case
of soulless movement, and so to associate time with that, while
ignoring succession and the reality of time in 'the Movement
from which the other takes its imitative existence' (III. 7. 13; 238).
It is the 'self-actuated movement' of Soul which provides the
basis for the reality of time, creating a sequence by which each
instant no sooner comes into existence than it passes into the
next. Whereas for Aristotle soul entered into the definition of
time only through the implicit reference to mind carried by the
idea of measurement, for Plotinus the time of the cosmos imitates
the movement of Soul, just as the latter in turn imitates the
eternal.

For Plotinus, then, time, as the life of the soul, is prior to the
time of the cosmos, the time of physical motion. There is a 'soul
movement' which constitutes time and hence cannot strictly be
said to be contained by it. Contrary to Aristotle, for Plotinus not
all being-in-time involves being contained by time. We treat the
cosmic movement as overarched by that of the soul and bring it
under time, he says. Yet we do not set under time that soul-
movement itself with all its endless progression. The explanation
of this paradox is simply that the soul-movement responds not to
time but to eternity, and the 'descent towards Time' begins with
this soul-movement which 'made Time and harbours Time as a
concomitant to its Act' (III. 7. 13; 238).

It comes easily to us to think of movement in the soul as merely
metaphorical – an analogue of the literal movement of bodies.
But for Plotinus the movement of souls – as well as that of the 'All-
Soul' in which they participate – is prior to the movement of
bodies. He makes it clear that this applies to movements in the
individual soul no less than to the 'All-Soul' in an interesting

'supplementary observation' at the end of his discussion of time in the seventh section of the third *Ennead*. Take a man walking, he says, and observe the advance he has made. That gives us the 'quantity of movement he is employing' and when we know this, represented by the ground traversed by his feet, we know also the movement that exists in the man himself before the feet move. We must relate the body, carried forward during a given period of time, to a certain quantity of movement causing the progress and to the Time it takes, and that again to the movement, equal in extension, within the man's soul. He then goes on to consider the 'movement within the Soul', asking to what we are to refer it. Let your choice fall where it may, he says. From this point there is nothing but the unextended primarily existent, 'the container to all else, having no container, brooking none'. And as it is with the human soul, so it is with 'the Soul of All'. 'Is Time, then, within ourselves as well?', he asks, and responds: 'Time is in every Soul of the order of the All-Soul, present in like form in all; for all the Souls are the one Soul.'

Plotinus's shift from physical motion to the movement of the soul as the paradigm for the understanding of time is an extension of the Platonic idea of physical motion as imbued with soul. But he gives a special status to meaningful bodily movements, and especially speech, as illustrative of the idea of unity and the overcoming of fragmentation. His most famous example of bodily movement as a metaphor of the unity of the universe is the image of the dancer. Every soul, he says, has its hour – 'all is set stirring and advancing as by a magician's power or by some mighty traction'. 'Like is destined unfailingly to like, and each moves hither or thither at its fixed moment' (IV. 3. 13; 272). The configurations, by their varied rhythmic movements, make up 'one total dance-play', in which the limbs of the dancers are adapted to the overall plan. The whole universe is to be understood in terms of this image of unified action. It 'puts its entire life into act, moving its major members with its own action and unceasingly setting them in new positions', and brings the minor members under the system as in the movements of some one living being (IV. 4. 33; 317).

Plotinus elaborates the theme of soul's presence in the world through other analogies drawn from the spoken word which illustrate the unity and indivisibility of soul itself. He stresses, as Augustine will do later, the difference that form and meaning make to mere sounds. Speech is subject to measurement, but only in so far as it is sound. Its essential nature resides not in what makes it quantifiable like other sounds, but in its significance. As significant sound it involves both activity and passivity – both action and experience. In addition to the motion involved in the act of speech, there is also a counter-motion. We can think of speech as both action upon air as substratum and as experience within that substratum (VI. 1. 5; 447). These shifts between activity and passivity, action and experience make speech for Plotinus a fitting illustration of the unity in variety which characterizes the presence of soul. Whatever in the world is 'apt for soul' will possess itself of it, just as an ear within range will catch and comprehend a spoken word. From the one identical presence, meaning will be derived by more than one hearer. The spoken word is entire at every point in the appropriate space, every listener catching the whole alike. Its sound is evidently not 'strung along the air section to section'. Why then, he asks, should we not think of soul as omni-present, indwelling at every point in the totality of the All, rather than 'extended in broken contact, part for part?' Having entered into such bodies as are apt for it, soul is like the spoken word. Present in the air, before that entering, it is like the speaker about to speak. Even when embodied, it remains at once 'the speaker and the silent' (VI. 4. 12; 528–9).

These illustrations drawn from speech, imperfect though they are, carry, Plotinus thinks, a 'serviceable similitude' to soul. It is equally a 'self-enclosed unity' – the speaker silent – and a 'principle manifested in diversity' – the speaker speaking. The analogy of the reception of the spoken word shows how Soul can become present in some parts of the world and not in others, including the ambivalent presence of soul in individual human beings, just as, from a significant sound, some forms of being take sound and significance together, others only the sound, the 'blank impact'. The 'participant newcomer', the 'intruder', the 'thing of beginnings in time', has made human beings become a duality, winding himself about 'the Man that each of us was at first'.

Then it was as if one voice sounded, one word was uttered, and from every side an ear attended and received and there was an effective hearing, possessed through and through of what was present and active upon it: Now we have lost that first simplicity; we are become the dual thing, sometimes indeed no more than that later foisting, with the primal nature dormant and in a sense no longer present.

(IV. 4. 14; 530)

Plotinus's picture of mind, turning back to contemplate the eternal out of which it comes, and in the process understanding its own role in the constitution of time, answers – as the Aristotelian account cannot do – to the experience of time and consciousness as intimately connected. It is this which attracts Augustine to images drawn from Plotinus. If time were what Aristotle takes it to be, he thinks, time would be as nothing to me. If the substratum of time were thus outside himself, he could not understand what is involved in his consciousness being in time. The challenge Augustine sets himself is to give an account of time's nature which will answer to his own experience of the stretching out of consciousness. Just as Plotinus re-tells Plato's story of time as mimic of eternity, Augustine now re-tells Plotinus's story. As a bald statement of the nature of time, identifying it with the distension of the soul may seem preposterous. But as a variation on a literary story, it emerges as a profound insight into what it is to be in time. The twists in Augustine's version of the tale of time allow him to extract from it a legend of recovering unity of consciousness in a journey out of time back into eternity. Having in mind that Augustine is not merely engaged in timeless reflection on time, but is re-telling an inherited story of its nature, origins and power, let us now see what use he makes of the metaphors and analogies of the spoken word he took over from Plotinus.

## AUGUSTINE'S ANALOGIES OF THE SPOKEN WORD

The consideration of the spoken word preoccupies Augustine throughout the *Confessions*. In the early sections of the work he pictures the phases of life as stages in acquiring the power of speech. It is through his growing awareness of this power that he knows his infancy has receded into the past. The power of speech is here a model of autonomy. Learning to speak involves acquiring a capacity for spontaneity – a self-directedness which contrasts with following a set system of instruction, as he does in learning to read. Through the spoken word he expresses his own observations and wishes. But this new autonomy brings with it new responsibilities. Speech takes him more deeply into the realm of the social – 'a further step into the stormy life of human society' (I, 8; 29).

The freedom associated with the self-directedness of the spoken word has as its correlate a certain necessity. In Book III, verbal composition provides him with an analogy for the idea that things have from an inner necessity their own proper time. When he composed verses, he reflects, each verse was differently scanned. Although the act of poetry does not vary from one line to another, the location of each phrase is governed by rules. Through reflection on speech, Augustine is better able to understand how self-directedness and necessity can come together in the relations between individual life and the unfolding of time. Recalling his early griefs, he reflects that things have their appointed times, rising and setting like the sun, growing until they reach perfection, then growing old and dying.

> Not all reach old age, but all alike must die. When they rise therefore, they are set upon the course of their existence, and the faster they climb towards its zenith, the more they hasten towards the point where they exist no more. This is the law they obey.
>
> (IV, 10; 80)

The analogy of the spoken word provides the model of necessity and a unity which encompasses past, present and future. Just as a sentence is not complete unless each word, once its syllables have been pronounced, gives way to make room for the next, so changeable, mortal things continue on their course. And if the soul loves them and wishes to be with them and 'find its rest in them', it is torn by destructive desires. In these things there is no place to rest, for they do not last, passing away beyond the reach of our senses. 'Indeed, none of us can lay firm hold on them even when they are with us' (IV, 10; 80).

The most striking of Augustine's analogies between being in time and the spoken word comes towards the end of the discussion of time in Book XI. Here we see the full significance of his reflections on the measurement of time. Suppose, he says, I am going to recite a familiar psalm. Before I begin, my faculty of expectation is engaged by the whole of it. But once I have begun, what I have 'removed from the province of expectation and relegated to the past' now engages my memory. The scope of the action I am performing is divided between memory and expectation – the one looking back, the other forward to what I have still to recite. But my faculty of attention is present all the while; and what was future passes through it in the process of becoming past. The 'province of memory' is extended in proportion as that of expectation is reduced until it is all absorbed into memory. Augustine goes on to extrapolate from this illustration of a mind consciously active in time to the understanding of temporal reality generally:

> What is true of the whole psalm is also true of all its parts and of each syllable. It is true of any longer action in which I may be engaged and of which the recitation of the psalm may only be a small part. It is true of a man's whole life, of which all his actions are parts. It is true of the whole history of mankind, of which each man's life is a part.
>
> (XI, 28; 278)

The illustration is preceded by another in which the reader is asked to imagine three sounds (XI, 27; 275). In the first case, a noise is emitted by a material body. The sound begins and we continue to hear it until it finally ceases. When is it measurable? asks Augustine. Not now that it has ceased, for it is no longer there to be measured. While it was present, then – while it was gaining some extent in time? But not in present time, for the present has no extent. This leads to the consideration of the second case, where the sound has begun, but not yet ceased. It still cannot be measured; for we now lack a final point which could give us a measurable interval between beginning and end: '. . . we measure neither the future nor the past nor the present nor time that is passing. Yet we do measure time' (XI, 27; 275).

The beginnings of a resolution of the problem come when we move to consideration of not just any sound but sounds with meaning – speech. Consider, he says, the line 'Deus creator omnium.' He can measure the syllables as short or long, despite the fact that they are past. So what he measures is something that remains in memory. Reflection on the familiar experience of hearing significant speech shows him that the measurement of time goes on, not in the physical world, but in the mind. We are blinded to this by preoccupation with the idea of time as something objective – a feature of the physical world. The crucial shift which we have to perform is from the cosmological to the mental.

What we measure are 'impressions' that remain present despite the transition, whatever it may turn out to be, into the past. We measure the sound mentally, as though we could actually hear it. Even without opening our mouths, he points out, we can go over speech in our minds, and reflecting on this is supposed to bring about a turning away from the physical world to the mind, where we can hope to understand the true nature of time. Consideration of the spoken word helps shift attention away from the thought of physical motion in a changing world to our own being in time. Some of the points Augustine extracts from his psalm example are independent of the fact that it is a meaningful utterance rather than, say, a wordless melody. But the spoken word is for him the ultimate model of a unified temporal structure.

We will not resolve the problem of time, Augustine thinks, until we learn to examine our own consciousness, rather than treating it as the transparent performer of measurement of external change. What is problematic about our being in time is not resolvable through consideration of change in the physical world. But Augustine of course wants to go further than this. Understanding the relations between the spoken word and time is supposed to reveal also the true nature of time itself. All motion – not just the self-movement involved in speech – is to be seen as measurable only in the mind; and for Augustine this means that time itself is to be understood in terms of the distension of the soul. Here his attempt to turn the mind around to its own contemplation may well be seen to have over-reached itself. But it is important to see just what the shift achieves for understanding the soul's being in time. In moving from the Aristotelian external viewpoint on change to the consideration of what it is to be in the midst of understanding an act of speech, we move from a passive model to an active one; and this shift gives the mind some redress against the sense of time's onslaught. Its distressing passivity in the face of time's bewildering passage – out of a non-existent future through an extensionless present into an equally non-existent past – is transformed into an active relegating of the future to the past. 'All the while the man's attentive mind, which is present, is relegating the future to the past. The past increases in proportion as the future diminishes, until the future is entirely absorbed and the whole becomes past' (XI, 27; 277).

By shifting attention away from the world of bodies that move independently of him to the world of consciousness, Augustine gains a new perspective on time. Consciousness is no longer present as a mere observer of external change but located, as it were, within movement. Change is now located in its inner life. The upshot of this shift is, in a way, to eliminate change. Future, present and past are now accommodated into an encompassing presentness of the attending mind – a mental act which holds together a temporal reality which had previously been seen as having only the most tenuous of existences. Consciousness, rather than being located at a precarious vanishing point between the non-existence of past and future, is now seen as encompassing the passage of future into past.

The shift which Augustine has made is from seeing consciousness as in time to seeing time as in consciousness. It is a shift we will see undone and re-made throughout the subsequent philosophical tradition. In Augustine's version of this reversal of the relations between consciousness and time, a crucial structural role is assigned to God. If you would understand your self in relation to time, he is saying, you will do so not by looking to the external world, but rather by looking inward – to the inner world of consciousness where you can understand yourself in relation to God. If you would understand your own being in time, look not to the physical world of motion, but to your own self in relation to eternity. It is through the contrast between the stretching out of consciousness and God's eternal present that you will come to understand your own being in time. For Augustine, as for Plotinus, consciousness understands itself by looking back to what it has come from – to its unfolding out from a unitary presence. The spoken word is the metaphor through which this crucial relation between time as the stretching out of consciousness and God's eternal now is to be grasped.

## TIME AND ETERNITY

Augustine presents the process by which he gradually learns to turn away from the physical world to the world of consciousness as the story of his religious conversion. His turning away from the physical world to contemplate himself begins the process of turning towards God. But this is more than a tale of spiritual journeying into the ineffable. Let us look more closely at what Augustine has achieved. His way of thinking of the present is contrasted, on the one hand, with Aristotle's bounding instants –

the instantaneous presents which are mere limits of motion. On the other hand, it is contrasted with an 'eternal present' which escapes in a different way the dilemmas of the non-existent past and future. Aristotle's view of time, joining as it does the idea of what is measurable in motion with the idea of durationless instants by which it is measured, leaves no space for the Augustinian idea of the distension of the soul. Mind, as we have seen, enters the Aristotelian account only as the external observer and measurer of change – as the implicit presence of consciousness which is necessary to measurement. The kind of present associated with the distended soul brings time and soul together in a different way, and also makes possible a point of connection with the idea of eternity which was not possible on the Aristotelian view.

The fact that our present, ever moving on to become the past, cannot be always present, as Augustine points out, prevents it from being identified with eternity. He elaborates the contrasts between time and eternity – between the distension of the soul and the 'eternal now' of God's knowledge – through an extension of the recitation analogy. Let us suppose, he says, a mind endowed with such great power of knowing and foreknowing that all the past and all the future were known to it as clearly as we might know a familiar psalm. Such a mind would be 'awesome beyond belief' in its grasp of all that is to happen in ages yet to come. 'It would know all this as surely as, when I sing the psalm, I know what I have already sung and what I have still to sing, how far I am from the beginning and how far from the end' (XI, 31; 279). But such a mind would still be in time – spread, as it were, between past, present and future. When we recite or listen to a recitation, our feelings vary and our senses are divided because we are partly anticipating words still to come and partly remembering words already sung. It is far otherwise with God who is 'eternally without change', knowing changing things without any change in his knowledge. Such a knower is not in time and the eternal presence of his knowledge is quite different from the 'present of attention', through which the future passes into the past.

The content of Augustine's eternal present is elusive. But it is clear that this lack of past and future is a very different kind of lack from that involved in the Aristotelian bounding instant, which can allow for no past or future because there can be in it no mind or soul. Here, as Ricoeur points out in his commentary on Augustine in *Time and Narrative*, there is a conceptually unbridgeable gap separating Aristotle's instants from Augustine's present.[4] The Aristotelian instant requires only that a break be made in the continuity of movement – a break which can be made anywhere. Mind functions here as an external observer of motion which does not intrinsically involve itself. The lack of past and future which characterizes Augustine's eternal present, in contrast, arises from a fullness of presence which the human mind cannot achieve – not from absence of mind but from its presence in a superior form. Here again there are echoes of Plotinus. All progress of time, Plotinus says in the first *Ennead*, means the dissipation of a unity whose existence is in the present. Past and future are associated with this dissipation which is time's essence. To think of eternity is to think of a life not made up of periods but 'completely rounded, outside of all notion of time' (I. 5. 7; 54). And in the third *Ennead*, he associates eternity with the idea of a life ever varying, not becoming what it previously was not. Here there is no development but only actual presence – 'not this now and now that other, but always all; not existing now in one mode and now in another, but a consummation without part or interval' (III. 7. 3; 224). All its content is in immediate concentration 'as at one point'. The eternal remains identical within itself; what it is, it remains for ever. Nothing can make its way into this 'standing present' which excludes past and future. Any imagined entrant will prove to be not alien but already integral. No ground is left for its existence but that it be what it is. So eternity in contrast to time involves stable existence, neither in process of change nor having changed – 'pure being in eternal actuality'. Here there is no future, for every 'then' is a 'now'. Nor is there any past, for nothing here has ever ceased to be. Here 'everything has taken its stand for ever' – an 'identity well pleased, we might say, to be as it is'.

The idea of eternity plays not only a religious role in Augustine's thought on time but also a literary one. By projecting a construct of an alternative mode of presence, Augustine is able to sharpen his articulation of the temporal presence which characterizes human consciousness. Reflection on the idea of eternity serves to focus and intensify the experience of incompleteness and fragmentation that goes with being in time. The lack of eternity functions, as Ricoeur puts it, not simply as a limit that is thought but as a lack that is felt at the heart of temporal experience – 'the sorrow proper to the negative'.[5] The idea of the eternal present allows Augustine to integrate philosophical speculation on the nature of time with a more literary reflection on its power – on what is involved in the human experience of time. But it also serves to reconcile the mind by holding out an ideal of an alternative kind of consciousness with which the individual can identify. The distension of the soul which marks Augustine's separation from eternity also becomes through reflection the source of his deliverance from the distress of being in time. It becomes both the mark of the difference between human and divine consciousness and the reflection in him of the divine understanding. God's all-encompassing present becomes a model for the mind's act of attention, which overcomes the fragmentation of temporal experience. The extended present becomes the approximation in the soul of God's eternal now. It is through attempting to think of eternity that Augustine most strongly realizes the nature of time.

## THE PHILOSOPHICAL AND THE LITERARY

We have seen that Augustine's ideal for self-consciousness finds expression in the literary form of the *Confessions* as well as in its content – that its literary form is by no means incidental to its explicit treatment of time. The movement of time in the direction of eternity, as Ricoeur points out, is the very movement narrated by the first nine books of the work. The narrative activity accomplishes the itinerary whose conditions of possibility are reflected on in Books X and XI. And the narrative form, holding together disparate events in a meaningful unity, itself enacts Augustine's ideal of a consciousness which holds fragments together in a unity for which time is no longer a problem. The narrator, knowing what has been and what is to come, enacts his own life in the way the reciter goes through the psalm. The narrator has knowledge, denied to the protagonist, of how the story goes on. But the narrator of course is not simply 'reciting' this life. He is also in some ways creating it – bestowing unity and meaning on fragmented events. The autobiographical form of the work can in this way be seen as the vehicle of an attempt to achieve the elusive goal of a consciousness fully present to itself – a goal which being in time puts out of reach. For Augustine, as for

Plotinus, the distension of the soul is a disruption of unity. In contrast to God's fullness of presence to himself, we cannot have it all at once. But the distension of the soul, epitomized in memory, also functions, as we have seen, as a semblance in the midst of time of the standing present of eternity. Past, present and future can be held together in a unifying act of attention which finds its clearest expression in the form of autobiography.

Augustine of course believed that his 'resolution' of the problem of time was more than a literary device to give clearer philosophical articulation to the problem. What we call the present, for him as for Derrida, is implicated in the non-existence of past and future. But Augustine tries to resolve the problem through appeal to the encompassing act of attention. The extended present offers a safe haven which solves the problem of the non-existence of past and future by bringing them into consciousness. Derrida would see this as a false solution to a problem which arises only from the conviction of the primacy of the present, fed by preoccupations with the spoken word. For him, what we call the present is constituted out of what in fact never really was present. The alleged primacy of the present is an illusion. His deconstruction of the primacy of the present is at the same time the deconstruction of the self-presence of consciousness. Augustine's yearning for an illusory fullness of presence expresses a nostalgia for a supposedly lost unity of consciousness. *Différance* is Derrida's version of 'taking account of time' without the false reassurance of the limiting idea of eternity. Whatever is distressing in being in time cannot be allayed by aspiring to the self-presence of the eternal word. The distension of the soul, the extended notion of the present, and the idea of eternity can provide no resolution of Augustine's dilemma. But that dilemma is of his own making, generated by the pivotal role he gives the supposed primacy of the present – in his suggestion that 'wherever the past and future are, they are there not as past or future but as present'; in the idea of the act of attending which makes past and future present to the mind; in the complementary idea of the distended soul; and, finally, in the crucial idea of the standing present of God's eternity.

Because the idea of God and his eternal present clearly carry the force of theological belief in the *Confessions*, it is easy to overlook their literary role in the work – their function as 'fictions' which allow a clearer articulation of the experiential and emotional dimensions of being in time. In later chapters, where our discussion will focus on philosophers for whom religious belief is either non-existent or much less important, we will see more clearly the interactions between the philosophical and the literary. We will see many of the themes which give substance to Augustine's treatment of time – the self as fragmentation and as unity; the shifts from finding time in consciousness to finding consciousness in time; the primacy of the present; the 'loss' of the past; the aspiration to attain through writing a form of consciousness which escapes time. His version of the interconnections between time and consciousness is at first sight outrageous. But he is attempting to answer a serious and important question: how is time to be understood by a consciousness which is itself immersed in time? His answer – that if time were not integral to consciousness it would be as nothing to consciousness – is in some ways, as we shall see, not so very different from Kant's definition of time as 'the form of inner sense'. But Kant is able to give much more sophisticated expression to the interdependence of time and human consciousness, and the alternative idealized form of consciousness which he uses to clarify it lacks Augustine's explicit theological commitments.

Whatever may be its deficiencies, the eleventh book of the *Confessions* remains a work of great insight into the experience of time, its connections with speech, and its expression in narrative – a profound attempt to 'take account of time' and to engage philosophically with the ways in which it makes us a 'problem to ourselves'.

# Chapter 2

# The self: unity and fragmentation

On my reading of Augustine's treatment of time, his central concern was to repudiate the idea that it is only incidentally related to consciousness. Unless they are interconnected, he thought, it is impossible to understand what it is for consciousness to be in time – impossible to experience being in time as anything but fragmentation of selfhood and loss of the past. For Augustine, it is because time is constituted by a stretching out of consciousness that it can be lived as something more than fragmentation and loss. The divine mind, living in an eternal present, is the model for a much desired self-presence in the midst of time.

In the subsequent philosophical tradition the role of theological belief has been less straightforward. However, the role of an idealized form of self-consciousness in the literary structure of the *Confessions* has its echoes and its analogues in modern philosophical writing. In this chapter I will examine the transformation of themes of fragmentation – from Descartes's view of the self as thinking substance, through Hume's rejection of the substantial self, into Kant's 'unity of apperception'.

## DESCARTES: THE UNITY OF THINKING SUBSTANCE

Descartes too developed a model of idealized consciousness with which the individual mind can identify in its search for stability and self-knowledge. But the ideal now shifted from divine consciousness to mind itself, thinking exclusively clear and distinct ideas. It was an ideal no more attainable within the flux of time than was Augustine's idea of God's eternal presence; but it played a similar role in rescuing the self from fragmentation. In Descartes's *Meditations*, God became part of the mechanism of knowledge, assuring certainty; and the mind's reflection on its dependence on God becomes the source of another version of the idea of the 'stretching out' of the soul.

## DESCARTES AND AUGUSTINE

Central themes from Augustine's writings recur in Descartes's famous discussions of self and self-consciousness. Turning away as he did from Aristotelian models of knowledge and of the relations between mind and body, it is not surprising that his philosophy should echo some Platonic ways of thinking, startlingly novel though his transformation of them was. As Etienne Gilson says, Descartes, having rejected Aristotle, could not but follow the other great way of metaphysical speculation. Surrounded as he was by contemporary Augustinians, he was bound to meet Augustine on that Platonic way.[1] Augustine's efforts to establish certainty against the sceptics, and the spirituality of the soul against the Manichees, were being re-enacted in Descartes's intellectual milieu. Augustine's shift of focus from world to self is paralleled in Descartes's emphasis on the inwardness of knowledge, and in his dramatic view of 'ideas' as the proper objects of knowledge. The self, rather than being just a preferred object of contemplation, becomes the immediate object of knowledge, mediating even the knowledge of material things, in so far as that can be certain.

Rejecting the Aristotelian orientation of scholastic theories of knowledge, Descartes reversed the prevailing conception of the order of knowledge, giving precedence to the mind's awareness of its own thought rather than to its confrontation with the world through the senses. Whatever we clearly and distinctly perceive through pure intellect as belonging to a thing, he thought, can be taken as a real property of it – a principle through which he establishes both the limits of certainty and the utter separation of spiritual soul from material body.

Something of Augustine's yearning for stabilized self-knowledge can be discerned in Descartes's concern with the transparency of thought to itself. Moreover his most famous insight into self-consciousness – that from the indubitability of the act of thinking follows the certainty of the thinker's existence as a thing that thinks – had, as some of his contemporary readers pointed out, already been formulated by Augustine. Augustine's delight in finding in his own self the stability and security which had eluded him in his dealings in his search for knowledge and love in the world outside him, finds more systematic philosophical expression in Descartes's *Cogito*. But Descartes himself was sure that his own version went well beyond anything to be found in Augustine. When his contemporaries drew his attention to similarities to passages in Augustine, Descartes was not interested in the resemblance. Augustine, he thought, had put the point to very different use, lacking his own concern with articulating the radical separation of mind and body. In response to the Jansenist Arnauld, who was rather more preoccupied with the echoes of Augustine in Descartes's works, Descartes said, with a note of irony, that he would not waste time thanking Arnauld for bringing in the authority of Augustine to support him.[2]

Pascal endorsed Descartes's claim to be the real inventor of the *Cogito*, stressing the distinctive reflectiveness of Descartes's version. Descartes, he pointed out, drew out the consequences of the argument to distinguish spiritual from material natures and build an entire physics on it. In Descartes's writings, he suggested, the *Cogito* becomes as different from its occurrence in the works of others, who have said it in passing, as a man full of life and force from a dead man.[3] Gilson has argued against this that Augustine in fact put the principle to similar uses – to refute sceptical doubt and to shift the mind's attention from objects of sense to the intelligible order; and that Augustine too emphasised the soul's grasp of its own existence through an act of pure thought, immediately accessible to consciousness, in contrast to its mediated awareness of body.[4] Descartes's treatment of the self can be seen as retracing in a systematic way the Augustinian turning away from world to find God in the soul. For Gilson, Augustine is more Cartesian, and Descartes more Augustinian, than Pascal or Descartes himself would allow. But to recognize the Augustinian influence is, as Gilson acknowledges, in no way to deny the originality of Descartes's transformation of the master theses of Augustinian metaphysics, or the extraordinary depth with which he developed them. This is evident in Descartes's transformation of another theme we have already seen in Augustine – the dependence of the human mind on God.

The awareness of God as cause of the soul's existence played a crucial role in Augustine's efforts to stabilize consciousness in a self-presence modelled on God's eternal present. In Descartes's philosophy, self-knowledge becomes much more explicitly connected with understanding the mind's dependence on God as cause. The awareness of God as uncaused cause, and of the soul as finite thinking thing, are here seen as two sides of the same thought. It is the reflective awareness of this dependence, as we shall see, that generates Descartes's version of the 'stretching out' of the soul.

## SELF-CONSCIOUSNESS, TIME AND GOD

Descartes's *Meditations* is suffused with a sense of the tenuousness of the self's capacity either to integrate itself into the world or to maintain a secure relationship with its past. The Cartesian thinking self experiences its very existence as fragile. Time is involved in this distinctively Cartesian sense of the fragility of consciousness; and awareness of God is crucial to the mind's deliverance from it. Time poses a challenge even to the narrator's capacity to extract from the indubitable *Cogito* anything more than a momentary existence. 'I am, I exist – that is certain. But for how long? For as long as I am thinking. For it could be that were I totally to cease from thinking, I should totally cease to exist'.[5] For all that he can at present know, the certainty that comes from reflection on his own thinking cannot yield anything more than a momentary existence for this thinking thing. Perhaps it has no more relation to past or future than the stuff that dreams are made of.

The Cartesian self is rescued from being thus stranded in the present through reflection on its dependence on God. In knowing that God is its efficient cause it knows that its existence as a thinking thing stretches beyond the moment of present thought. Gilson has suggested that the simplest formula to capture the whole content of the *Meditations* is that they reduce to an exhaustive explication of the content of the *Cogito* by the principle of causality.[6] Although both dependence on God and the *Cogito* have a strong presence in Augustine's thought, Descartes brings them together in a way that yields a new sense of inwardness. God now is needed, not just to symbolize an alternative realm, which competes with the world as object of attention, but to ensure that the mind has access to that external world. The mind's capacity to know a world external to itself and its capacity to extend its consciousness beyond the present both depend on the power and veracity of God.

This dependence dramatizes both the fragility of the self's contact with the world and the tenuous continuity of its inner life. What goes on within is separated from what goes on outside by a gulf which only God can bridge. The truth of the *Cogito* is assured by confrontation with the inner stream of thought itself. Beyond that direct and indubitable truth, the meditation on the self can lead nowhere without God to bridge the gulf between inner and outer. Susan Bordo has commented on the implications of this for Descartes's conception of the continuity of consciousness.[7] When the immediacy of intuition passes, so too does our slender grasp on confidence in our own faculties. The mind's confidence in its past insights cannot survive the test of supposing that there is an evil genius intent on deceiving it. What it has perceived in the past is now seen as having been always open to doubt, although the doubt was not felt at the time. To attain certainty we must be convinced not only beyond present doubt, but also beyond the shadow of any future doubt. Descartes's God is needed not only to provide our continued existence as enduring things, but to provide an assurance of continuity to our inner life as well. The mind's continued existence depends on God; but there is a correlate of this in its inner life. Its understanding cannot reach beyond the present instant without the certainty that God exists, any more than its existence itself could persist without his sustaining force. Without knowledge of God, certainty could be sustained only by constant mental vigilance. Each idèa that presented itself would have to be confronted and interrogated anew – a requirement that would make the progress of science impossible.

What the Cartesian thinker lacks in the second Meditation is supposed to be given in the third by the proof of God's existence, where Descartes makes explicit the connections between time, self and God. Time plays a central role in this proof. He cannot, he says, escape the force of arguments for the necessity of a cause of his existence by supposing that he has always existed as he does now. A lifespan can be divided into countless parts, each completely independent of the others, so that it does not follow from the fact that he existed a while ago that he must exist now, unless there is some preserving cause which, as it were, creates him afresh at this moment. Descartes then goes on to make what seems a strange claim – that the necessity for such a cause is quite clear to anyone who attentively considers the nature of time. It will, he says, become apparent that the same power and action are needed to preserve anything at each moment of its duration as would be needed to create it anew if it were not yet in existence. Hence, he concludes, it is evident by the natural light that the distinction between preservation and creation is only a conceptual one.

Despite Descartes's claim that they would be apparent to attentive consideration, the supposed connections between the nature of time and the soul's dependence on God were by no means obvious to Descartes's contemporary critics. The objections raised by Gassendi bear most directly on the theme of continuity of consciousness. Far from thinking that the parts of our duration are separable, he says, he is tempted to ask whether we can think of anything whose parts are more inviolably linked and connected.[8] The later parts seem inevitably to be closely tied to and dependent on the earlier. But what difference, he asks, does this issue of the dependence or independence of the parts of our duration make to our creation or preservation? Surely those parts are merely external to the self, following on without playing any 'active role'. They make no more difference to our creation and preservation than the flow or passage of the particles of water in a river makes to the creation and preservation of some rock past which it flows. Although it is true that my future existence does not follow from the fact that I exist now, that is not because a cause is needed to create me anew, but rather because there is no guarantee that there is not some cause present which might destroy me, or that there may not be some unnoticed inner weakness which could bring about my demise.

Descartes's response to Gassendi makes it clearer what exactly the preservation of existence is supposed to have in common with creation with respect to causality, clarifying in the process both his idea of efficient causality and his treatment of time. The point is not that each phase of a thing's existence should be thought of as a fresh beginning to exist, as if it were a new event that had to be explained. It concerns being rather than beginnings: '. . . the sun is the cause of the light which it emits, and God is the cause of created things, not just in the sense that they are causes of the *coming* into being of these things, but also in the sense that they are causes of their *being*; and hence they must always continue to act on the effect in the same way in order to keep it in existence'.[9] Being demands efficient causality no less than does beginning to be. Descartes insists again that this can be plainly demonstrated from the independence of the divisions of time. The argument cannot be evaded, he says, by talking of the necessary connection which exists between the divisions of time 'considered in the abstract' for this is not the issue: '. . . we are considering the time or duration of the thing which endures, and here you would not deny that the individual moments can be separated from those immediately preceding and succeeding them, which implies that the thing which endures may cease to be at any given moment'.[10]

The exchange illuminates how Descartes thinks of the continuity of consciousness. For Gassendi, the parts of a mind's duration are external to the being of the mind. So it makes no difference to me whether those parts are necessarily connected or independent of one another. His picture of the relations between mind and time is in this respect like that of Aristotle. Human minds, like other temporal things, are contained by time. Gassendi's image of the rock is revealing. It suggests that my duration is external to me, just as the flow of water around the rock is external to its being. So the relation between parts of my duration is irrelevant to my being and hence irrelevant to my creation or preservation. In Descartes's picture my duration is not in that way external to my being. I do not stand in time like a rock in a river; what is true of my duration must be true of me. If the moments of my duration can be separated it must also be true that I myself will cease to exist in the lack of an external cause.

Descartes thinks that the point is fundamentally the same, whether we think of it in terms of the thing with duration or in terms of the duration of the thing, although it may be more easily grasped in the latter formulation. Gassendi, he says, is thinking of time 'in the abstract' rather than in the 'concrete'. At first sight this response is puzzling. What, we might ask, could be more concrete than the mind's experience of its own past? Gassendi is saying that to a mind looking back on its past – from an autobiographical perspective, as it were – the parts of its duration seem to display a necessary connectedness. But Descartes is addressing a different contrast between the abstract and the concrete. He is concerned with duration as an aspect of a thing's very existence. Descartes stresses that his point is not that each moment of being must be thought of as literally a fresh beginning. Rather it is that the being of created things – the being of duration – stands in need of an efficient cause no less than does a new beginning. To say that the parts of my duration are separable is to say that my being is durational – a prolongation of existence. The being of created things, no less than their beginnings, depends on an external cause. As he sums up the point in the *Principles* version of the argument, because the nature of time is such that its parts are not mutually dependent and never coexist, from the fact that we now exist, it does not follow that we will exist a moment from now, unless there is some cause which originally produced us and 'continually reproduces us, as it were, that is to say, which keeps us in existence'.[11]

The case of God is different for Descartes, not because he acts as his own efficient cause, but because for his kind of being no efficient cause is needed. Nothing is needed to preserve God in existence, for his being is not that of duration. Arnauld's objection to this part of the *Meditations* invokes the Augustinian distinction between time and eternity. He takes Descartes to imply that God, in contrast to the human soul, somehow preserves himself in time, as if his existence involved prolongation of being rather than the lack of division between past, present and future appropriate to eternity. Arnauld cites against Descartes the authority of Augustine's 'worthwhile and sublime' remarks on God's eternal presence.[12] Descartes responds that he did not mean to suggest that God was the efficient cause of himself, but only that in contrast to lesser beings he has no need of a preserver.

What is important in all this is the close connection made by Descartes between thinking of the duration of a finite thing and thinking of it as existing. In the *Principles*, he says that we should regard the duration as 'simply a mode under which we conceive the thing in so far as it continues to exist'.[13] Spinoza takes over the point and develops it in his *Thoughts on Metaphysics*. There is for God, he says, no possibility of the kind of 'existence in stages' appropriate to finite conditioned things which depend on a force not their own for a prolongation of existence and hence can be said to 'enjoy' existence.[14] Descartes regarded the preservation of things as differing 'only conceptually' from their creation. Spinoza makes the connections between causal dependence and existence even closer. Duration is distinguished only 'by reason' from the existence of finite things. In the *Ethics* he gives up even the 'distinction of reason' between them, defining duration as the existence appropriate to modes – an 'indefinite continuation of existence' – in contrast to eternity, the existence appropriate to substance.[15]

Having separated himself radically from the Cartesian philosophy which had been his starting point, Spinoza came to see the mind's dependence on God for the prolongation of existence as incompatible with the status of substance. However, the seeds of the collapse of the mind's status as individual substance were already there in Descartes's thought. In the *Principles* he distinguished two senses of substance. The primary sense – involving totally independent existence – applies only to God. The second – involving an existence so complete that it depends on nothing but God – applies to the human soul.[16] Spinoza repudiated this secondary sense of substance: anything which depends on a force not its own for the prolongation of existence can, he argued, be only a mode of God as substance. The individual mind loses its status as substance and becomes a finite mode of substance under the attribute of thought – an idea in the mind of God. We will see the outcome of this loss of the status of substance in Hume's picture of the self as a bundle of fragments of consciousness. But even in Descartes's thought the idea of intellectual substance comes under strain. Whatever the extension into the past of the Cartesian mind might amount to, it seems to be something quite different from the status of an individual substance enduring through and contained by time.

Descartes's discussion of the mind's dependence on God moves with apparent unconcern between an impersonal, third-person formulation, in which the mind is treated no differently from other finite things, and a first-person perspective, in which its dependence is experienced as an imperfection, a lack in its very existence. This more experiential aspect of the argument is more conspicuous in the *Principles* version, where Descartes reasons that a thing which recognizes something more perfect than itself could not be the source of its own being, for if it were it would have given itself all the perfections of which it has ideas.[17] But it is in the *Meditations* that Descartes explores most fully the integration of principles of causality and the direct experience of himself as a thinking thing.

## ATHEIST DREAMERS AND MATHEMATICIANS

The soul, unlike other finite things, is able to understand and reflect on its dependence on God for continued existence. This reflection has consequences both for self-knowledge and for the possibility of a science founded on certainty. The reflective mind becomes capable of reaching through time in a way that differs from the duration it shares with other finite things. It can attain to a reflective, first-person analogue of the prolongation of its existence through time. This is an aspect of Descartes's treatment of self-consciousness which puzzled his contemporary critics and continues to perplex modern commentators – the alleged difference between the knowledge of the world available to those who believe in God and the more limited knowledge available to the atheist.

All minds are maintained in existence by God; but those which understand their dependence are capable, Descartes thinks, of an enduring state of certainty which is denied to others. The mind of the believer knows itself to be a structure of necessarily connected clear and distinct ideas, although inevitably it does not achieve a continuous state of attentive awareness of those ideas. The waters of consciousness are muddied by the presence of body. Knowledge of God's existence is supposed to make the mind aware that, underlying that surface confusion, the deepest waters of self flow pure and clear. Without that knowledge, the mind has only a series of disconnected episodes of clear and distinct thought, each carrying a momentary certainty. By following Descartes's method, enacted in the *Meditations*, the individual mind makes contact with the deeper levels of mind in which the separate occurrences of clear and distinct ideas are connected. Cartesian meditation makes it understand both that its ideas correspond to the real natures of existing material things and that it has an essential continuity, beneath the fragments of experience, as thinker of the clear and distinct.

Descartes's critics were puzzled about what exactly he thought was lacking in the atheist's knowledge of things other than God. He says in one of his replies to Mersenne that the knowledge of God's existence is needed to assure us of those conclusions which can be recalled when we are no longer attending to the arguments from which we deduced them. My awareness that I am a thinking thing is in contrast a 'primary notion' whose self-evidence is recognized by a 'simple intuition of the mind'.[18] By direct experience of my own thinking I understand that it is impossible to think without existing. In response to Mersenne's incredulity that an atheist should be thought incapable of being clearly and distinctly aware that the three angles of a triangle equal two right angles, Descartes elaborates on what the atheist lacks. Indisputably, he says, the atheist can be aware of mathematical truth while perceiving it; but this certainty can change to doubt and hence is not to be called knowledge. Even on matters which seem most certain to him the atheist cannot be certain that he is not deceived. He will always be vulnerable to doubt, either from external sources or when he looks into the matter himself. Descartes makes a similar point in his replies to the sixth set of objections.[19] The atheist's knowledge, he says there, can easily be shown not to be immutable and certain; for the less power he attributes to the author of his being, the more reason he will have to suspect the imperfection of his nature, so that he may be deceived even in what seems most evident. He will never be free of doubt until he recognizes that he has been created by a truthful God.

Although the atheist can know clearly in isolated intellectual acts, he cannot attain well-grounded, systematic knowledge, and this inability to extend certainty through time has consequences also for his own self-consciousness. The mind of the atheist, like all other finite things, is preserved through time by God; but, confined to episodic clarity, it lacks the reflective analogue of this prolongation of existence. This becomes clearer in Descartes's exchange with Hobbes about the competence of atheists to know that they are not now dreaming. In the sixth Meditation, Descartes had used the knowledge of his dependence on a veracious God to allay the central doubt from which his Meditations began – the possibility that he is dreaming even while feeling certain that he is awake. He can now, he thinks, distinguish dreams from waking life by the fact that they are never linked by memory with all the other actions of life. Consider, Hobbes replies,[20] someone who dreams that he is in doubt as to whether or not he is dreaming. Could not such a man dream that his dream fits with his ideas of a long series of past events? Could not the actions he believes to belong to his past life be themselves dreams? If, as Descartes claims, certainty depends on knowledge of the true God, an atheist would not be able to infer that he is awake on the basis of memory of his past life. But the atheist, surely, can know he is awake without knowledge of the true God. Descartes responds that a dreamer cannot really connect his dreams with the ideas of past events, although he may dream that he does: everyone admits that a man may be deceived in his sleep; but afterwards, when he wakes up, he will easily recognize his mistake.[21] His reply to Hobbes parallels his discussion of the atheist mathematician. An atheist can infer that he is awake on the basis of memory of his past life. But he cannot know that this criterion is sufficient to give him the certainty that he is not mistaken if he does not know that he is created by a non-deceiving God.

Atheist dreamers and mathematicians are capable of episodic certainty; but they cannot with justification extend that certainty beyond the moment of clear and distinct perception. They lack the assurance of continuity – the reflective, self-conscious certainty that reaches through time. Whatever ease they may find in stretching out in time as reflective clear and distinct thinkers must be ill-founded. Atheist dreamers and mathematicians exist through time. Their lack of belief in God does not change the fact that he sustains them in existence. But they lack a first-person perspective, as it were, on their temporal extension. They lack understanding of what is involved in their being in time – of their duration, which Descartes comes close to identifying with the very being of the mind. That crucial dimension of the existence of conscious mind remains inaccessible to them.

Atheist dreamers and mathematicians thus lack a certain capacity for unified consciousness. They do not have access to the sustained continuity of certainty. But what this involves for Descartes is not a connected narrative of episodes making up the daily experience of consciousness. Necessary connections between ideas hold only at the level of the underlying unity of clear and distinct ideas. This is not the stream of consciousness of ordinary life, which contains much that is not clear and distinct, and hence much that is not, in Descartes's sense, necessarily connected. But for Descartes the easy inhabiting of that everyday world rests on the capacity to separate out the clear and distinct from the intrusions of the body, even if that cognitive possibility is rarely realized. The sensuous confusion of the realm of inter-mingling of mind and body becomes intellectually manageable through the assurance that there are reliable criteria for dis-tinguishing it from the realm of clear and distinct ideas. The necessary unity of consciousness holds only below the surface of ordinary unreflective consciousness. Let us now see how these Cartesian themes of dependence on God, unity of consciousness and continuity in time are reinforced by the literary structurę of the *Meditations*.

## TIME IN THE LITERARY STRUCTURE OF THE MEDITATIONS

The transition from doubt to certainty involves for Descartes a transformation of the confusion of mind-body intermingling into the clarity of pure thought. It involves also a transformation of unstable, disorderly mental movement into the steady state of intellectual contemplation. This theme of the transformation of the mind's relations to time runs through Descartes's work. It is built into the argumentative structure of the *Meditations*; and it is enacted in metaphors of motion which interact with the more commonly noticed metaphors of light. Images of darkness and sleep interact with images of restlessness and turmoil. Whirl-pools tumble the mind around as it labours in darkness without a firm foothold. The intrusions of body through the senses and imagination put the mind into a state of fluctuating, unstable, erratic motion. Its self-movement in assent to clear and distinct perception is contrasted with its giddy motion under the influ-ence of body – motion which is really a form of passivity rather than true activity. Cartesian method involves learning to dis-tinguish these two kinds of mental motion. On the one hand there is the restless impulse to assent to what is not clearly and distinctly understood; on the other, the irresistible movement of rational assent which is the true activity of the mind.

In his *Rules for the Direction of the Mind*, Descartes described the transformation of deduction into intuition. In deduction we are aware of a 'movement or sort of sequence' and this sequence is bound up with memory.[22] But with practice the movement of deduction can come to approximate to the superior state of intuition. We can enlarge the capacity of our 'sluggish' intel-ligence by practising a continuous uninterrupted movement of imagination, until we learn to pass from one intuition to others so quickly that memory is left with practically no role to play, and we seem to intuit the whole thing at once.[23]

The passage from deduction to intuition is echoed in the *Meditations* in transitions from fragmentation to continuity and from instability to stasis. Reflection on its dependence on God as cause for its continued existence, as we have seen, plays a central role in Descartes's reasoning about the mind's relations with time. It also plays a central role in the literary structure of the work. At the end of each Meditation, Descartes pauses to reflect, fixing in his mind the truths which have emerged. The reader is guided through a series of pauses in which self-awareness is progressively articulated in the light of what each Meditation has brought to consciousness. Together these reflective moments yield a narrative from the most tenuous to the most secure of holds on self-knowledge and certainty. Their succession gives a sequence of clear and distinct thoughts which enact the mind's transformation from episodic to continuous thinking thing – a transformation centred on its deepening understanding of dependence on God. They also offer a series of shifts between passivity and activity. The mind moves through reflection on the passivity it experiences under the influence of body to an active understanding of itself and of its relations with matter.

In the first Meditation, the narrator's dependence on God is just one belief among others, a firmly rooted and long-standing opinion that there is an omnipotent God who makes him the kind of creature he is. At this stage the belief in God threatens certainty as much as it potentially guarantees it. For all he yet knows, the omnipotent creator could be intent on deceiving him. The rational course is to resolutely withhold assent from all opinions – to actively embrace passivity. But the narrator finds himself at the mercy of his past; the readiness to give assent is habitual. He must not merely note the necessity of withholding assent but must also endeavour to remember it. Habitual opinions keep coming back, capturing belief which is bound over to them as a result of long occupation and the law of custom. To break the grip of habit, turning passivity into activity, he must turn his will completely in the opposite direction and 'deceive himself' by pretending for a time that these former opinions are utterly false and imaginary, until the weight of habit no longer prevents his judgement from perceiving things correctly. Descartes resolves to 'stubbornly and firmly' persist in this Meditation which supposes that some malicious demon of the utmost power and cunning is employing all its energies to deceive him. He enacts the hypothesized state of helpless passivity. But to persist in this withholding of assent is an arduous undertaking; a kind of laziness brings him back to normal life. He is, he reflects, like a prisoner enjoying an imaginary freedom while asleep. Suspecting that he is asleep, he dreads being woken up and goes along with the pleasant illusion as long as he can, for fear that he will have to live not in the light but in the 'inextricable darkness' of the problems he has raised.

At the beginning of the second Meditation, Descartes compares the state of unresolved doubt to the experience of falling into a deep whirlpool which tumbles him around so that he can neither stand on the bottom nor swim to the top – a state of movement with no fixed point. His reflection at the end of the second Meditation conveys a more secure sense of self. In his previous state of mental fluctuation he had only a tenuous hold on existence as a thinking thing. Lacking the ability to hold his intellectual perceptions steady, he could not withhold assent, as reason dictates he should, without lapsing back into the dream-filled sleep of normal mental life. He now knows, however, that his knowledge of bodies comes through intellect rather than sense; and this assures him that he can have an easier and more evident perception of his own mind than of anything else. He finds this easier to impress on his memory than his first hard-won truths. The will's torpor in the face of old habits has receded. Increased self-knowledge brings increased confidence in his capacity for stable certainty. Mind has now learned to separate itself from body, but it does not yet understand its relations to God as sustaining cause, and to this extent self-knowledge remains unstable.

At the end of the third Meditation, his gaze shifts from himself to God. The shift is supposed to occur as a natural outcome of self-reflection. When he turns his gaze on himself, he understands that he is 'a thing which is incomplete and dependent on another'. Reflection on his own imperfections leads him to gaze with wonder and admiration on the perfections of God, so far as the eye of his 'darkened intellect' can bear it. From the knowledge of his own dependence and incompleteness there arises a clear and distinct idea of God's independence and completeness, and he now sees a way forward to the knowledge of other things.

By the end of the fourth Meditation, his newly acquired capacity for sustained attention has given Descartes confidence that he can counter the weakness of mind which has thrown him into turmoil. Out of 'attentive and repeated meditation' comes the habit of avoiding error. This new-found confidence is grounded in the knowledge that his clear and distinct perceptions come from a truthful God. He now knows it is impossible to fall into error, provided he restricts his assent to what is clearly and distinctly perceived; for every such perception is 'undoubtedly something' and hence must have God for its author. Since God is supremely perfect he cannot make the mind capable of undetected error; what is clearly and distinctly perceived must be true.

By the end of the fifth Meditation Descartes is confident that he can extend this certainty back to what he remembers having clearly and distinctly perceived. Certainty can now reach through time. He is no longer pushed into doubt by knowing that he has in the past regarded as true and certain many things he later recognized to be false; for none of those things were clearly and distinctly perceived. Even his former objection – that he might be dreaming – cannot shake his new-found certainty through time. Even though he might be dreaming, he reflects, anything evident to his intellect is wholly true. He now sees that truth and certainty depend on God in such a way that he was incapable of perfect knowledge of anything else until he knew him. He now knows with certainty the nature of all things whose nature is intellectual, and also the whole of that corporeal nature which is the subject matter of pure mathematics. But he does not yet know the existence of matter. This is the last bastion of doubt, which falls in Meditation Six, when reflection on the mind's shifts between activity and passivity comes together with reflection on dependence on God. If his mind could be rendered passive by sensation without the existence of bodies, he reasons, God would have to be a deceiver. The passive faculty of sensory perception demands a correlated activity, either in him or in something else which produces those ideas. Clearly they involve no intellectual activity on his part. Nor could they be produced by God independently of bodies, since the veracious God has given him no faculty to recognize this, and a great propensity to

believe that they come from corporeal things. Descartes's concluding reflections express an easy confidence about the
reliability of sense, memory and intellect, which finds expression
especially in his confidence that he is not dreaming. He can safely
use both memory – connecting present and past experience – and
intellect, which can be relied upon to detect the causes of error.
He need have no further fear then of the falsity of what his senses
tell him every day. On the contrary, his exaggerated fears of the
last few days should be dismissed as laughable. He now sees a
vast difference between dreams, which are never linked by
memory, and waking life. When he can connect his perceptions
with the whole of the rest of his life without a break, he can now
be quite certain that he is awake, although 'the weakness of our
nature' under the pressures of 'things to be done' may often leave
us unable to make such meticulous checks and leave us open to
mistakes about particular things.

Descartes's *Meditations* enact the transition from discontinuity
to continuity, from fragmentation to the unity of consciousness.
In response to Hobbes's objection that he might merely dream
that his present links up with a real past, Descartes insists that
such a dream would give him not a real certainty as a thinking
thing, but only a dreamt one. It would remain a mere episode of
thought. The continuity of consciousness of which Descartes
thinks he is assured at the end of the *Meditations* is not internal to
the content of a thought. That continuity can be given even in
dreams. Nor is it the mind's continuous existence through time;
for that belongs even to atheist thinkers. Nor can it be equated
with memory; there is no suggestion that Descartes thinks that
atheists characteristically have bad memories, any more than
that they are incapable of clear and distinct perception of mathematical truths. What Descartes has found his way to is a different
relationship between consciousness and time. But it is difficult to
articulate it within the restraints of his view of the mind as an
enduring individual intellectual substance.

The Cartesian mind seems to undergo a shift in the course of
the *Meditations* from an individual thinking thing, enduring
through time, to a timeless structure of necessarily connected
clear and distinct ideas. Each of us is invited to participate, as an
individual consciousness, in the process of self-discovery
through the Cartesian method. But to the extent that the reflections that make up the *Meditations* are successfully performed, all

individuality seems to collapse into an unindividuated, timeless chain of clear and distinct ideas. It is not clear then how this underlying unified self is supposed to ground the individual mind's assurance of its continuity of consciousness. Having started as an individual sequence of mental states, the mind – to the extent that it attains to clear and distinct ideas – becomes a timeless universal structure of entailments. By the end of the *Meditations*, the mind is supposed to understand itself as stretching back in time, extending its certainty back from the present into the past. But this is not a sequence of clear and distinct ideas necessarily connected. That, to the extent that it is achieved, disappears into the timeless structure of entailments making up a unified science.

What is the 'connecting up' which Descartes, in response to Hobbes, is so confident about? From the perspective of later developments in the articulation of the problem of unity of consciousness, we can see distinctions here of which Descartes himself was not aware. It is not a sequence of mental states that might be thought to make up a narrative of a life. For that, since it does not consist entirely – or even very much at all – of clear and distinct ideas, is not necessarily connected. Why then is Descartes so confident that his consciousness does indeed reach into the past? And what exactly is this unity of consciousness which can be equated neither with endurance through time nor with an internal content of a single thought? The question finds no satisfactory answer within Descartes's philosophy. But, given that it is not clear that Descartes was really aware of the nature of the question, this is hardly surprising. There are, in effect, two kinds of self about which we are supposed to feel assured by the end of the *Meditations* – the timeless structure of necessarily connected clear and distinct ideas to which each of us has access through the Cartesian method, although it is achieved only in rare moments in the course of normal human life; and that individual continuity of consciousness whose certainty stretches back from present into past. The second is supposed to be grounded in the first. Knowledge that this is the true nature of the self is supposed to assure us that our present consciousness does in fact connect up with a real past. But what is the nature of the connections between the present of this stretched out consciousness and its past? Descartes's necessary connections can yield no such unity of consciousness, for they hold only between clear and distinct ideas. Nor is it clear that the mind's status as individual substance can ground this unity of consciousness. For that would seem to assure only the existence of mind through time of the kind granted even to atheist dreamers. Hume, having rejected both necessary connections and substance, struggles unsuccessfully with the problem of unity of consciousness. But it is a problem even within the Cartesian philosophy. Kant, we will see, offers a kind of resolution, in his transcendental deduction of the categories, by relating the unity of consciousness more closely than Descartes did to the necessary connections of ideas. In the process Kant greatly sophisticates the understanding of the relations between time and consciousness.

## HUME'S LABYRINTH AND THE PAINTING OF MODERN LIFE

### HUME AND THE UNITY OF CONSCIOUSNESS

For Descartes, the fragmentation of self-consciousness is overcome at the level of clear and distinct ideas, necessarily connected – the universal deep structure of the mind, revealed by Cartesian method beneath the confusion of its intermingling with body. However there are unresolved problems, as we have seen, about how the unity of this idealized structure of clear and distinct ideas grounds the unity of past and present consciousness. For Hume, the unity of consciousness is located nearer the surface of everyday thought. It has less to do with intellect than with passions and imagination. But he too has difficulties in providing a coherent account of how it is secured.

It may at first sight seem strange to think of Hume as at all concerned with the problem of the unity of consciousness. In the famous sections on personal identity in the *Treatise*, after all, he insists that the self is a mere bundle of impressions and ideas – connected not by necessary connections, but only by habit and custom operating in accordance with 'principles of association'. For Hume there can be no necessary connections between discrete episodes of consciousness. Nor is there any mental substance in which they could be unified. The mind is 'but a bundle or collection of different perceptions, which succeed each other with an inconceivable rapidity, and are in a perpetual flux and movement'.[1] The unity of consciousness is to be thought of not through analogies of unified dance movements, but through the famous metaphor of the theatre 'where several perceptions successively make their appearance; pass, re-pass, glide away, and mingle in an infinite variety of postures and situations'.[2] We must not be misled by the comparison, he insists, even into thinking of the mind as a permanent place within which scenes are represented. It is 'successive perceptions only' that constitute the mind.

Despite his confident assertion of the bundle theory in the sections on personal identity, however, Hume himself was aware of a deep problem in his treatment of self-consciousness – a problem about which he expresses dismay in the appendix to the work,[3] and which has since perplexed commentators. He had entertained some hopes, he says, that however deficient his theory of the intellectual world might be, it would be free from those contradictions and absurdities which seem to attend every explication that human reason can give of the material world. But, upon a more strict review of the sections on personal identity, he finds himself involved in such a labyrinth that he must confess he knows neither how to correct his former opinions, nor how to render them consistent. All our perceptions, he has claimed, are distinct existences, which form a whole only by being connected together. But he has also claimed that no connections between distinct existences are ever discoverable by human understanding. We only feel a connection or determination of thought to pass from one object to another. It follows that 'thought alone finds personal identity'. When we reflect on the 'train of past perceptions that compose a mind', the ideas of them are 'felt to be connected together' and 'naturally introduce each other'.

The idea that personal identity arises from consciousness, and that consciousness is nothing but a 'reflected thought or perception', Hume remarks, is not a philosophical novelty. But it poses, he now sees, a serious difficulty for him. All his hopes now vanish, he says, when he comes to explain the principles that unite our successive perceptions in our thought or consciousness. He cannot discover any theory which will allow him to reconcile two principles, neither of which he can renounce: the first, that all our perceptions are distinct existences; the second, that the mind never perceives any real connections among distinct existences. He would be saved, he thinks, if it were the case that our perceptions inhered in something simple and individual, or if the mind perceived some real connection among them. In the lack of either of these escape routes, he must 'plead the privilege of a sceptic' and confess that this difficulty is too hard for his understanding. 'I pretend not, however, to pronounce it absolutely insuperable. Others, perhaps, or myself, upon more mature reflexions, may discover some hypothesis, that will reconcile those contradictions.'

Hume's 'dismay' is evident. But it is by no means clear what exactly his problem is. As commentators have pointed out, Hume's two propositions – that all our perceptions are distinct existences, and that the mind never perceives any real connections between distinct existences – are not themselves contradictory. And together they seem in fact to amount just to the view of the self as a mere bundle of perceptions, held together only by principles of association – the view he has so confidently asserted in the discussion of personal identity in the text. What exactly is the problem he now sees? The fact that Hume addresses the issue of the unity of successive episodes of thought in the context of the consideration of personal identity may give us a false lead here. For the real issue is how we are to understand the relations between consciousness and time: in the lack of both substance and necessary connections, how can distinct episodes of consciousness form a unity?

The fact that Hume raises the issue in relation to the adequacy of his treatment of personal identity can here distract us from the real nature of his problem. There is more at stake here than finding the correct criteria for the application of the concept of personal identity. Hume's analysis of concepts typically involves telling the story of their origins – the story of how we come by them. His problem concerns the possibility of telling such a story at all in the case of personal identity. There are difficulties here of a kind which do not beset his accounts of our beliefs about other things that endure through time. For the general form of Hume's account of how we come by a belief is in terms of the operation of principles of association between perceptions. But being able to tell that kind of story presupposes that there is unity of consciousness within which those principles of association operate. In offering an account of how we come by the belief in personal identity, Hume seems involved in an unavoidable circularity.

This aspect of the problem was perceptively diagnosed by Barry Stroud in his book *Hume*.[4]

In Stroud's formulation of the problem, Humes's dissatisfaction expresses a profound sense of some conflict or obstacle at the very heart of the concerns of the *Treatise*. It is as if something written into the theory of ideas itself renders impossible his task of explaining the origin of all our fundamental ideas. The whole enterprise presupposes the centrality, the ineradicability of the idea of 'one self or mind' in Hume's science of human nature. So there is an important question about self-consciousness in relation to which Hume now seems to realize his inability to say anything – something to which the theory of ideas and its consequences make an answer impossible. Hume must take it as simply a basic inexplicable fact that for any one of us a survey of past perceptions will not extend to all the perceptions there have ever been. It must be taken as a given fact about the universe of perceptions that the range of reflective vision of any one of them does not extend to all the rest. And it is only because one's gaze is thus restricted to a subset of the totality of perceptions that it is possible to get an idea of one's self.

Hume's problem, on Stroud's diagnosis, thus arises at a deeper level than how we get from the data of perception to particular beliefs. It is the problem of why the data are divided into different 'bundles' in the first place. For Hume's science of human nature to be workable, he argues, it would have to be somehow discernible that perceptions occurred only as members of particular series – as if they came already tied together into bundles, so that no member of a particular series could be a perception of any outside that series. But how could that be, on Hume's theory? For all perceptions are for him distinct existences; and so each of them could exist independently of every other and of everything else in the universe. There is nothing intrinsic to a perception that connects it with one series rather than another. So why do perceptions present themselves, so to speak, in separate bundles? If there were either spiritual substances in which sets of perceptions inhered, or some 'real' connections between the subsets, this would perhaps explain why each of us is presented with only some perceptions. Perceptions would then really come in separate bundles. So Hume's explanation of our belief in personal identity seems to depend on a fact which must remain inexplicable in terms of the theory –

that the scope of one's experience does not extend to all the perceptions that there are.

Although Stroud's diagnosis takes us in the right direction, there is, I think, an important dimension of Hume's problem which it does not capture. As Hume sees it, his problem is one that could be resolved either by inherence of ideas in a substance or through necessary connections between ideas. This suggests not only that it is not a problem about the analysis of the concept of personal identity, but also that it is not really a problem about the distinction between individual selves at all – that it is a different problem about the unity of consciousness.

In rejecting necessary connections, Hume is rejecting the relations of entailment which the rationalists saw as binding ideas together. Those necessary connections between ideas do not of themselves yield any distinction between different selves. For Descartes, that was provided by the different intellectual substances in which ideas occur, although all such intellectual substances share a common structure, given by the innate ideas which pertain to their nature. For Spinoza, too, the necessary connections between ideas in no way yield a difference between individual minds. For him, that is provided by the distinctions between the individual bodies of which our minds are ideas. Personal identity, if that is construed as an issue of the differentiation of individual selves, is not what is at issue in the unity of consciousness which Hume is trying to secure. His problem is about the relations between consciousness and time – how successive perceptions come together to form one consciousness. The problem concerns not how we individuate temporally coexisting consciousnesses, but rather how consciousness reaches through time.

Even if Hume thought there were only one self in existence – although of course as a good sceptic he could not claim to know that – the problem which reduces him to dismay in the appendix would remain. His real problem lies in getting a workable distinction between the intellectual world – in which all our beliefs can be, if not justified, at least explained in their origins – and that other world, supposedly there as independent object of knowledge, the world philosophers have been unable to describe without contradictions and absurdities. The science of human nature demands this shift of focus, to the realm of mental life, which we have some hope of understanding and exploring without incoherence.

> Let us fix our attention out of ourselves as much as possible: let us chace our imagination to the heavens, or to the utmost limits of the universe; we never really advance a step beyond ourselves, nor can conceive any kind of existence, but those perceptions, which have appear'd in that narrow compass. This is the universe of the imagination, nor have we any idea but what is there produc'd.[5]

When Hume says, early in the appendix, that what has deserted him is the hope that he might avoid in this intellectual world the contradictions and absurdities of the supposed other one, he means the distinction to be taken quite seriously. What dismays him is that he seems to have found an absurdity in the intellectual world, an absurdity which seems indeed to undermine the very existence of that world and hence the very possibility of the crucial shift of focus on which the whole enterprise of the *Treatise* depends. For here the story of how we come by a belief cannot coherently be told.

In telling Humean stories of the origin of beliefs, we must presuppose that principles of association operate to ensure that subsets of impressions and ideas coalesce within the wider totality. It all presupposes a unifying frame – a unifying 'subject', as we might now say. And this is what Hume cannot presuppose – an intellectual world within which the principles of association could operate to produce subgroups of perceptions. Principles of association can bring about a coalescing of impressions and ideas into subsets, groupings which stand out within the bundle. But how could such a story be told of the belief in unified consciousness itself, within which the operations of principles of association must go on? The central problem is not about the distinction between individual minds. It is rather about that idea of an intellectual world which is for Hume prior to our beliefs in any enduring objects – the 'world', within which supposedly enduring objects are constructed. On what – or in what – do those principles of association operate?

The 'cement of the universe' may, as Hume suggests in the *Inquiry*, be habit. But what gives unity to the intellectual universe presupposed by the principles of association? It would be all very well if Hume thought the bundle which is an individual mind were accommodated into a wider intellectual whole – as in Spinoza's version of the mind of God, the totality of thought. But the coherence of that model – even if Hume wanted it – demands necessary connections between ideas. The point is that we need thought or mind within which the bundles can form. If there is no wider totality of thought within which individual bundles might coalesce, standing out as sub-unities, does not the whole picture fall apart? Without the unity of mind, we cannot make sense of the operations of the principles of association. But all that Hume has allowed himself to account for this unity is the operation of such principles of association.

Hume has internalized the 'external world' into his intellectual world. But rather than yielding the great advance in knowledge which he had hoped – the end of absurdities and contradictions – this new world has provided a site for a fundamental absurdity at the heart of things. We can talk coherently of the formation of certain kinds of self-consciousness within the 'bundle'. Thus Hume is able to show in Book Two how pride can produce a form of self-consciousness which involves how others perceive us. What he cannot do is account for a prior form of self-consciousness – the 'unity of apperception', as Kant later called it – within which imagination and passions can carry out their productive role. Hume's problem is not so much about how he can be one self among others, but about how his experiences come together as a mental world. The possibility of making connections within a mental world presupposes that there is already a kind of unity of consciousness. And it is in accounting for this unity that Hume has difficulty. Descartes, we have seen, considered the possibility that the projection of his self-consciousness back in time might amount, not to any real continuity of consciousness through time, but only to an internal and perhaps delusory content of a single episode of thought. And he thought this doubt could be resolved through the mind's acceptance of its dependence on a veracious God. For Hume, of course, any such resolution of the doubt would conflict with his embargo on the application of ideas beyond the limits of what can be derived from the content of impressions. To get clearer about the problem, it will help to look at the section on the immateriality of the soul, immediately preceding that on personal identity – Hume's discussion of Spinoza,[6] which is echoed in his puzzling remarks in the appendix.

In this section, Hume makes explicit the shift to the mental world, which is the cornerstone of his scepticism. Having found such contradictions and difficulties in every system concerning external objects, and in the idea of matter, which 'we fancy so clear and determinate', we might, he says, expect still greater difficulties in hypotheses concerning the nature of the mind, which we are apt to imagine so much more obscure and uncertain. But in this we should deceive ourselves. The intellectual world, though involved in 'infinite obscurities', avoids the contradictions we discover in the natural. 'What is known concerning it, agrees with itself; and what is unknown, we must be contented to leave so.'

It is this confidence about the intellectual world – achieved through the shift from concern with a supposedly external reality to the study of human nature – that is shaken in the appendix. The intellectual world must be subject to the same stringent standards of coherence and consistency that we apply to the supposed external world. Otherwise we would be applying to ideas something that cannot be found in impressions – in breach of Hume's fundamental principles of empiricism. Hume makes the point, with trenchant irony, in his discussion of the doctrines of the 'infamous' Spinoza, comparing the doctrine of the theologians – that all perceptions inhere in a spiritual substance – with the Spinozistic doctrine that all material things are modifications of one substance. Since whatever is in an idea is derived from a corresponding impression, whatever is intelligible or consistent with regard to objects must be so with regard to perceptions. But it is intelligible and consistent to say that this table and that chimney exist separately. So we must be able to say that with regard to perceptions. If such independence is to be the definition of substance, then all our perceptions would satisfy the criterion. The consequences for the theory of the self as substance are devastating.

The doctrine of a substantial self in which perceptions inhere, Hume argues, has the same structure as Spinoza's atheistic view of the material world. He goes on to cunningly present the theological belief in the soul as 'a true atheism which will serve to justify all those sentiments, for which Spinoza is so universally infamous'. There is only one substance in the world, says Spinoza, and that substance is perfectly simple and indivisible. Everything else is nothing but a modification of the one, simple and necessarily existent being, lacking any separate or distinct existence. But the doctrine of the theologians is comparable to these 'gloomy and obscure regions of Spinoza's thought'. Spinoza's 'hideous hypothesis' is almost the same as that of the immateriality of the soul which has become, in contrast, so popular. We are presented then with two different systems of being, to which we are expected to assign some 'substance, or ground of inhesion'. He observes, first, he says, the universe of objects or of body, including both natural and artificial things. 'Here *Spinoza* appears, and tells me, that these are only modifications; and that the subject, in which they inhere, is simple, uncompounded, and indivisible.' He then considers the other system of beings, the 'universe of thought', of impressions and ideas. There he observes another sun, moon and stars and everything he can discover or conceive in the first system. Upon his enquiry concerning these, theologians present themselves, and tell him that these also are modifications of one simple, uncompounded and indivisible substance. 'Immediately upon which I am deafen'd with the noise of a hundred voices, that treat the first hypothesis with detestation and scorn, and the second with applause and veneration.'[7] When he tries to discover the reason for this partiality, Hume complains, he finds that they have the same fault of being unintelligible, and that they are so much alike it is impossible to discover any absurdity in one which is not common to both.

The second 'system of beings' – the mental realm of impressions and ideas – is properly understood, Hume thinks, as a collection of distinct and separable mental items, held together in accordance with principles of association. This provides his great hope of deliverance from futile attempts to know an 'external' world. Hence his dismay at the eruption of contradictions and absurdities in the mental realm. Its very existence as a collection of distinct items seems to make it impossible for it to provide the unity of consciousness in which principles of association might operate. The other system of beings – the external world – is supposed to be generated out of this one by the coalescing of perceptions in accordance with the principles of association. But the coherence of that story demands a real unity of consciousness which the framework is unable to support.

The central problem, then, is not the distinction between individual selves. In terms of Kant's distinction, to be discussed in the next section, Hume's problem concerns not the 'empirical' self, but the 'unity of apperception'. But Kant's distinctions between the different aspects of selfhood were not available to Hume. Nor can Hume's empiricism accommodate the Kantian claim that representations can stand together in a unified consciousness only on the assumption that they are held together by necessary connections. Kant's synthetic *a priori* judgements can forge the crucial distinction between 'subjective' consciousness and 'objective' world which eludes Hume. His hope, expressed in the appendix, that later thinkers might resolve his dilemma is in some ways realized, as we shall see, in Kant's reinstatement, in a more sophisticated form, of a metaphysics of the self. But here I want to try another response to Hume's plea for help, which takes us in a different direction from the metaphysics of selfhood.

## NARRATIVE UNITY AND THE ASSOCIATION OF IDEAS

Hume's discussion of the association of ideas in the third section of the *Inquiry* begins – perhaps strangely – with a discussion of conversation. Even in our 'wildest and most wandering reveries', he says, even in our very dreams, we find that the imagination 'ran not altogether at adventures'. There is always a connection among the succession of ideas. 'Were the loosest and freest conversation to be transcribed, there would immediately be observed something which connected it in all its transitions.' Here Hume's concern with principles of association is framed by an interest in the unity connecting threads of discourse. And his treatment of what makes that unity gives us a very different picture of our mental life from the one associated with rationalism. The view of mental life offered in Descartes's *Rules for the Direction of the Mind*, as we have seen, is of a sequence of clear and distinct ideas necessarily connected – a chain of deductions which, in the well-functioning mind, can come to approximate to the unity of a single, clear and distinct perception – what Descartes calls an intellectual 'intuition'. Even for Descartes, of course, our ordinary mental life is not like that. Rather it is a buzzing confusion of sensation, images, passions, resulting from the intermingling of mind and body – a confusion to which we must bring order by following the Cartesian method. But for Descartes nonetheless it is that order of clear and distinct ideas, necessarily connected, that constitutes the true structure of the mind. This is mental life as it would be, if only mind could operate in the way that accords with its own nature, unobstructed by the intrusions of body. Hume is saying that the unity of our mental life is not like that, even at the ideal level. What makes it all hang together is not the grasp of necessary connections, but rather principles of association of the kind that govern the art of conversation.

We have here a shift from the kind of question Hume asked about the self in the sections on personal identity in the *Treatise*, or at any rate a shift of emphasis, which points away from the metaphysics of the self towards the articulation of the experience of selfhood in the sociable world. His concern here is with that world of 'conversation' in which we come to self-consciousness. The question now is: what are the principles of connection that operate in mental life, as instanced in our conversation, our thinking – even perhaps our dreaming? Hume's suggestion is that we try to understand the unity of mental life on the analogy of the unifying associations which operate in conversation. The task is to understand our mental life – how it is organized, how it all hangs together, its distinctive style. For Descartes of course there was only one way in which mental life could hang together, once the distorting intrusions of body were shed. True mental life must follow necessary connections grasped in processes of deduction. For Hume, space opens up to consider the contingency of our mental. life.

In an intriguing section which appears in only some versions of the text,[8] Hume goes on to elaborate the point with reference to the principles of unity which operate in different kinds of written narrative. Different principles of association – resemblance, contiguity or cause and effect – have primacy in different kinds of narrative. Unity takes different forms in different literary genres. This is a 'field of instruction more entertaining and perhaps more instructive', he suggests, for understanding the principles of association than in the abstract. The question is how 'unity of action' is achieved in narrative composition – how events or actions are to be brought together under one 'plan or view'. Hume presents himself as trying to bring the accuracy of philosophy to bear on understanding the principle of unity of action which has been talked of by critics since Aristotle. The connecting principles vary according to the different designs of the poet or historian. For Ovid's narrative of metamorphoses, the connecting principle is resemblance. For an annalist or historian writing the history of Europe, in contrast, it is the connection of contiguity in time and place. But the most usual species of connection among different events which enter into any narrative composition is that of cause and effect.

Hume uses the analogy of the different forms of narrative to make the point that there is a variety of ways in which the mental world can be unified. There is no one way in which perceptions must come together, any more than there is just one form of narrative unity. The demand for unity of action applies just as much, he says, to a biographer of Achilles, connecting events by showing their mutual dependence and relation, as to a poet describing Achilles's anger.

> Not only in any limited portion of life a man's actions have a dependence on each other, but also during the whole period of his duration from the cradle to the grave; nor is it possible to strike off one link, however minute, in this regular chain without affecting the whole series of events which follow.[9]

But the application of unity of action in biography differs from its application in poetry. Here the interaction of passions and imagination, inflaming the one and enlivening the other, demands a stricter and closer attention to unity in the narration. And it is in his discussion of epic poetry that Hume draws the most interesting connections between narrative unity and the unity of consciousness.

Poetry, says Hume, is a species of painting. It brings us nearer the objects than any other species of narration, throwing a stronger light on them, and delineating more distinctly those minute circumstances which, though they may seem superfluous to the historian, 'serve mightily to enliven the imagery and gratify the fancy'. Because of the greater demands it places on the reader's imagination and passions, poetry cannot comprehend such a great compass of time or series of events without wearying the reader. The agitation of imagination and passions would induce overload. The reader's imagination and passion must flag long before the period of narration and must 'sink into lassitude and disgust from the repeated violence of the same movements.' So the epic poet must both restrict his 'canvas' to avoid emotional overload, and also ensure that the connections between events are preserved. For the connections between the events, grasped by the imagination, emphasize the easy transition of the passions from one to another. Our sympathy and concern for Eve prepares the way for a like sympathy with Adam. But if the poet introduced new actors, in no way involved with the familiar ones, the imagination, feeling the discontinuity, would 'enter coldly into the new scene, would kindle by slow degrees; and in returning to the main subject of the poem would pass, as it were, upon foreign ground'.

The poet must take care not to break the course of the passions – to see that the emotional force of one scene is transferred easily to the next until the whole produces that 'rapidity of movement which is peculiar to the theatre'. If we are suddenly introduced to new personages in no way related to those already present, the steady course of passion is interrupted, extinguishing this 'warmth of affection'. Instead of carrying sympathy from one scene to the next, we are obliged every moment to excite a new concern and take part in a new scene of action. Narrative poetry, in contrast to drama, demands an authorial plan or design, comprehending the subject in some 'general aspect or united view'. There is an authorial presence in the narrative which contrasts with the way the author is 'entirely lost' in dramatic composition, where the spectator is taken into a direct presence, as it were, at the actions represented. On the stage, any dialogue or conversation may be introduced, provided it could, without improbability, be imagined to have occurred in that determinate portion of space represented by the theatre. Thus, Hume comments, the unity of action is never strictly observed in English comedies. It is enough that the characters be related to one another by blood or living in the same family. They are allowed to display their 'humours or characters' without advancing the main action. What is permissible turns, again, on the level of emotional involvement demanded. Relative indifference to unity of action is all very well in comedy, but is inappropriate to tragedy, where the passions aroused are more intense.

Hume stresses that the restraints of unity of action apply to the writing of history as well as to other kinds of narration, although it requires a less close attention to unity than narrative poetry because of its less intense involvement of imagination and passions. In the historical narrative what unites events is cause and effect, as in the case of the epic poem. But poetry requires a closer attention to unity. 'The Peloponnesian War is a proper subject for history, the siege of Athens for an epic poem, and the death of Alcibiades for a tragedy.' But what separates history and poetry is only a matter of degree. So it may be objected to Milton that he traces his causes to too great a distance, that the connection of events by cause and effect is tenuous. The creation of the world, which Milton relates at length, is no more the cause of Adam's fall than it is of the battle of Pharsalis. But there are nonetheless, Hume ironically suggests, some relations of resemblance and contiguity in Milton's narration: they are all miraculous; and there is enough contiguity in time between the creation of the world, the rebellion of the angels, the fall of man, for the work to satisfy the demands of unity of action. Even Milton, it seems, satisfies the principles of unity of action, although Hume implies that the operation of association is somewhat tenuous here.

Hume presents this discussion of the unity of action in narrative as 'loose hints' towards understanding the dependence of the human mind on principles of association. It illustrates especially, he stresses in conclusion, the remarkable sympathy between the passions and the imagination. In Descartes's treatment of the unity of consciousness, what is crucial is the necessary connections grasped through intellect. Passions and imagination belong to mind's intermingling with body, rather than to the unified structure of pure thought. For Hume, in contrast, passions and imagination become crucial to understanding the principles of unity of consciousness. In Book Two of the *Treatise* Hume presented the interactions of passions and imagination as a powerful force in the production of beliefs. Pride, he says there, both presupposes and produces the idea of the self.[10] My awareness of myself as owner of a beautiful house – without which pride could not operate – is transformed into a different form of self-consciousness, centred on how others perceive me. Through pride I pass from a focus on the house, as object of my ownership, to myself as its owner. In these passages in the *Inquiry*, Hume directs his readers to another feature of the interactions of passion and imagination – its role in that form of self-consciousness which is presupposed by pride, as distinct from the one that is produced by it. The interaction of passion and imagination is crucial in the constitution of the mental world which is presupposed by the formation of the individual self-consciousness related to pride and shame.

The discussion of association in the *Inquiry* allows us to separate out more clearly the two kinds of concern with self-consciousness – on the one hand, the unity of mental life; on the other, the question of the self as one among others. In these intriguing passages on literary genres, we are invited to consider the forms of our shared mental life – to position ourselves within a continuing 'conversation' and try to apprehend the principles of connection that operate within it. Hume invites us to consider the constitution of our mental life, on the model of writing a narrative, subject to the restraints of unity of action.

The theme of conversation is a favourite one in Hume's *Essays*, and is indeed central in his conception of essay-writing itself as a literary genre. In the essay on 'Essay Writing' he talks of the essay as bridging the regrettable gulf between the 'learned' and the 'conversable' worlds. Even philosophy, he complains there, has been wrecked by this 'moping recluse method of study', becoming as chimerical in her conclusions as she is unintelligible in her style and manner of delivery – all of which is what we should expect from thinkers who 'never consulted experience in any of their reasonings, or who never searched for that experience where alone it is to be found – in common life and conversation'.[11] The concern with 'experience', which is the touchstone of Hume's empiricism here, has as its context the social enactment of mental life in conversation.

The shift from the attempt to know an 'external' world to the understanding of the intellectual world is, as we saw earlier, crucial to Hume's science of human nature. It is the basis of his version of scepticism. The 'loose hints' of the *Inquiry* passage reinforce what is distinctive about that scepticism. We can tell stories about the origins of particular beliefs. But we cannot tell the same kind of story about the origins of the intellectual world. Here we cannot ask even how we came by it. There is no answer to the question in that form. We should not ask about its origins or about its supposed reference to something 'external'. We must take it as it comes. But we can try to understand from within how it works. We always find ourselves within the mental, the 'conversable' world. Understanding its operations becomes not a matter of the metaphysics of selfhood, but a question of style – of grasping the characteristic features of our mental life.

Seen in this light, Hume's concerns with the unity of consciousness can be seen as having affinities with some of those
later writers on the time-consciousness of modernity which I
mentioned in the Introduction. They too stressed the relations
between time-consciousness and the interactions of passion and
imagination. Hume's collapse of the rationalist distinctions between inner and outer worlds echo in Simmel's talk of the
essence of modernity as psychologism with its dissolution of
fixed contents into the fluid elements of the soul. Simmel's and
Baudelaire's talk of the fragmentation of consciousness has to a
philosophical reader striking affinities with the fragmented self
of Hume. There are resonances of Hume in these later writings on
the self-consciousness of modernity, although it may be an
overstatement of these similarities to cast Hume in the role of
Baudelaire's 'painter of modern life'.

Hume's 'loose hints' on the interaction of passion and imagination in different forms of mental life can be seen as offering a
potential resolution of his own problem about the *Treatise*,
though what we get – as so often in the history of philosophy – is
not so much an answer to the question as a reformulation of it.
The unresolvable problem of the *Treatise* – 'how can the fragments of consciousness form a unity?' – gives way to a less
metaphysical question: 'what are the principles, the characteristic forms of association which bring ever-reforming patterns of
coherence to our mental life?' There is no one unity of consciousness, but as many as we can provide through the narratives in
which we weave the scattered fragments of our consciousness.
Baudelaire and Simmel both stress the contingency of the self-
consciousness of modernity – the distinctiveness of consciousness at a particular period of time. Simmel talks of 'dropping a
sounding' into the depths of the psyche, finding in the most
banal externalities of life connections with its ultimate meaning
and 'style'.[12] Baudelaire talks of uncovering in the present the
unique 'gait, glance and gesture' which distinguishes a period of
history.[13] Hume's 'loose hints' do little more than gesture at these
issues. But in them we can see the 'science of human nature'
begin to shake off the legacy of the aspiration to timeless truth
about the nature of mind and world and move towards the more
historical self-consciousness of modernity.

# KANT: THE UNITY OF APPERCEPTION

The philosophical problem of unity of consciousness is different from the more familiar one of personal identity, although it is not readily extricated from it. Personal identity is an issue of individuation – how to identify a self as one among others. The problem of unity of consciousness concerns rather how a consciousness understands itself as unified. The relations between time and consciousness are central to this issue. For Descartes it took the form of extending certainty beyond the immediacy of the present. Once a mind is assured of the truth of its clear and distinct ideas even when it is not attending to them, its certainty stretches through time. The cramped consciousness of the atheist in contrast is stranded – as far as certainty is concerned – in the present. The Cartesian mind's capacity to know itself as a unified consciousness depends on its capacity to render its ideas clear and distinct and to link them in necessarily connected deductive chains. The necessity of these connections transcends time. But unless clear and distinct consciousness can transcend the present, there can be no such deductive chains, no true knowledge and no true self-consciousness. Descartes's version of the unity of consciousness can, I suggested, be seen as a reflective analogue of the soul's existence through time as an individual substance through being sustained by the preservative force of God.

Hume, having repudiated both necessary connections and the idea of substance, found himself with an irresolvable difficulty in accounting for the unity of consciousness. Although Hume's formulation of the problem does not explicitly relate it to time, it is clear that the issue for him too concerns the capacity of consciousness to transcend the immediate awareness of a present state. Let us now see what becomes of this problem in the more complex theoretical framework of Kant's treatment of self-consciousness and its relations to time in the *Critique of Pure Reason*.[1]

## SELF-CONSCIOUSNESS AND NECESSARY CONNECTION

Kant regarded Humean association of ideas as useless for securing unity of consciousness. Hume himself, as we have seen, had come to this view by the time he wrote the appendix to the *Treatise*. But whereas Hume claims the dilemma is too much for him, Kant tries to resolve it by reasserting a version of the rationalist necessary connections which Hume rejected. Kant's 'unity of apperception' is possible only on the assumption of necessary connections between mental representations. But his version of these necessary connections leaves intact Hume's conviction that they cannot yield any genuine knowledge of objects.

In the *Critique of Pure Reason* Kant offers a 'transcendental deduction' of the categories which necessarily organize our experience, arguing that their necessity is a presupposition of our experiences occurring in a unified consciousness (A96–130/B 130–169; K.S. 130–75). In the course of that argument, Kant distinguishes between a merely 'empirical' association of mental items – a 'synthesis of reproduction in the imagination' – and a higher exercise of the imagination which it presupposes – a 'pure transcendental synthesis of imagination', which conditions the very possibility of all experience. The empirical synthesis resembles Humean 'association'. Representations which have often followed or accompanied one another finally become associated, so that one can, 'in accordance with a fixed rule, bring about a transition of the mind to the other'. If there were no possibility of reproducing appearances, experience would be impossible. But in the lack of the higher 'transcendental' synthesis, Humean association of ideas would never find opportunity for 'exercise appropriate to its powers'. The power to associate ideas would remain concealed within the mind as a 'dead and to us unknown faculty' (A100; K.S. 132). This higher synthesis involves the subjection of appearances to rules – to necessary order, articulated in the categories. If there were no objective order governing the manifold of appearances, neither could we have the operation of merely empirical association. Without necessary connections, our perceptions would not belong to any experience and would consequently be without an object, merely a 'blind play of representations, less even than a dream' (A112; K.S. 139).

Hume's problem is dissolved. The question as to how associations of ideas yield a unified consciousness can arise only on the assumption that there are necessary connections governing our representations. Otherwise there would be no 'empirical' associations of ideas to consider. The unity of consciousness and the necessity of the categories stand or fall together. It is necessary that in my knowledge all consciousness should belong to a single consciousness – that of myself. But that unity demands an 'objective ground' for the association of appearances – that they fit necessarily into a 'connected whole of human knowledge' (A122; K.S. 145). A consciousness in which a multitude of perceptions existed in a state of separation would not belong to a consciousness of myself. But for Kant that is impossible; for it is only because I ascribe all perceptions to one consciousness that I can say that I am conscious of them. What Kant calls the 'unity of apperception' really amounts, he says, to just the same thing as the interconnected unity of thought. To say that representations are 'mine' is really just to say that they stand together in thought. To assert that they are in this way 'one and all in me' – that they are 'determinations of my identical self' – is only another way of saying that there must be a complete unity of them in one and the same apperception (A129; K.S. 149).

Kant's treatment of self-consciousness also points forward from the unresolved obscurities in Descartes's treatment of the relations between time and the self. We saw the essential Cartesian self emerge as a strangely unindividuated thinking thing which has nonetheless the status of individual substance; and it remained unclear how Descartes's ideal of a unified structure of necessarily connected ideas was supposed to assure the continuity of consciousness stretching back from present into past. For Kant the individual self becomes the determined self of inner sense, while the 'transcendental' self ceases to be anything that could fall under the category of substance. Because this 'I think' is presupposed by all objects of knowledge, it cannot itself be known as object. To see how this transformation of the Cartesian thinking thing occurs, and the important ramifications it has in the understanding of time and consciousness, we must first look at some of the most obscure, but also richest, sections of Kant's Transcendental Deduction.

Kant's argument for the interconnection of the unity of consciousness and the necessity of the categories rests on a 'fundamental observation' about the relations between consciousness and time: that all our representations, whether they be due to the influence of 'outer things' or produced through 'inner causes', belong to the mind's inner experience – to what he calls 'inner sense'. Earlier, in the Transcendental Aesthetic, he argued that time is the formal condition of inner sense, necessarily structuring all our experience. All our knowledge is thus 'finally subject to time' (A99; K.S. 131). If we could not distinguish time in the sequence of one representation upon another, the single representations would be useless for knowledge. For each of them in so far as it is contained in a single moment can never be anything but self-contained unity. That we can grasp representations in time is thus essential to all knowledge; but this in turn, Kant argues, demands a synthesis – a 'running through' and 'holding together' of the given manifold.

Kant's 'act of synthesis' is crucial to his versions of the unity of apperception and of the relations between consciousness and time. But its nature, and especially its status as an act, are obscure. Through it, Kant conceives the unity of consciousness as having the status of an act. Experience would be impossible if appearances were not reproducible; and this demands not just the passive retention of traces of former experience, but also a capacity to enact a mental process. Synthesis involves the mind's attention – not just as passive observer of change but also as participant in a process. This act, like others, involves time. The representations that figure in it must be apprehended by thought, one after another. But it is also a precondition for our experience even of time itself. Synthesis makes possible the representation of time. If a manifold of representations is to form a whole, it must have a unity which allows us to be conscious that what we think is the same as what we thought a moment before.

In the second edition version of the transcendental deduction, Kant goes into more detail on the important notion of synthesis. The 'I think' which marks the unity of apperception must be able to accompany all my representations. Otherwise something would be represented in me which could not be thought at all – a representation which would be 'nothing to me'. Unless I can grasp the manifold of representations in one consciousness, calling them one and all 'mine', I should have 'as many-coloured and diverse a self as I have representations of which I am conscious to myself' (B134; K.S. 154). But, because it must accompany all representations, this 'I think' cannot itself be accompanied by any further representation. It could yield an object of knowledge only if our understanding were 'intuitive', rather than having to depend on sensibility. But for intuition we must look to the senses. Human understanding of itself knows nothing whatever but merely 'combines and arranges the material for knowledge'. We discern its synthesizing activity only in its outcome. The act of synthesis is therefore as inaccessible and as unable to provide its own objects in the case of the mind itself as with regard to the rest of reality. Here the Kantian self seems to be disintegrating into paradox. But its tensions take us into new depths in understanding the relations between consciousness and time. Inner sense represents to consciousness even our own selves only as we appear to ourselves, not as we are in ourselves (B153; K.S. 166). We intuit ourselves 'only as we are inwardly affected' – that is, under the form of time. Here the self seems to be put into a contradictory state – a passive relation of active affection towards itself. How could a self be passive in relation to its own activity? Kant resolves the apparent contradiction in this idea of self-affection by distinguishing between two aspects of the idea of determination. On the one hand, we have active determining by a subject; on the other, the resulting determination in subjectivity. The understanding, under the title of a transcendental synthesis of imagination, performs this act upon a passive subject whose faculty it is, affecting inner sense to yield determinate representations. Apperception is distinguished from inner sense by this active role. Kant's resolution of the apparent paradox – that the self can be passive in relation to its own activity – is through the mediation of a determining act whose effects are then grasped in inner sense.

The crucial point here is that Kant's embargo on the understanding providing its own objects – and hence being able to know things as they really are, rather than as mere appearances – applies just as much to the inner experience of temporal succession as to the outer experience of appearances in space. In outer sense, according to Kant's transcendental idealism, we know objects only in so far as we are externally affected. So too in inner sense we intuit ourselves only in so far as we are affected by ourselves. So we know our own subject only as appearance, not as it is in itself. But in knowing it we do not know the self as determining in the act of synthesis, but only as determined by it. With respect to the act of determining, I am conscious of myself 'not as I appear to myself, nor as I am in myself, but only that I am' – a representation which is not an intuition but a mere thought (B157; K.S. 168). So, in so far as self-consciousness can be construed as self-knowledge, it is restricted to knowledge of myself as I appear to myself – that is, as I am determined in inner sense. I cannot know myself as I would if my intuition were intellectual, but only as I must appear to myself; and this appearance, like all others, is subject to time, the limiting condition of inner sense.

Kant has here separated out the act and object poles of self-consciousness which formed a unity in Descartes's *Cogito*. The 'I think' expresses the act of determining my existence. But the determination of this existence demands self-intuition, and that belongs to 'the receptivity of the determinable (in me)' (B158, footnote a; K.S. 169). Since time is the form of inner sense, in which alone the determination produced by synthesis can be apprehended, it would seem that the act of synthesis itself cannot be construed as in time. Time, for Kant, is nothing but the form of inner sense, in which the effects of synthesis are apprehended. But this puts the act of synthesis into a puzzling relationship with time. Although not itself in time it can, it seems, be apprehended only through its effects which are in time.

Kant's description of synthesis shifts between activity and passivity. Sometimes it is presented as an act which 'cannot be executed except by the subject itself' (B130; K.S. 152). Sometimes it seems rather to be a representation of a unity which already exists. It seems to slide between being an act of bringing together and a recognition of connection. The representation of time itself involves synthesis. Yet it also seems that synthesis can only be apprehended through its temporal effects. In a later section on the 'paralogisms' of pure reason – inherently fallacious forms of argument which purport to yield knowledge of the real nature of the self – Kant elaborates on the complex relations between time and self-consciousness.

Kant's general concern in these sections is to show that knowledge of the unity of consciousness does not yield any knowledge of the self as a unified ego. In the third paralogism, of the 'personality' of the soul, Kant links the soul's consciousness of its identity with its consciousness of being in time. It really says nothing more, he says, than that 'in the whole time in which I am conscious of myself, I am conscious of this time as belonging to the unity of myself'. It comes to the same, he says, whether I say that 'this whole time' is in me as 'individual unity' or that I am to be found as 'numerically identical' in all this time (A362; K.S. 341). To be self-conscious is to be conscious of self in relation to time. With respect to this self-awareness, the perception of time as 'in' me comes to the same thing as that of myself as 'in' time.

There is, Kant continues, a more familiar kind of perception of myself as 'in' time for which that equation seems not at all to hold. In this latter sense, it is an outside observer who first represents me in time; and the time in which the observer sets me belongs to his sensibility rather than to mine. I can consider myself as in time in this way by taking on this third-person perspective, looking at myself from outside. I then apprehend my being as framed by time – as something which, within time, began and will cease to be. But there is a projection in the opposite direction which is for Kant more fundamental – the projection of my first-person perspective to an outside consciousness. The identity which is necessarily bound up with my consciousness is not thereby bound up with the consciousness which contains the 'outer' intuition of my subject. And it is the priority of this first-person perspective on consciousness that allows us to see the intimate connections between the idea that time is in me and the idea that I am in time.

For Kant, the awareness of another consciousness cannot be understood as a relation between the knowing subject and the known object. It takes the form rather of a projection from my self-consciousness. In his discussion of the second paralogism, on the simplicity of the soul, Kant argues that we must assign to objects all the properties under which alone we think them. But I cannot have any representation whatsoever of a thinking being through any outer experience, but only through self-consciousness. Objects of this kind are therefore nothing more than the transference of this consciousness of mine to other things. 'It is obvious that, if I wish to represent to myself a thinking being, I must put myself in his place, and thus substitute, as it were, my own subject for the object I am seeking to consider (which does not occur in any other kind of investigation)' (A354; K.S. 336).

So what I am calling the 'first-person' perspective takes priority for Kant in our understanding of selves. That perception of myself as in time which is available from an outsider's perspective – whether occupied by another or by myself – presupposes a prior apprehension of my own consciousness. From this more fundamental perspective, time is in me. In apperception, Kant says, time is represented, strictly speaking, only in me. And it is in relation to this awareness of myself through apperception that we are to understand Kant's point that it amounts to the same thing whether I say that I am in time or that time is in me. What this means is to be understood through Kant's idea of self-affection – the strange but fruitful idea of the determining act of synthesis yielding a determinate sequence of representations. The idea that consciousness is in time is the idea of self as determined. The idea that time is in consciousness is the idea of self as determining. Each captures from a different direction the same idea of self-affection.

By pursuing this idea we can find in Kant an answer to the question we asked of Descartes – how the individual self's stretching out in time is to be understood in relation to the necessary connections between ideas. Kant's answer is that if self did not affect itself – if there were no determining act of synthesis – there would be no separating out of past and present and no problem of the self's being in time. The elusive stretching out of the Cartesian self in time was, it seemed, neither memory nor the existence through time which the mind shares with other finite things. For Kant it is time itself, as internal to the mind, as distinct from the externally perceived being that mind, like other things, has in time. Time's being in me amounts to the same thing as my being in time because both claims are to be understood through the same fact of self-affection. Let us look in more detail at this crucial Kantian idea.

## SELF-AFFECTION

Whatever underlies Kant's unity of apperception is not in itself knowable, any more that what underlies the appearances we apprehend through outer sense is known. We know neither what underlies outer sense nor what underlies inner sense. In his discussion of the third paralogism, Kant makes the point in a striking way. The thinking subject might for all we know be constantly replaced, each successive subject retaining the thought of the preceding one and handing it over to the subsequent one in a way analogous to the communication of motion through a series of impinging plastic balls. From the unity of consciousness we cannot infer permanence of thinking substance. In the fourth paralogism, on ideality, this theme of the unknowability of whatever might underlie the unity of consciousness is taken even further. Not only might the thinking subject be constantly replaced, but also – Kant claims – for all that the understanding of the 'I think' can show, there might be no difference between whatever it is that underlies our inner experience and what underlies outer spatial appearances. The 'empirical object' is called 'external' if it is represented in space, and 'inner' if it is represented only in its time relations. Neither space nor time, however, is to be found save in us. Whatever produces appearances in space cannot be known to be different in kind from whatever it is that underlies our own inner states. The 'I' represented through inner sense in time is a distinct appearance from objects in space outside me. But they are not on that account to be thought of as different things. Neither the 'transcendental object' which underlies outer appearances nor that which underlies inner intuition is in itself either matter or a thinking being, but a ground that is to us unknown of both kinds of appearance (A380; K.S. 352).

There is, then, no privileging of inner sense over outer sense as regards the status of appearances; and nor can there be any privileging of time as the form of inner sense over space as the form of outer sense. The experience of temporal succession, no less than that of spatial relations, involves the self being affected. The empty form of time stands to determinate appearances in time as determining to determinable. But there is something which stands to that form itself in a relationship of determining act; and to this we have no direct access. We cannot discern the act of synthesis except through its determinate results. The experience of time, no less than that of space, involves the self being affected; and we are in no position to know whether what does the affecting in the case of time is different from what does it in the case of space. The empty form of time – first one thing then another – determines particular states of consciousness; and is itself determined by the act of synthesis. But there is, Kant tells us, nothing which stands to the act of determining in that relation in which the empty form of time stands to determinate states of consciousness in time. I cannot determine my existence as that of a self-active being. All I can do is represent the spontaneity of my thought. My existence is determinable only sensibly, as the existence of an appearance.

Although Kantian inner sense is 'determined' no less than outer sense, it is more difficult to grasp the distinction between determining act and determined sensibility here than with outer sense, where the distinction between knowing subject and object of knowledge provides a grid on which we can impose the distinction. What is given to the mind comes from outside; the determining act which produces determinate spatial appearances comes from within. In the case of inner sense, the whole drama must be played out within the notion of the knowing subject. The relation between 'affected' and 'affecting' must be seen as self-affection.

The apparent paradox, we have already seen, is supposed to be resolved through the distinction between the determining act and its resulting determination. We can now see more clearly how this resolution of the paradox of self-affection involves time. Different representations must be apprehended by me one after the other. But if I were always to drop out of thought the preceding representations and did not reproduce them while advancing to those that follow, Kant argues, a complete representation would never be obtained. No thought – 'not even the purest and most elementary representations of space and time' – could arise (A102; K.S. 133). If a manifold of representations is to form a whole, it must have 'that unity which only consciousness can impart to it'. This dependence on synthesis holds for the representation of time no less than for other cognitive states. It demands a 'running through' and 'holding together' of a manifold – a 'reproductive synthesis of imagination'. But knowledge demands, in addition to this capacity to retain and hold together discrete representations, also a 'figurative' use of imagination. We cannot think a line without drawing it in thought, or a circle without describing it. If we want to represent the three dimensions of space, Kant says, we must set three lines at right angles to one another from the same point.

In a passage which has sparked much discussion, Kant extends the point to the representation of time.

> Even time itself we cannot represent, save in so far as we attend in the *drawing* of a straight line (which has to serve as the outer figurative representation of time) merely to the act of synthesis of the manifold whereby we successively determine inner sense, and in so doing attend to the succession of this determination in inner sense.
>
> (B154; K.S. 167)

It is motion, Kant reasons, that first produces the concept of succession through which inner sense is determined. But this is motion as an 'act of a subject' rather than as a 'determination of an object' (B155; K.S. 167). The point is subtle and important. We have, at one level, a succession of mental states independent of any act of the mind: different representations can be apprehended only successively. But that succession, Kant insists, is nothing to the mind without a 'reproductive synthesis' which holds the successive representations together and makes possible the experience of succession. That reproductive synthesis in turn gives way to the 'figurative' synthesis, in which the mind enacts the synthesis of successive representations into a unity – a line, a circle which it draws in thought.

The passage has sometimes been taken as suggesting that time can only be apprehended through the representation of a line – that time must be construed in spatial terms. But Kant's point is subtler. What he asks us to attend to here is an act abstracted from content – the act of determining, which produces a determinate object of inner sense. He does, it is true, say that the line serves as the 'outer figurative representation of time'. But his emphasis is on the act of drawing the line in thought – on the activity of the mind, rather than on awareness of the line as a determinate spatial object: '. . . we cannot obtain for ourselves a representation of time, which is not an object of outer intuition, except under the image of a line, which we draw . . .' (B156; K.S. 168).

This shows more clearly how the apparent paradox of self-affection is resolved. I produce a describable mental configuration of successive elements by producing in thought a determined spatial configuration. This detour is the necessary mediation between self as affecting and self as affected. By construing a determined space I am conscious of the successive character of the activity of understanding. But I know it only to the extent that I am affected by it, not in so far as I do the affecting. Kant's resolution of the apparent paradox – that I can be passive in relation to my own activity – is through the mediation of a determining act, whose effects are then grasped in inner sense. The determination which it produces provides the means through which I can come to grasp the determining act as something with successive stages.

The crucial point is the lack of any privileged position for our awareness of time with regard to what is given through inner sense. We cannot obtain for ourselves a representation of time except through spatial representation – under the image of a line which we draw. But this is in no way to assimilate time to space. It is the line as drawn in thought which gives us the representation of time – not the line as mere spatial representation. The determinations of inner sense must be arranged as appearances in time, in precisely the same manner, says Kant, in which we arrange those of outer sense in space. The act of drawing the line in thought makes us aware of this arranging in time – of the determining act which underlies our experience of succession.

The distinction we saw in Descartes – between mind existing like other things from moment to moment through time and, on the other hand, the mind's stretching back with the ease of certainty into the past – is replaced for Kant by a threefold distinction. We have, first, the mere succession of representations. This would be as nothing to the mind without its accompanying activity, the 'reproductive' synthesis which runs through and holds together the successive representations. Third, there is the 'figurative' act of synthesis through the determinate effects of which the mind can apprehend the act of synthesis as a succession of stages. One might wonder how Kant can assert the possibility of a mere succession of states for which there is no accompanying mental presence. But this would be to misunderstand the relations between the three kinds of 'succession'. To the extent that mind is ever aware of temporal succession, the determining effects of synthesis are already in place. The state of mere succession is not the initial stage in a process, but an abstraction – a fiction of how things are not, through which we understand better how things are. That Kant talks of it need not mean that he believes in an 'objective' time sequence independent of the mind.

## TIME: SUBJECTIVE OR OBJECTIVE?

We can now see just how complex is Kant's treatment of the relations between time and consciousness. On the one hand, time is internalized. It is, as he says in the Transcendental Aesthetic, 'nothing but the form of inner sense, that is, of the intuition of ourselves and of our inner state' (A33/B50; K.S. 78). If we abstract from our mode of inwardly intuiting ourselves, taking objects as they may be in themselves, time vanishes. It is, he says, 'a purely subjective condition of our (human) intuition'; of itself 'apart from the subject' it is nothing (A35/B52; K.S. 78). It is to be regarded as real, not as 'object' but only as 'the mode of representation of myself as object'. But the manner in which time is for Kant 'subjective' does not at all make it less objective than the 'outer' world of spatial objects. The mind's awareness of temporal succession must indeed, as we have seen, be mediated through its awareness of outer appearances. We can get at succession only through the mediating role of representations in outer sense, which are, despite their status as representations, thoroughly 'objective'.

Time and objectivity, Kant stresses throughout the *Critique*, are interdependent. Objective existence is understood through time; and time can be grasped only through the objectivity that comes from the unification of representations through the categories. Time as the form of inner sense is 'subjective' – a condition of our experience of the world, rather than a feature of things as they might be in themselves. But our experience of it presupposes an 'objective', necessarily connected ordering of representations in accordance with the categories. Without such objective order the experience of succession would be 'less even than a dream' (A112; K.S. 139).

The dependence of temporal experience is accentuated too by the need for an objective correlate of permanence in relation to which we can grasp the reality of change. Inner experience cannot provide this, since it is a constant flux. The permanent is not to be found in consciousness; but without it we cannot grasp succession. Kant elaborates on this aspect of the interdependence of the experience of time and that of space in the section called 'The Refutation of Idealism'. Self-awareness, he argues there, has no priority over the awareness of outer objects. Descartes moved from the immediacy of inner experience to the certainty that the external world existed only by a circuitous path through the existence of a veracious God. For Kant the gap is never allowed to open. Without 'outer' experience I could not be aware of my own existence. Applied to the experience of time, the interdependence of inner and outer means that I can be conscious of the determination of time in inner sense only through awareness of a 'permanent' in outer spatial experience.

The experience of succession in consciousness thus presupposes a sense of permanence which temporal experience cannot provide. Kant elaborates on this in other sections of the *Critique*. In the 'Schematism', he argues that time enters into the reality of things. Only through it can objective existence be understood. Reality and negation are to be understood with reference to being or non-being in time. Their opposition rests on the distinction of one and the same time as filled and as empty (A143/B183; K.S. 184). But relations in time involve relations in 'the permanent'. 'Permanence,' he says in his discussion of substance in the Analogies, 'as the abiding correlate of all existence of appearances, of all change, and all concomitance, expresses time in general' (A183/B226; K.S. 214). All determinations of time presuppose something permanent in perception; and that must be provided through the perception of things 'outside' me.

Ricoeur has argued that this dependence of time on outer spatial experience makes Kant's view of time – for all its transcendental ideality – akin to Aristotle's definition of time as having something to do with motion.[2] The 'ancient dialectic' which sets into opposition to each other a time of the soul and a time of motion, he suggests, is here added to a 'modern dialectic' between subjectivity and objectivity. For Ricoeur, although it might seem at first sight that the assertion of the transcendental ideality of time brings us closer to Augustine than to Aristotle, the function of the Kantian 'transcendental' is in fact exhausted in establishing the conditions of objectivity. The Kantian subject is wholly taken up in 'making the object be there'. Time, despite its subjective character, is wholly defined by the categorical apparatus of the mind. It does not cease to be on the side of nature rather than that of the soul; indeed, the side of the soul is no more. The conditions under which internal phenomena can be known objectively are the same as those to which external phenomena are themselves subjected. There is here no notion of a past or future connected to a present that is the instant of its own utterance, and hence nothing of Augustine's sense of the mind's immersion in time.

However, Kant's treatment of the status of time is more complex than is suggested in Ricoeur's picture of a transcendental framing of a time which remains thoroughly objective. It is true that some dimensions of time's subjectivity disappear into the objective world constituted out of the apparatus of the categories. But Kant's emphasis on the many ways in which the mind must enact time – some of which are highlighted by Ricoeur himself –

can be seen as dissolving the opposition between the time of the soul and the time of the world, rather than opting for the world side of the ancient opposition.

The role of mental activity in the experience of time appears in many guises throughout the *Critique of Pure Reason*. Sometimes the activity is experiential, as in the recurring mental drawings of lines and circles through which the mind provides itself with representations of spatial objects and temporal succession. Sometimes it is a transcendental act, as in the non-sensory synthesis which is presupposed in the representation even of space or time (B160 and footnote; K.S. 170). Synthesis, as it occurs in the arguments of the Transcendental Deduction, is both a figuration and a finding of combination. But even in the Transcendental Aesthetic, Kant stresses the role played by our own mental acts in the awareness of time. Although time is the form of inner sense, because our inner intuition yields no shape through which we might perceive it, we endeavour to make up this want by analogies, representing the time-sequence by imagining a line progressing to infinity. The understanding of time is bound up with reflection on mental activity; and this inevitably takes a transcendental turn. The resources of inner sense yield very little in the understanding or even the perception of time. The full non-dream-like experience of time waits upon the synthesis of representations in accordance with the categories. This synthesis is, as we have seen, inaccessible to direct perception. But this does not mean that it should be relegated to a mental apparatus behind the scenes which leaves the Aristotelian time of the world intact. Ricoeur sees Kant's emphasis on the interdependence of subjectivity and objectivity as giving his treatment of time an Aristotelian twist. But it can just as well be seen as a more sophisticated version of the emphasis on the activity of the soul which took Plotinus and Augustine away from the Aristotelian view.

Can the Kantian treatment of time be seen as a resolution, of the kind Ricoeur claims to be impossible, of the tensions between subjective and objective approaches to time? By showing that neither subjectivity nor objectivity can be understood without the other, Kant can be seen as undermining an opposition. But the resolution does not amount to a reconciliation of Ricoeur's 'time of the world' and the 'time of the soul'. Rather, for Kant time itself is neither subjective nor objective, if those terms are regarded as excluding one another. His transcendental idealism destabilizes the opposition. Nor is this the only point of resemblance between Kant's philosophy and more recent strategies of deconstruction. His notion of synthesis, as David Wood has pointed out, plays in some respects a role similar to Derrida's *différance*.[3] It makes possible all determination, but cannot itself be pinned down to a determinate concept. Kant's talk of the impossibility of treating it, or the self which is its subject, as object of knowledge, however, sometimes conjures up the idea of an inaccessible presence which Derrida would repudiate. Despite Kant's concern to show that knowledge of the unity of consciousness does not yield any knowledge of the self as unified object, he insists that the 'I' here is something real – that 'in the consciousness of myself in mere thought I am the *being itself*, although nothing in myself is thereby given for thought' (B429; K.S. 382). Where Derrida is content to point to *différance*'s slides between activity and passivity, Kant ties the similar shifts in synthesis to an elusive self-affection of the subject, in relation to which both inner and outer experience are to be seen as passive effects.

## KANTIAN JUDGEMENT AND THE FICTIONS OF SELFHOOD

The richly suggestive but elusive concept of a self-affection, which produces both the inner experience of temporal succession and outer experience of a material world, allows the conceptualization of temporal experience to cut across older dichotomies between mind and matter, between thinking and extended beings. But Kant consciously leaves the relations between individual selfhood and the transcendental subject mysterious. As selves we find ourselves at the nexus of the phenomenal and the noumenal – within time, but also mysteriously participating in the unknowable process by which it is produced out of the self-affection of consciousness. The Kantian self is both determined by time and mysteriously behind the scenes of its production.

In his discussion of traditional beliefs in the immortality of the soul in the concluding sections of the Paralogisms, Kant hints at the idea of an alternative form of consciousness whose possibility cannot even be coherently formulated from within the consciousness we in fact have. The thought of the soul as continuing to think after the cessation of all communion with the material world is here formulated as the idea that the 'thinking subject' might continue to apprehend in another form the unknown 'transcendental objects' which now appear to it as bodies. There can be no ground, Kant stresses, even for thinking such an assertion is possible. We can know nothing of the absolute inner cause of outer corporeal appearances. So we cannot know either that the condition of all outer intuition of the thinking subject itself will cease at death, or that it will not. Such speculation takes on for Kant the character of an 'imaginary science', which lures us through an 'imagined felicity' to the bondage of theories and systems; and, in a different metaphor, to a vexatious, tedious and ultimately hopeless voyage of reason beyond the coastline of experience (A394–6; K.S. 360–1).

Such speculations take us beyond the legitimate exercise of human reason. But there is also, Kant thinks, something inevitable, even natural about them. The tendency to engage in such imaginative speculation is not an individual idiosyncratic aberration but an inherent disposition of reason. Speculation on what exactly the 'knowing subject' might be like beyond its effects, which we grasp through our experience of time and space, is inherent to the mind, although the illusoriness of this desired knowledge must be constantly exposed.

How does this 'imaginary science' compare with other exercises of the imagination? How do the fictions of pure reason compare with the fictions of literature? And how do both compare with the legitimate stories which Kant himself tells in the Critique of Pure Reason – the stories of unknowable transcendental acts of synthesis; of alternative forms of consciousness which give themselves their own objects; of the transcendental objects which might, for all we know, underlie both mind and matter? There is no direct answer to these questions in the Critique of Pure Reason. But there are clues to a possible answer in Kant's extended account of judgement in his third Critique. In the Critique of Judgement Kant talks of a kind of reflective judgement which he contrasts with the 'determinant' judgements he describes in the first Critique.[4] Determinant judgements take us from a given universal to a particular subsumed under it. Reflective judgements take us in the opposite direction, finding universals for given particulars. Reflective judgements relate to the finality of nature, to the purposive character we ascribe to things in attempting to get a 'thoroughly interconnected whole of experience'. These ascriptions of purpose are fictions, though grounded in the nature of the mind and in the harmony mind postulates between its objects and its faculties of cognition. This anticipated harmony of fit between mind and world is not a 'given' of human knowledge, but another of those Kantian conditions – a way in which we must proceed in our reflections on nature, a way in which we must tell the story of nature.

For Kant, understanding amounts to the faculty of judgement. In the third Critique he defines 'judgement in general' as 'the faculty of thinking the particular as contained under the universal'. Although the affinities between judgements and fictions are closer in reflective judgement, even the determining judgements of the first Critique bear some resemblance to the telling of a story – the drawing of disparate fragments of experience into a unified whole. Ricoeur comments on the similarities between Kantian judgement and the idea of narrative as a configurational act which draws the manifold of events together into a temporal unity. Judgement, on Kant's account, consists not so much in joining a subject and predicate as in placing an intuitive manifold under the rule of a concept, bringing together a number of representations into a single necessarily unified representation. Judgements are functions of unity among our representations. The creative narrative act likewise extracts a 'configuration' from a mere succession. Kantian judgements can thus be seen, Ricoeur suggests, as incipient narratives, through which the mind transforms the rhapsody of disconnected experience into a unified consciousness.[5] The capacity for narrative is the condition which makes possible all experience that is more than a dream – even the experience of temporal succession itself.

Kantian judgement is the making of a structure, the mental figuration of a unity of representation. In it, time and necessity draw together. The subjectivity of mere succession is structured by the necessary categorial connections which yield experience of an objective world. The dreams, the mere rhapsodies of experience, are left behind. Philosophical insight into the conditions and the limits of our understanding allows us to grasp the differences between such dreams and knowledge of an objective world. But such insight rests on grasping the contingency of human understanding; and that already involves an imaginative exercise in speculating on how a different kind of knowing subject might think and know. Philosophy, according to Kant, is always at risk of toppling out of constructive fiction into unproductive theorizing. To the extent that mind attempts to judge beyond the limits of the coastline of experience, we are taken into the realm of 'imaginary silence' – into another dimension of the realm of dream, where fiction and truth cannot be reconciled. But even in attempting such judgements about mind's self-affection, contradictions though they may be, the mind, for Kant, shapes up to a reality it cannot know. The illusion resides not in thinking that the questions can meaningfully be asked but in thinking that answers are to be found. In asking the questions the mind comes to a clearer understanding, both of the limits of its knowledge and of its relations with time.

# Chapter 3

# The past: loss or eternal return?

Augustine's 'problem' of time arose from its apparent passage into non-existence – a relentless flight which the passive self could only experience as loss. If the past is non-existent, this is indeed a problem for the self which is in time. Augustine's response was to secure the existence of the past through the distension of the soul – the holding together of future, present and past in an act of attention approximating to God's eternal 'now'. Both lacks – the loss of the past and the fragmentation of the self – are supposed to be met by redefining time in terms of the soul's stretching out. In this chapter I want to focus more closely on the idea of the past as 'lost', exploring it through Bergson's philosophy of time. I will then examine a stark alternative posed by Nietzsche's idea of 'eternal return' – that, far from thinking of the past as lost, we might think of ourselves as never able to leave it behind.

## BERGSON: TIME AND LOSS

We have already seen some of the elements that go to make up the sense of the past as 'lost' – the sense of fragmentation, the connection between presentness and actual existence, and between pastness and negation; the tendency to conceptualize time through space. Bergson draws these themes together in an unusual reassessment of the role of intellect in the understanding of the human experience of time. Intellect, he argues, rather than being the key to the reunification of consciousness, is the source of its disintegration from continuity into discontinuity, from unity into fragmentation. For him, the question is not how consciousness brings unity to the temporal succession of experience but rather how the continuity of becoming is dissociated into successive mental states. Rather than looking to intellect for a synthesis of the successive atoms of consciousness given by experience, we should try to understand how intellect has produced discontinuity and how mind might transcend it, inserting itself back into 'real duration'.

Plotinus's story of time as arising from a lost unity – a descent into fragmentation – has echoed in many of the philosophical treatments of time and consciousness we have so far looked at. Bergson too talks of a natural 'return of the mind' to an undivided unity of perception. In *Matter and Memory*, he sees the tendency of every memory to gather to itself others as a reflection of this desire for a lost unity.[1] And in *Creative Evolution*, he says of philosophy that it can only be 'an effort to dissolve again into the Whole'.[2] Philosophy attempts to regain in the unity of 'becoming' the perception of a lost truth – real duration which is the very stuff of our life. According to Bergson, mind, rather than falling away from timelessness into duration, has fallen from duration into the false conceptions of time generated out of practical concerns. Intellect has broken down into fragments an original unity, producing a juxtaposition of simple atoms of consciousness, misleadingly excised from the continuity of becoming. Practically oriented intellect cuts up all progress into phases and then solidifies them into things. It is a tendency which feeds, Bergson thinks, misleading associationist theories of mind. Such theories substitute for the living reality of becoming a discontinuous multiplicity of inert elements. They construe mental life as a succession of independent entities floating, like the atoms of Epicurus, in an inward space, drawing near to each other and catching hold of each other when chance brings them within the sphere of mutual attraction'.[3]

Intellect, rather than transcending the errors of associationism, is complicit in them. Having 'stiffened' individual memory images into ready-made things, given cut and dried in the course of our mental life, associationism is reduced to postulating mysterious attractions between these objects. But this independent image is in fact a later and artificial mental product – a result of mind moving from the continuous whole to discontinuous parts. Intellect, for the greater convenience of practical life, breaks up the continuity of the real, taking snapshots as it were of a changing reality which it then mistakes for ready-made things.

Bergson sees intellect as closely connected with practical concerns, with the need to cope with the world. If we want instead to understand how things really are, we must cultivate intuition – the mental activity which can grasp duration and becoming. Duration overflows the intellect. It is a reality with which the clear distinctions of intellect cannot reckon.

In Bergson's picture of mind and knowledge, the Platonic Forms are just as much snapshots of a changing reality as the mental atoms into which intellect divides up the flow of consciousness. Their apparent timelessness is part of the illusion which mistakes the work of intellect for the discovery of what is really there. Rather than seeing time as a degradation, a falling away from eternity, Bergson sees eternity as an abstraction from change. Eternity is not the ultimate reality underlying time, but an unreal abstraction hanging over it. From the standpoint of ancient philosophy both time and space, he says, can be 'nothing but the field that an incomplete reality, or rather a reality that has gone astray from itself, needs in order to run in quest of itself'.[4] For Bergson, in contrast, duration is the ultimate reality. This gives it a very different status from space, with which it is more commonly seen as symmetrical, and very different relations with the idea of existence.

Bergson criticizes Kant for failing to recognize any difference between the status of time and that of space. By calling attention to how action has taken over the mind's speculative interest, Bergson attempts to open up an alternative between Kantian transcendental idealism and the commitment to 'absolute' homogeneous space and time, which should, he thinks, be seen as principles of division and of 'solidification' imposed on reality with a view to action rather than knowledge.[5] The mind constructs homogeneous space to assist its practical dealings with reality. For Bergson space is not a 'ground on which real motion is posited'. Rather, it is real motion that 'deposits space beneath itself'.[6] Homogeneous space has no reality other than that of a diagram or symbol.[7] Having constructed that symbol, we throw space beneath matter to bring it within our grasp, as he puts it in *Creative Evolution*. We then construct homogeneous time on its model. 'Once in possession of the form of space, mind uses it like a net with meshes that can be made and unmade at will, which, thrown over matter, divides it as the needs of our action demand.'[8]

Homogeneous space is thus for Bergson a mental construction. But it is not a *mis*construction: space is by definition
'outside us', always there, implying juxtaposition and consequently possible division. The homogeneity of space, though a
construction, has a basis in reality. 'Abstract space is, indeed, at
bottom, nothing but the mental diagram of infinite divisibility.'⁹
That divisibility is neither fiction nor illusion. With duration,
however, it is quite otherwise. Here there is no 'real' infinite
divisibility. Whereas homogeneous space is a convenient construction, homogeneous time is for Bergson an illusion which
masks the perception of movement, suggesting that the parts of
movement are somehow there independent of the process which
divides them. 'Movement visibly consists in passing from one
point to another, and consequently in traversing space.'¹⁰ The
space which is traversed is infinitely divisible. And as the
movement is, so to speak, 'applied' to the line along which it
passes, it appears to be one with the line and, like it, divisible.
'Has not the movement itself drawn the line?' It has, it would
seem, traversed in turn the successive and juxtaposed points of
that line. But these points have no reality except in 'a line drawn,
that is to say motionless'. By the very fact that we represent the
movement to ourselves successively in these different points, we
necessarily arrest it in each of them. The 'successive positions'
are 'at bottom, only so many imaginary halts'. 'You substitute the
path for the journey, and because the journey is subtended by the
path you think that the two coincide.'

Homogeneous time is a fiction. The illusion is facilitated,
Bergson thinks, by the fact that we distinguish moments in the
course of the duration, like halts in the passage of the moving
body. We then think that the moving body must occupy at that
precise moment a certain position, which thus stands out from
the whole. The line, through which we so readily symbolize the
passage of time, is here the source of its illusory spatialization. A
line AB can symbolize the duration, already elapsed, of the
movement from A to B already accomplished. But, being motionless, it cannot represent the movement in process. It cannot
represent duration in its flow. The line is divisible into parts and
ends in points. But we cannot conclude from this that the
corresponding duration is composed of separate points or limited by instants.

Accompanying this illusion of time as divisible into instants is a 'cinematographic' model of knowledge. Rather than seeing duration itself as the fundamental reality, Bergson says in *Creative Evolution*, we 'take snapshots, as it were, of the passing reality', stringing them on an abstract, uniform and invisible 'becoming', situated at the back of the apparatus of knowledge.[11] Much of Bergson's writing is devoted to conveying a sense of the indivisible unity of movement, echoing, sometimes explicitly, Plotinus's fascination with the unity of action and the spoken word. Discussing movement in relation to the idea of creation, he stresses that the trajectory of a gesture is created 'in one stroke', although a certain time is required for it. Once the trajectory is created, we can divide it at will. But we cannot divide its creation, which is not a thing but 'an act in progress'.[12] The movement of my hand, seen from without, is the course of a curve in which I can distinguish as many positions as I please. But the positions have sprung from the indivisible act by which my hand has gone from one point to another. Movement gives the appearance of conscious order when it is seen in its completeness – a complex structuring of elements. But the process of its completion is an undivided whole.[13]

In *Creative Evolution*, Bergson attributes the process of disassociation of consciousness to a falling away from the concentrated unity of action into 'dreaming'. His description of this fall echoes again Plotinus's talk of the stages by which mind falls away from unity into fragmentation. But for Bergson the fall is not from eternity into time, but away from the undivided unity of becoming into a spatialized fragmentation of consciousness – a scattering of the self in which our past, which had been 'gathered together into an indivisible impulsion to action', is broken into externally related 'recollections'. As these recollections lose their interpenetration and become 'fixed', our personality 'descends in the direction of space'.[14]

Mind falls from unity into fragmentation by losing the concentrated unity of action, whether its own action or in the experience of following another's action. When I follow with interest a poet reading his verses I put myself into his feelings, living over again the simple state he has broken into phrases and words, following it with a continuous movement which is, like the inspiration itself, an undivided act. But I need only relax my attention, let go the tension in me for the sounds, hitherto swallowed up in the sense, to appear to me distinctly, one by one in their materiality. If I go further 'in the direction of dream' the letters themselves will become loose and be seen to 'dance along, hand in hand, on some fantastic sheet of paper'. Hovering over this multiplicity of elements into which it has been decomposed by the scattering of attention, is the undividedness of the real whole. Bergson himself at this point makes an explicit comparison with Plotinus's treatment of space as an enfeeblement of original Being.[15]

What Bergson sees as the fundamental illusion about time is to think of it on the model of space. This illusion has two levels: the belief that time's relation to human experience is symmetrical with that of space, and the construction of 'homogeneous' time on the model of infinitely divisible space. To dispel the illusion, he confronts us with the undivided unity of action, and with the reality of becoming, which eludes the practical concerns of intellect. Here he draws on Plotinian analogies with action and speech similar to those through which Augustine found his resolution of the problem of time. But the consequences Bergson draws from them give a very different picture of the relations between mind and time from Augustine's distension of the soul. Where Augustine saw past and present as accommodated into the unity of an attentive mental presence which overcomes the passage of time into the non-existence of the past, Bergson sees past and present as coexisting, not as a result of some intellectual feat, but as a result of their very nature. The past is 'preserved' not because mind is able to counter the flight of the present into non-existence, but because it is only through an illusion that we think of the past as separate from the present at all. Bergson's idea of the 'coexistence' of past and present is in this way very different from Augustine's juxtaposition of them in an encompassing act of mental attention. For Bergson the coexistence of past and present is not a matter of the holding together in unity of a succession of discrete states, but rather a coexistence of different elements within the one state. The past is not 'lost'; for it is never really separated out from a present whose existence excludes it. Why then do we think of it as lost?

## TIME, EXISTENCE AND NEGATION

The idea that only the present really exists is, in Bergson's diagnosis, a product of a number of misleading pictures – of the relations between subjective and objective, of the relations between space and time, and of the relations between the speculative and the practical interests of mind. Because we think of 'objective realities' existing without relation to consciousness, and of states of consciousness existing without relation to objective realities, we readily think of the whole spatial series as existing unperceived, whereas in the case of time only the present exists. Space appears to us as preserving things indefinitely while time in its advance devours the states which succeed each other within it. But we misunderstand the past in seeing it as separated from the present by the divide which separates non-existent from existent. The distinctions between past, present and future are to be understood, Bergson argues, not in terms of different relations to existence, but in terms of different relations to action. The past no longer has any interest for us. It has exhausted its possible action. The immediate future, on the contrary, consists in 'an energy not yet spent'.

The contrast spills over into different attitudes to temporal and spatial distance. The unperceived part of the material universe has a reality for us 'big with promises and threats', which unperceived periods of our past cannot possess. And this unavoidable distinction, which is entirely relative to practical utility and to the material needs of life, takes on in our mind 'the more and more marked form of a metaphysical distinction'. Material objects have an apparently solid reality, available to us for continuing action. Our memories in contrast seem 'so much dead weight that we carry with us, and by which we prefer to imagine ourselves unencumbered'. The same 'instinct' in virtue of which we open out space indefinitely before us prompts us to shut off time behind us as it flows. So in our inner life that alone seems real which begins with the present moment. The rest is 'practically abolished'. For Bergson then the past has not ceased to exist, but has only ceased to be useful.[16]

As well as severing the link between the present and actual existence, Bergson also breaks another connection which we have seen to be central to Augustine's treatment of time – that between temporal and psychological presence. Unreflectively we think of the present as given by perception, the past by memory.

Bergson attempts to break down this apparently straightforward association between perception and the present. '*Practically we perceive only the past*, the pure present being the invisible progress of the past gnawing into the future.' Consciousness illumines not the present but 'that immediate part of the past which, impending over the future, seeks to realize and to associate with it'.[17] If we never perceive anything but our immediate past, our consciousness of the present is already memory. Strictly we never perceive the present, but only remember it. To understand this paradoxical but important breaking of the nexus between perception and the present, we must look at Bergson's distinction between two kinds of memory and at his idea of the 'virtual coexistence' of past and present.

## THE TWO KINDS OF MEMORY

For Bergson the past survives in two distinct forms – 'motor mechanism' and 'independent recollection'.[18] The first form of memory consists in a set of intelligently constructed mechanisms which ensure the appropriate reply to immediate practical demands – a 'habit' memory which allows us to adapt ourselves to the present situation. This is a form of memory which resides in sensori-motor response. It 'acts' our past experience but does not call up its image. The second kind of memory is, in contrast, a 'recollection' memory – summoning up specific images. This 'pure' memory, however, cannot function without the more basic habit memory: '. . . that a recollection should reappear in consciousness, it is necessary that it should descend from the heights of pure memory down to the precise point where *action* is taking place'.[19] It is from the present that comes 'the appeal to which memory responds'. Memory borrows the 'warmth that gives it life' from the sensori-motor elements of present action. Both forms of memory are needed for effective action, engaging with the present without being confined there. Effective action is not the impulsive response of those who live only in the present. Nor is it consistent with living in the past for the mere pleasure of being there. Habit memory is associated with the life of action, recollection memory with the life of dreams. And good sense is poised between the two.

Habit memory continues the past in present action. As far as this kind of memory is concerned, what is 'lost' is what of the past is not thus continued. Here memory, with the totality of our past, is continually 'pressing forward, so as to insert as much of itself as possible into the present action'.[20] This underlies the 'concrete feeling' that we have of present reality – our conscious-ness of 'the actual movements whereby our organism is naturally responding to stimulation'.[21] In completely uninterrupted sensori-motor response we would have a present in which the past is 'truly given', because each moment is the equivalent of the preceding one and may be deduced from it. In conscious beings that immediate deductive connection between past and present is disrupted. The past of a conscious, creative being cannot be read off from its present. But even here movement involves a solidarity between past and present through the prolongation of the past into present action by habit memory. It is this aspect of memory which is central for Bergson. Memory is not a 'regres-sion' from the present to the past – a fading of an image – but rather a 'progress' from the past to the present, to be defined in terms of sensori-motor response and action. The present is that which acts on us and makes us act and, above all, the state of our body. And our past is 'that which acts no longer but which might act, and will act by inserting itself into a present sensation of which it borrows the vitality'.[22]

However, more is involved in the idea of the past as 'lost' than misconstruing its 'uselessness' as non-existence. Might not a 'useless' past be just as 'lost' as a non-existent one? The thought of the past as lost involves more than its simply not being there, available to action, except in so far as it is carried forward by habit memory. It is here that 'recollection' memory becomes important. The 'loss' of the past involves, Bergson suggests, the idea of 'replacement' or 'substitution'. And this in turn involves turning our back on the reality which flows from past to present, advancing from behind. We then see change as a traveller would see the course of his carriage if he looked out behind, and only knew at each moment the point where he had ceased to be. For a mind which followed purely and simply the 'thread of experi-ence', there would be no void, no possible negation. It would see only things existing, states appearing, events happening. It would live in the actual and, if it were capable of judging, it would never affirm anything except the existence of the present.[23] To see anything more than the present state of a passing reality – to represent the passing as a change and therefore as a contrast between what has been and what is – the mind must be able to dissociate and distinguish. It must have memory and, especially, the desire to dwell on the past. To represent that a thing has disappeared, it is not enough to perceive a contrast between the past and the present. It is also necessary to turn our back on the present, to dwell on the past, thinking of it without letting the present appear in it. The idea of annihilation is therefore not a 'pure idea'. It implies that we conceive the past as regrettable, that we have reason to linger over it. 'Suppress all interest, all feeling, and there is nothing left but the reality that flows, together with the knowledge ever renewed that it impresses on us of its present state'.[24] From annihilation to negation there is then only one step. All that is necessary is to represent the contrast of what is, not only with what has been, but also with all that might have been. The links between the past and negation are negotiated, not through the distinctions of intellect, but through our emotional responses to time. But for Bergson there is an alternative to this alignment of the past with negation – to recognise the virtual coexistence of past and present.

## PAST, PRESENT AND BECOMING

For Bergson, duration poses to consciousness an irreducible reality. We perceive it as a 'stream against which we cannot go' – as 'the foundation of our being', as 'the very substance of the world in which we live'. It is not just the 'infirmity of a mind that cannot have everything at once' – not, as Leibniz thought, a confused perception, relativized to the human standpoint: 'a perception which would vanish, like a rising mist, for a mind seated at the centre of things'.[25] There are misunderstandings about time from which we can be delivered through a better understanding. But duration itself is not something from which mind could be delivered. Real duration 'gnaws on things, and leaves on them the mark of its tooth.'[26] It is a consequence of this solidity of Bergsonian duration that the same concrete reality never recurs. Where Nietzsche, as we shall see, wishes to affirm everything as eternally recurring, Bergson argues that nothing singular can recur. Repetition is possible 'only in the abstract'. What is repeated is some aspect that our senses and intellect have singled out from reality because action can move only among repetitions. Intellect, preoccupied with generalities, focuses on repetition, 'welding the same to the same'. Intellect turns away from the vision of time – away from what is fluid, 'solidifying' everything it touches. 'We do not *think* real time. But we *live* it, because life transcends intellect.'[27] The unrepeatable cannot be grasped through intellect, whose proper function is the organization of the material world for action. The intellectualizations of science can work only on what is thus withdrawn from the action of real time. What can be repeated is by that very fact excluded from real time. But the unrepeatable can, we are told, be grasped through intuition, which, in contrast to intellect's division of the world into 'mental snapshots', has access to becoming, to duration itself. 'Anything that is irreducible and irreversible in the successive moments of a history eludes science.'[28] This is only what we should expect, given that science and intellect focus on what can fall under general laws. It is the task of intuition to provide insight into becoming. To get a notion of it we must break with science, doing violence to the mind by going counter to the 'natural bent of intellect'. This 'violence' Bergson sees as 'the function of philosophy'.

What is it, then, that we are supposed to grasp through intuition? And how does this non-intellectual perception overcome the idea of the past as lost? If the reality of duration involves non-repeatability, what do we know of the real past, as distinct from the 'repeatable', generalizable past grasped through intellect? Bergson's answer is that we understand what is real and 'living' of the past only because it is not strictly separated out from the present. The past is 'virtually' existent in the present.

This difficult aspect of Bergson's treatment of time is explored by Gilles Deleuze in *Le Bergsonisme*.[29] For Bergson, on Deleuze's reading, it is not the past but the present that 'is not'. In thinking of the past as having ceased to be, we confuse being with being present. But the present, being 'pure becoming', is indeed *not*. It is 'always outside itself'. The proper element of the present is not being but rather the active or the useful. The past, on the other hand, although it has ceased to act or to be useful, has not ceased to be. 'Useless and inactive, impassive, it IS, in the full sense of the word. At the limit, the ordinary determinations are reversed: of the present, we must say at every instant that it "was", and of the past, that it "is", eternally for all time. This is the difference in kind between the past and the present.'[30]

If we are to make sense of the passage from present to past, Deleuze suggests, we must, according to Bergson, think in terms of a coexistence of past and present – of a virtual existence of the pastness in the heart of the present. Our accustomed ways of thinking of the relations between past and present privilege the present. We think of the past as being constituted only after it has been present and also as reconstituted in some way by the new present whose past it now is. Bergson reverses our normal ways of thinking of past and present. 'We do not move from the present to the past, from perception to recollection, but from the past to the present, from recollection to perception.'[31] In the grip of the privileging of the present we believe that a present is only past when it is replaced by another present. If a present is to pass it must be past at the same time as it is present. The past must be constituted as the past at the same time as it is present.

The most profound paradox of memory, Deleuze suggests, lies in the fact that the past is '"contemporaneous" with the present it *has been*'.[32] It would never be constituted if it did not coexist with the present whose past it is. So past and present do not, as we are accustomed to think, denote two successive moments, but rather two elements which coexist: the present, which does not cease to pass, and the past, which does not cease to be but through which all presents pass. Rather than following the present, the past is presupposed as the pure condition without which the present could not pass. Bergsonian duration is thus defined less by succession than by coexistence. 'Duration is indeed real succession, but it is so only because, more profoundly, it is *virtual coexistence*.'[33] To say that past and present 'co-exist' is to say that each must be thought through the other. Rather than thinking past and present through the model of successive moments, we are to see them as different aspects under which each moment must be thought if we are to apprehend the reality of duration. Bergson extends to the past the movement of the present; and to the present the determinacy of the past.

## NIETZSCHE: 'ILL WILL TOWARDS TIME'

At first sight nothing could be further from Bergson's insistence on the uniqueness and unrepeatability of the past than Nietzsche's famous doctrine of eternal recurrence. For Bergson, as we have seen, unrepeatability is a consequence of the reality of

duration. Repeatability belongs with general concepts. It is possible only 'in the abstract'. To specify an event is to render it
unrepeatable. What is repeated is some aspect that our sense and
intellect have singled out from reality because action can move
only among repetitions. The two pictures of time seem diametrically opposed. But there are in fact a number of connections
between them. Both involve a commitment to the coexistence of
past, present and future. Both give centrality to the immediate
sense of movement. And the appearance of a contradiction
between Bergson's claim – that nothing can be repeated – and
Nietzsche's – that everything must be – may dissolve on closer
inspection. For Nietzsche, as for Bergson, 'becoming' loses its
traditional subservience to 'being'. The idea of recurrence as
deliverance from time's relentless onward passage involves an
affirmation of transience rather than a denial of its reality. And,
while it is true that he talks of eternal return in terms of redemption, this is not a redemption from transience but from 'ill will'
towards time – from the attitude which makes the passage of time
seem destructive.

Before Nietzsche had developed his mature doctrine of eternal
return, he himself endorsed the unrepeatability of all that happens. 'In our heart', he says in *Schopenhauer as Educator*, 'we all
know quite well that, being unique, we will be in the world only
once and that no imaginable chance will for a second time gather
into a unity so strangely variegated an assortment as we are.'[1]
Even in his mature thought Nietzsche seems to see no real
inconsistency between eternal recurrence and uniqueness. Indeed, he seems to see the juxtaposition of unrepeatability and
recurrence as the core of the doctrine. It is in their very uniqueness that he wants to see individual events as eternally recurring
– not in some remote future time where the 'variegated assortment that we are' is reformed, but in the here and now.

How seriously can we take the idea of eternal recurrence?
There are various statements of the idea throughout Nietzsche's
work. In some, he seems to present it as a serious thesis about the
real nature of time. In others, he seems to see it rather as a fiction,
a thought experiment which inculcates a certain attitude to being
in time – as if the point of the doctrine were not to explain the real
nature of time but rather to articulate an ethical attitude towards
the events of a life – a role which can be extricated from consideration of its truth or falsity. In an early critique of the doctrine,

Georg Simmel suggested that it is analogous to Kant's idea of universalizability as a test of the moral worth of an action. Whereas Kant places action into the dimension of infinite repetition in the 'one-alongside-the-other-of society', Nietzsche has action repeat itself in the 'infinite-one-after-the-other of the same person'. Both multiplications of action serve the same goal of getting beyond the 'accidentality' that colours representations in their 'only-now and only-here'.[2] The effect of the mental experiment of thinking of an action as if it were eternally repeated is to focus our attention on its inner value, on that for which we can take responsibility – something which is in itself beyond time and number, where and how often. To think of an act as if it were always repeated has a similar effect to thinking of it as if it were done by everyone. Eternal recurrence on this way of looking at it is, Simmel suggests, a symbol. Unjustified though Nietzsche was in going beyond the symbol, to assert eternal return as a reality, that unwarranted move makes no difference, he thinks, to its function as a regulative idea of ethics.

Simmel's Kantian parallels capture an important aspect of the doctrine – the way it focuses our attention on the content of the moment. Separated out from its temporal position, what happens is considered without regard for whether it is past, present or future. But in emphasising this timeless aspect of Nietzsche's way of thinking of events as 'eternal', Simmel sets aside others. His account obscures the way the idea brings together delight in transience with more traditional aspirations to eternity. Nor does his assimilation of Nietzsche's ethical vision to Kantian ideals of moral responsibility do justice to the novelty of the dramatic extension of the idea of 'taking responsibility' to things that lie outside the power of the human will to affect the course of events. And, although the connection with Kantian universalizability is supposed to be only an analogy, by detaching the event from the self's own temporal perspective, Simmel's version of the idea takes us in the direction of a focus on kinds of action, rather than acts or events in their particularity.

It is not clear that Nietzsche could accept Simmel's distinction between cosmological theses and ethical 'fictions'. What is more important, however, is that his reconstruction fails to capture one of the most important and interesting aspects of Nietzsche's version of eternal return – its peculiar juxtaposition of uniqueness and recurrence. But is what it leaves out intelligible? Simmel is scornful of the 'deep emotion and devotion' with which Nietzsche speaks of it – a fervour which, he suggests, must rest on imprecise logical conceptualization.[3] The point is an important one. From a logical viewpoint, as Simmel says, there is no importance inherent to repetition. A succession of repetitions remains of no significance unless it can be synthesized in our experience. The actual repetition of an experience matters for me only if I remember the previous instances. If the second instance finds me in exactly the same state as when the first occurred, my reaction the second time would be the same as it was initially. The repetition would then be without significance. We are thus forced into a dilemma. If the recurrence happens without my being conscious of it as a repetition, it can have no significance to me. If, on the other hand, I am aware of it as a repetition, what 'recurs' is, by virtue of that consciousness, not exactly what originally occurred.

Simmel's response to the idea of eternal return reflects an incredulity that what Nietzsche envisages as recurring should be, not a similar kind of experience, but the very present experience itself. Eternal recurrence, in his Kantian reconstruction of it, becomes a 'functional ideal': thus should we live in every moment as if we would live that way for ever – as if the content of each moment has eternal worth. What slips through the net in his interpretation of eternal return as a regulative ethical idea is the mind-numbing conjunction of recurrence and uniqueness which Nietzsche found such an awesome thought. Simmel's reconstruction also reflects a failure to grasp just how radical is Nietzsche's repudiation of traditional views of the self as a subject of traits and experiences. Comparing recurrences, Simmel suggests, demands a persisting ego, capable of checking the repetition against the original. Eternal recurrence could have import only for someone who watches, reflects on and unites the many returns in his consciousness. As an 'external' reality it is nothing. Although his argument on that point is convincing, he concludes too swiftly that Nietzsche's eternal recurrence can only be made coherent by postulating a transcendent ego which does not itself recur – a self able to stand above and compare different instances of the same kind of event.

What Nietzsche offers in the idea of eternal return is, not an edifying injunction to a transcendent will as to what kinds of thing are worthy of its choice, but rather a perception of the weight of eternity in the midst of transience. 'Being' and 'becoming' do indeed come together in Nietzsche's perception of eternal recurrence. But their conjunction is not a projection of the will, choosing what *kinds* of event it will endorse. It is a matter rather of seeing everything that happens – whether it be grand or unbearably petty – as integral to the being of a self which, if it were to recur at all, could do so only in its entirety. The perception, as we shall see, has to do both with the relations between self and time and with the bearings on both of the idea of narrative.

Because Simmel sees Nietzsche as intending, however mistakenly, a cosmological theory, his interpretation of eternal return retains an external perspective. It fails to engage with Nietzsche's radical transformation of the traditional treatment of the self as a permanent substance confronting a changing reality. Nietzsche's 'reverence' for the idea can then only appear as a confusion. The ego, for Simmel, must exclude itself from the thought experiment in which everything recurs. It must remain outside the hypothesized repetition, in order to be able to reflect on it. But what is in fact involved in Nietzsche's idea is a convergence of time and consciousness even more radical than what we saw with Kant. Obscure though this convergence is, it is clear that themes of selfhood are central to Nietzsche's version of eternal recurrence. It is its application to the facts of one's own existence, its implications for self-knowledge, that give it the awesome dimensions which Nietzsche ascribes to it. In his first formulation of the idea, in the fourth book of *The Gay Science*, Nietzsche refers to it as 'the thought of thoughts', the 'greatest burden', the thought that is 'hardest to bear'. The prospect of recurrence is here put in the mouth of a demon who steals near in the self's 'loneliest loneliness' to say:

> This life as you now live it and have lived it, you will have to live once more and innumerable times more, and there will be nothing new in it, but every pain and every joy and every thought and every sigh and everything unutterably small or great in your life will have to return to you, all in the same succession and sequence – even this spider and this moonlight between the trees, and even this moment and I myself.[4]

The question in each and every thing – 'Do you desire this once more and innumerable times more?' – is here presented as lying upon the self as 'the greatest weight' precisely because it is envisaged not as an external truth about the nature of time but as something the mind understands with reference to itself.

This essential self-reference becomes more explicit in the most famous formulation of the idea in *Thus Spake Zarathustra*. In 'The Vision and the Riddle',[5] Nietzsche presents the idea in the context of a conversation between Zarathustra – the poetic creation of the thinker capable of thinking 'the most terrible of thoughts' – and the dwarf he has been carrying on his shoulders, representing the spirit of gravity and small-mindedness. The conversation occurs at a gateway where two paths meet. Here Zarathustra gets the dwarf to jump off his shoulders by taunting him with the prospect of hearing the most abysmal of thoughts, the thought the dwarf himself is not strong enough to think. The long lane behind us, says Zarathustra, goes on for an eternity. And the long lane ahead likewise into another eternity. The opposed paths meet at the gateway, which is inscribed 'Moment'. If we were to follow them further, Zarathustra asks the dwarf, would they be in eternal opposition? All truth is crooked, the dwarf responds disdainfully; 'time itself is a circle'.

The dwarf's response is dismissed by Zarathustra as too light a version of the most unthinkable of thoughts. The dwarf misses what is 'abysmal' in it, reducing it to a platitude. The dwarf talks of recurrence as if it were a theory of the nature of time, externally perceived. He construes the circle without any essential reference to his own temporal perspective, his own immersion in time. Zarathustra's grasp of the doctrine eludes the dwarf, who can perceive it only in a small-minded way. He does not grasp the import of the fact that his own mind is part of the recurrence or that it is the very moment in which they are talking which will recur. Must not whatever can walk have walked this lane before? asks Zarathustra. Must not whatever *can* happen have happened, have been done, have passed by before? Must not this gateway too have been there before? And are not all things bound together so firmly that this moment draws after it all that is to come? Whatever *can* walk, in this long lane out there too, it must walk once more.

> And this slow spider that creeps along in the moonlight, and this moonlight itself, and I and you at this gateway whispering together, whispering of eternal things – must we not all have been here before? – and must we not return and run down that

other lane out before us, down that long, terrible lane – must we not return eternally?[6]

The narrative continues to a description of Zarathustra's vision of the shepherd and the snake which he can dislodge from his throat only by biting off its head. He then sees the frightened shepherd transformed in light and laughter, such as no one has ever laughed. The vision leaves Zarathustra longing for that joy. But his reaching it of course lies on the other side of his own endeavour to bite the head off the snake, symbolizing his acceptance of the recurrence of all that is small and evil for the sake of all that is great. The vision of the shepherd and the snake is a prefiguring of Zarathustra's own confrontation with the abysmal thought of eternal recurrence, which is recounted in a later section, 'The Convalescent'.[7] Here the thought leaves him in a death-like stupor, from which his attendant animals coax him back to life. The version of eternal recurrence which the eagle and the serpent sing to the convalescent Zarathustra, although it is presented with more charm and subtlety than the dwarf's platitudes, initially also falls short of Zarathustra's vision. It also misses the way the idea affects the self's grasp of its own relations with time. 'Everything goes, everything returns,' they say, 'the wheel of existence rolls for ever. Everything dies, everything blossoms anew; the year of existence runs on for ever. . . . The path of eternity is crooked.'[8] It is a version of the doctrine appropriate to 'buffoons and barrel organs', Zarathustra tells them. It has 'made a hurdy-gurdy song' of the profound and overwhelming idea of eternal recurrence. They have not grasped the long twilight limping in front of him – the death-intoxicated sadness which speaks with a yawn, the thought of all that is small and petty recurring eternally. And the animals respond with an acknowledgement of Zarathustra as he who must become the teacher of the external recurrence, his greatest danger and sickness. 'Behold, we know what you teach: that all things recur eternally and we ourselves with them, and that we have already existed an infinite number of times before and all things with us.' And if he should die now, they know what he would say.

I shall return, with this sun, with this earth, with this eagle, with this serpent – *not* to a new life or a better life or a similar life.

I shall return externally to this identical and self-same life, in the greatest things and in the smallest, to teach once more the eternal recurrence of all things.[9]

What exactly did the animals' 'hurdy-gurdy' version of the doctrine miss? Zarathustra's complaint is, of course, partly directed at the thoughtless way in which they recite it. But, from the context of Nietzsche's development of the idea here and elsewhere, it would seem that the animals miss at least two things that are central to its content. First, they fail to grasp fully that what recurs is not an abstract or general 'kind' of thing but each thing in its very uniqueness. The model of the 'year of existence' fails to grasp just how radical is the idea of recurrence. The tension in the conjunction of utter uniqueness and endless repetition is too easily removed in the animals' conversion of the idea into the relatively unthreatening cycle of death and renewal. The deeper formulation involves the 'return' of the same in its specificity. The second thing which the animals fail to capture is the essential reflexiveness of Zarathustra's idea – that it is to be understood with reference to the self and the moment. Nietzsche dramatizes the contrast between Zarathustra's comprehension of the idea and that of the animals by presenting them as blissfully singing of eternal recurrence to the exhausted Zarathustra who has lapsed again into a coma-like state. Now, however, they have sufficient insight to respect the great stillness around him and to withdraw discreetly.

Its essential reference to the present moment is an aspect of Nietzschean eternal recurrence which is stressed by Heidegger in his commentary on these two sections of *Zarathustra*.[10] The dwarf turns the doctrine into a cosmological idea which does not engage with the significance of the moment, identified with the gate at which the two paths collide. The dwarf has in fact eliminated the 'collision' between past and future which is essential to the thought. And the animals too grasp the application of the doctrine to themselves only at a level of detached external perception, rather than in the immediacy of the present. In missing the crucial role of the present moment, the superficial versions of the doctrine also miss its full implications for self-consciousness. On Heidegger's interpretation, the 'collision' of the two paths is something accessible only from within the temporal, only through reflection on our own being in time. Zarathustra thinks the thought of eternal recurrence from within time and with reference to himself, in a way that the dwarf cannot. From an outside perspective which does not grasp eternal return from within time and selfhood, the two avenues, future and past, do not collide at all, but merely pursue one another. The 'not yet now' becomes the now, and forthwith becomes a 'no-longer-now' in a perpetual 'and so on'.[11] This is a spectator's view of time; and to abandon it, Heidegger suggests, is to become oneself 'the Moment', performing actions directed towards the future, while at the same time accepting and affirming the past. A mind with such a perspective cultivates and sustains the 'strife' between what is assigned it as a future 'task' and what has been given it as its 'endowment' from the past. 'To see the Moment means to stand in it.'[12] The perception of the dwarf, in contrast, 'keeps to the outside'. For Heidegger it is this experience of real 'collision' between past and future, bound up with the sense of agency, that carries the weightiness of the doctrine of eternal recurrence. 'That which is to come is precisely a matter for decision, since the ring is not closed in some remote infinity but possesses its unbroken closure in the Moment, as the centre of the striving.' What is 'hardest to bear' in the doctrine is that eternity is in the Moment – 'that the Moment is not the fleeting "now", not an instant of time whizzing by a spectator, but the collision of future and past'.

We can see here something that was not present in Augustine's repudiation of the Aristotelian model of time. Aristotle's 'instants' arbitrarily marked off temporal intervals in a way that had no essential reference to the observing mind's own temporal position, whereas Augustine's 'now' was firmly anchored within the temporal. But Heidegger's description of instants 'whizzing by a spectator' – the 'now's continuous pursuit of the 'not-yet-now' – does nonetheless capture some aspects of Augustine's picture of time. It fits those passages where Augustine talks of 'the future' as passing through the present on its way to become the past. In the fuller, but also more elusive, development of Augustine's view of time, as we have seen, this passive, spectator model of mind's relations with time gives way to a more active model of mind 'stretching out' to encompass past and future in an act of attention which brings them into a kind of co-presence. But precisely because the contradictory characters of past and present are reconciled in this mental coexistence, there is in Augustine's picture nothing that answers to what

Heidegger described as the 'collision' of past and future in the moment. For Heidegger this 'collision' is action – the coming together of an orientation towards the future with the 'endowment' from the past. Action is the past breaking into the future, the future drawing the past behind it – a moving into the future which, unlike Bergson's unreflective 'habit' memory, is fully conscious.

Heidegger's picture of past and future 'colliding' in the present thus involves a dimension of activity which Augustine's more passive model lacked. Despite their co-presence in the mind's act of attention, Augustine's 'past' and 'future' remain external to one another. For Heidegger, in contrast, they interpenetrate in action. Even Augustine's elaboration of the speech analogy involves a passivity in contrast with Heidegger's stress on agency. What is still to come passes through the mind's presence into the past – a 'pursuit' rather than a 'collision' of future, present and past. This sense of past and future as 'colliding' in the experience of human action is what for Heidegger gives content to the 'weightiness' Zarathustra ascribes to the idea of eternal return. The stress on mind's orientation towards the future in action is in keeping with his own treatment of time in *Being and Time*. The present moment is momentous in being the site of the interpenetration of past and future in which action – and hence selfhood – resides. The dread with which Zarathustra approaches the idea of the presence of eternity in the moment is for Heidegger bound up with the weightiness this gives to human action. The awesomeness of the present is largely a matter of its being, as it were, the gateway from the 'endowment' of the past to the 'task' of the future. Heidegger stresses that the temporality of eternal recurrence is something that pertains distinctively to human being in time. It is a feature of human temporality – the characteristic way in which human beings, 'resolutely open to what is to come and preserving what has been, sustain and give shape to what is present'.[13]

## BEING, BECOMING AND ETERNITY

In desiring that everything recur eternally, Zarathustra does not desire to escape from time into a reality which somehow transcends becoming. Nietzsche attempts rather to undermine the ancient Greek downgrading of becoming. Eternal recurrence does not take us into a realm of timeless being. Where Heraclitus claimed that we can never step twice into the same river, on account of its perpetual and ineluctable onward flow, Nietzsche envisages a redemption from the eternal flux. Becoming is to be stamped with the character of Being, as he puts it in *The Will to Power*. That everything recurs is 'the closest approach of a world of Becoming to a world of Being'.[14] It offers a redemption not from time but from 'the will's ill will towards time' with its ceaseless 'it was'.[15] 'Ill will' towards time degrades all that passes away, treating the transient as a form on non-Being, in contrast to the true Being of the permanent. The idea of eternal recurrence offers redemption from this ill will – an affirmation of transience, suffusing it with the ideal of eternity which was traditionally reserved for the permanent. The fullness of Being resides not in timelessness but in the eternal return of the same. Eternity is to be detached from its associations with remaining the same. The fullness of Being no longer resides in timelessness but in eternal recurrence.

Heidegger's interpretation of this convergence of being and becoming is coloured by his emphasis on orientation towards the future. To escape from time would also be to escape from the possibility of action. Ill will towards time is transcended in the affirmation of the present moment as the momentous site of human agency. But there are other, less action-orientated aspects of Nietzsche's picture of the present, which bear more on the relations between present and past than on those between present and future. Eternal recurrence concerns both past and future in their relations to the present. Although the orientation towards the future is important in the longing for eternal return, there are also some aspects of this longing which turn away from the future. The 'higher men' do not long for something better, says Zarathustra in the section towards the end of the work, called 'The Intoxicated Song'. Their longing is not for something 'remoter, higher, brighter' as in the longing for heirs, which is actually the expression of present suffering: 'all that suffers wants to live, that it may become ripe and joyous and longing – longing for what is farther, higher, brighter. "I want heirs" – thus speaks all that suffers. "I want children, I do not want *myself*".' The desire for eternal return is, rather, the longing that is implicit in joy, with its delight in the present. 'Joy, however, does not want heirs, or children, joy wants itself, wants eternity, wants recurrence, wants everything eternally the same.'[16] The affirmation of eternal return is an affirmation of the present, a refusal to let it drain away in the hope of a better future or a release from present suffering. Eternity enters the moment in the refusal to see the present teleologically, as if it were just a gateway to the future. Eternity is in the moment, not beyond it as the goal towards which mind moves. No moment exists for the sake of another.

Nietzsche's image of the moment as gateway conjures up not only the onward path to the future, but also the relentless passage of future into past. The moment not only draws past into future but also future into past. So bound together are all things that what is to come can be seen as having already been. The shaped, determinate character of the past lurks in the apparent indeterminacy of the future. This extension to the fluid future of the determinacy of the past is crucial to understanding the connections between Nietzsche's version of eternal return and the idea of narrative, and also to seeing how these connections bear on his understanding of immortality. For if the future takes on something of the fixity of the past in this Nietzschean convergence of being and becoming, it is no less true that the past loses some of its separation from the life and vivacity of the present.

## ETERNAL RETURN, IMMORTALITY AND NARRATIVE

What does eternal recurrence have to do with immortality? In a passage in the *Notebooks* (vol.12, section 730 of the Grossoktav edition) Nietzsche remarked that the most immediate impact of the idea of eternal recurrence is as a substitute for the belief in immortality. But this is presented as a superficial way of thinking of the doctrine. Anything true, he says, must suffer this fate – that it wins to itself the highest human beings last. The deeper understanding of the idea of eternal return does not find in it the promise of a personal immortality. In some ways, indeed, the idea suggests precisely the opposite – that our lives are not to be seen as moving towards future happiness, towards anything 'remoter, higher and brighter'. The hope of future immortality is inconsistent, not only with Nietzsche's rejection of temporal teleology, but also with its repudiation of all thought of the self as an ego transcending his present properties and experiences. But there is a version of immortality which Nietzsche does endorse and which is closely connected with the idea of eternal return.

In some passages in *Human, All Too Human*, Nietzsche draws together themes of immortality, eternal return, movement and the activity of writing. The context is a discussion of books and writing in a section called 'From the Souls of Artists and Writers'.[17] Some of Nietzsche's points here are similar to those he makes in repudiating the teleology of time. Just as youth and childhood possess value in themselves, and not merely as bridges and thoroughfares, he says, so 'incomplete thoughts' also have their value. The thoughts of poets are not to be tormented with subtle exegesis, as if they must be complete. 'The poet anticipates something of the joy of the thinker at the discovery of a vital idea and makes us desire it, so that we snatch at it; he, however, flutters by past our heads, displaying the loveliest butterfly wings – and yet he eludes us.' Nietzsche retains the analogy between thought and the movement of insects in an exploration of the way a book, once detached from its author, can, to the author's surprise, go on to live a life of its own as if it were part of an insect that had come free.

That author has drawn the happiest lot who as an old man can say that all of life-engendering, strengthening, elevating, enlightening thought and feeling that was in him lives on in his writings, and that he himself is now nothing but the grey ashes, while the fire has everywhere been rescued and borne forward.

The idea of writers living on in their books is a familiar one. But Nietzsche goes on to suggest that this kind of immortality can be extended to all movement.

If one now goes on to consider that, not only a book, but every action performed by a human being, becomes in some way the cause of other actions, decisions, thoughts, that everything that happens is inextricably knotted to everything that will happen, one comes to recognize the existence of an actual *immortality*, that of motion.

In a powerful and intriguing comparison, he adapts the insect analogy: 'what has once moved is enclosed and eternalized in the total union of all being like an insect in amber.' Nietzsche's image of the insect in the amber seems at first sight static – as if transient life had been deprived of its fragile vitality, pathetically frozen in an enforced immobility. But the point is precisely the opposite.

Nietzsche's emphasis is not on present immobility but on past motion. It is in respect of its having moved that the insect is thought of as eternalized. The bearer of immortality is the movement, caught by another impressionable substance, the amber. It is not the immobilized body of the insect – here analogous to the substantial ego – that is supposed to be immortalized, but rather the movement itself – caught by and continued in other movements, knotted into the encompassing unity of things which transcends the transience of each of its constituents. But the paralysing viscosity of the amber, catching and petrifying a moving transient thing, seems to pull against the intended import of Nietzsche's image.

There is something of the same tension in Nietzsche's idea of eternal recurrence as in the image of the insect in the amber. The idea is supposed to suffuse the transient with something of the eternal – to undermine the privileging of being over becoming. The idea of eternal recurrence shakes us from thinking of the ideal of eternity in terms of something remaining always the same, in favour of a new focus on transience – a delight in what passes. But this seems to be counterbalanced by the awesomeness of the picture of the moment as something that will never be done with, something never to be left behind. Past delights are, it seems, forever caught in the ossifying amber of eternity. The image of the insect in amber is all too reminiscent of specimens bottled in preserving fluid – dead insects to be inspected on dusty shelves. The passing moment – rather than being a source of delight in its very transience – becomes subsumed into the permanence of the eternal. But I think this is to miss the full force of Nietzsche's juxtaposition of becoming and eternity, which has its effects on the concept of eternity no less than on that of becoming. Nietzsche thinks of eternity not in terms of static permanence but in terms of happening – in terms of what always recurs. Eternity itself is to be thought of in terms of movement.

What exactly does the idea of eternity add then to the transience of happening? This amounts to the question as to what exactly is added to the awareness of happening by the elusive thought of eternal recurrence. Let us try to think it through in relation to the relations between past and present. It involves, on the one hand, thinking of the present in the mode of the past – as if it has already happened. The thought of eternal recurrence gives to the present something of the finality of the past.[18] The present loses its fluidity, and takes on determinate shape. It can be understood, articulated. Hence the connections between the idea of eternal return and narrative. Through the idea of eternal return we are able to lay hold on the fleeting present, to give it fixity, to suffuse it with the pastness which is already within it. On the other hand, the idea of eternal return has its effects too on the way we think of the past. The past takes on something of the character of the 'not yet done with' that we normally associate with the present. In thinking of eternal return, we break down the barriers between past and present, thinking each in the mode of the other.

Is it a fiction, this reconstruction of the past as if it had the vitality of the present, and of the present as if it had the finality of the past? In one sense, yes; for it is the stuff of narrative – fictional as well as biographical. Both transformations have connections with the idea of narrative. Through being seen with the finality of the past the present takes on determinate shape, caught in its movement, taken up into the amber of consciousness where it can reverberate with other experience, reach out into other selves. The transformation of the past through the idea of eternal return is rather more complex. Through bringing to the past the fluidity, the lack of fixity, of the present, we are able, in a certain sense, to change it. The past becomes less determinate, less final.

Alexander Nehamas elaborates on this aspect of the connections between eternal return and narrative in his chapter on the eternal return in *Nietzsche: Life as Literature*. This 'willing backward', of course, cannot literally undo the past. Yet, he points out, it is not easy to say what *the* past is in the first place. The events of a past are necessarily located through and within a narrative, and different narratives can generate quite different events.[19] How I see my present self crucially affects my past. The significance of the past – what it amounts to – depends on its relations to the future. The character of each event depends on its eventual implications for the whole of our constantly changing self. An important dimension of Nietzsche's idea of eternal return is that in this way it bestows on the random details of a life the coherence and unity of a narrative. That no event is for the sake of any other – that there is no natural teleology ordering events in relation to each other – leaves the way open for a multiplicity of narratives to give significance to events in a variety of ways. This is not to say that any interpretation of an event is as adequate as any other. The challenge is to integrate all the events of a life into a coherent whole. Nietzsche, Nehamas suggests, models his ideal case, in which if anything is different, everything is different, on his conception of the perfect narrative, the perfect story. The ideal person is assimilated to the ideal literary character and the ideal life to an ideal story.

Nehamas uses Proust's *Remembrance of Things Past* as a model to bring out this aspect of eternal recurrence. Here we see the apparently random details of a life acquire significance in the context of a unified narrative. The novel is a fictional autobiography in which the narrator relates what happened in his rambling efforts to become an author. Unconnected chance events take on a unified pattern, the result of which is his determination to begin at last his first book – the book he has yet to write but which his readers have just finished reading: 'the framework supplied by this perfect novel which relates what, despite and even through its very imperfections, becomes and is seen to be a perfect life, and which keeps turning endlessly back upon itself, is the best possible model for the eternal recurrence'.[20] Proust's 'paradoxical interplay' between creation and discovery, knowledge and action, literature and life, is here offered as an illustration, not of a direct influence of Nietzsche, but of the ideas at the centre of Nietzsche's conception of the self.[21] Through literature, perhaps, we can regain lost time or, at least, learn how to leave it behind.

# Chapter 4

# Life and literature

## PROUST: 'LIFE REALIZED WITHIN THE CONFINES OF A BOOK'

The role of explicit intellectual reflection in creative writing is itself a subject for reflection throughout Proust's *A la Recherche du Temps Perdu*,[1] especially in its extraordinary closing sections. The novel as a whole narrates the process by which its hero becomes its narrator. In the closing sections, the narrator reflects on the literary ideal embodied in the work whose genesis is finally revealed as the substance of the novel itself, now drawing to its close. The truths which the intellectual faculty finds lying in its path 'in full daylight' may, the narrator says, be of very great value, but they are 'like drawings with a hard outline and no perspective'. No depths have had to be traversed in order to reach them. They have not been 'recreated', but 'educed by intellect directly from reality' (III, 935). Such truths are not to be altogether despised. But it is clear that for the narrator they are to be judged by a standard quite different from that of philosophy's traditional exaltation of intellect over senses. There is no question here of intellect being given the highest status in a hierarchy of faculties. Its value resides in its capacity to give a different access to the 'essences' recovered from lost time. In going direct to reality, intellect bypasses the only true path to these essences, whose recovery forms the central thread in the *Recherche*. But those preferred impressions, accessible through 'involuntary memory' rather than intellect, are too rare, we are told, for a work of art to be constructed exclusively from them. Through the reflections of intellect, they may be enshrined in 'a matter less pure indeed, but still imbued with mind' (III, 935).

There is, of course, a self-referential dimension to these con-cluding remarks. They are themselves intellectual reflections, inserted as auxiliary reinforcement into a narrative which gives priority to a 'more pure' treatment of the essences common to past and present sensation. But although the novel is centrally concerned with the regaining of lost time through 'involuntary memory', its treatment of that theme is itself a highly sophistic-ated exercise of intellect no less than of imagination. Through the novel runs a sequence of philosophical reflections that parallels its quasi-autobiographical story – reflections on the process by which writing transforms particular events and experiences into something no longer restricted to their particularity – something akin to universals.

This is a different process from the universalized abstractions of philosophical reason. 'A writer reasons', the narrator says, 'that is to say he goes astray, only when he has not the strength to force himself to make an impression pass through all the succes-sive states which will culminate in its fixation, its expression' (III, 916). The Proustian ideal of writing clearly involves rigorous intellectual activity, though it culminates in 'fixation' and 'ex-pression' rather than 'abstraction'. It involves a process of detachment from the particular, bringing one experience to-gether with another through metaphor or analogy. This artistic process concerns time both in its explicit subject matter and in its formal techniques.

To see the full dimensions of Proust's treatment of the relations between time, self and narrative, we must consider not only the explicit philosophical reflections in the novel, but also the work-ings of 'involuntary memory' which provide the foundations for those reflections, and the narrative techniques through which the deliverances of involuntary memory are transformed into a work of art which 'recovers lost time'. These different levels cannot be kept entirely separate. As Ricoeur points out, even the narrator's philosophical reflections on involuntary memory and time have an irreducibly narrative character.[2] And metaphor itself here has temporal dimensions, bringing together into a unity different experiences relating to different times. The com-ing together of two objects despite their differences, raised to their essence, acts as a form of liberation from the contingencies of time. This is accentuated when the items brought together are themselves 'moments'. Time is regained – as Ricoeur sums it up –

as 'time lost eternalized by metaphor'.[3] Let us now look at the philosophical dimensions of Proust's crucial notion of 'involuntary memory' and the role it plays in relation to this recovery of lost time through the creation of a work of art.

## PROUST AND BERGSON

Clearly Bergson's philosophy is in the background of Proust's variations on themes of time and self-consciousness. But even in its explicit intellectual reflections – and much more in its subtle use of narrative techniques – the novel resists any straightforward summing up of its connections with Bergsonian thought. The novel cannot be presented either as a literary application of Bergsonian philosophy or as consciously offering an opposed view of time. But Bergsonian motifs reverberate throughout the work.

Proust himself acknowledged the influence of Bergson on his thought. In an article published shortly before the appearance of *Swann's Way*, he commented on the similarities and differences between his own treatment of memory and that of Bergson. Just as there is a geometry of planes and a geometry in space, he says, so for him the novel is not just a psychology of 'plane surfaces'; but a 'psychology in time'. He must present experience as having duration in order to isolate the 'invisible substance of time'. This makes it appropriate, he suggests, to see his novel as belonging with 'novels of the unconscious', even perhaps – since at every epoch literature tries to attach itself retrospectively to the reigning philosophy – with 'Bergsonian' novels. But such an assimilation to Bergsonian philosophy, he continues, would not be exact; for his own work is dominated by the distinction between 'involuntary' and 'voluntary' memory – 'a distinction which not only does not figure in Bergson's thought, but is even contradicted by it'.[4]

Is Proust right in thinking that his distinction is incompatible with Bergson's philosophy? How does it relate to Bergson's own distinction between the kinds of memory associated with 'habit' and 'recollection'? Although Bergson's 'recollection' memory cannot always be produced at will, it differs from Proustian involuntary memory in being a product of intellectual effort – a determined turning away from the future to 'go backwards towards the past'. In Proust's narrative, this kind of determined intellectual effort to remember is identified with 'voluntary' memory, which never yields the desired recapturing of past in present. Nor can 'involuntary' memory be identified with Bergson's 'habit' memory. For that is a disposition, developed through repetition of patterns of motor activity, whereas Proust's involuntary memory is not subject to the will. It may well appear then that, as Proust suggests, it cannot be located in Bergson's classification of the kinds of memory. But is it inconsistent with it?

There are some aspects of 'involuntary' memory which do seem to be diametrically opposed to the Bergsonian picture of memory. Bergson's distinctions are governed by his emphasis on action. In *Matter and Memory*, as we have seen, 'motor mechanism' and 'independent recollection' are the two distinct forms in which the past survives. What gives sense to this survival of the past is its prolongation into future action. Memory is, for Bergson, fundamentally 'the utilization of past experience for present action', a utilization which can lie in the 'automatic setting in motion of a mechanism adapted to the circumstances', but can also imply an 'effort of the mind, seeking in the past representations which can be appropriately applied in the present'. Even 'recollection' memory is for Bergson ultimately directed towards action, although, unlike 'habit' memory, it involves a turning back to the past in order to find the representations which will assist future action.

This emphasis on action underpins what is, for Bergson, the radical difference between present and past, ensuring that the difference is not one of degree. It is the motif of action that underlies the difference between past and present. My present is what 'summons me to action', whereas my past is essentially powerless. The present, as we have seen in the previous chapter, is for him given by the possibility of action. It is, 'in its essence', sensori-motor. It consists in the consciousness I have of my body as locus of action. The present is associated with sensation as a source of movement. What I call my present is my impending act. Pure memory, in contrast, does not in any degree share the nature of sensation.

Proustian concern with memory is oriented towards the finding of past in present rather than towards a subsuming of both in the onward movement towards the future. It is not action but contemplation that provides the rationale of his distinctions. His 'involuntary' memory is not subject to the exigencies of action. It is oriented towards the past; and the only concern for the future it elicits is through the creative act which will attempt to give it permanence. Proust's picture of the difficulties in pinning down the elusive intimations of the past given through the experience of involuntary memory nonetheless strongly echoes Bergson. To call up the past in the form of an image, Bergson says, we must withdraw from the action of the moment. And the past captured by this backward-turning memory is fugitive, readily thwarted by the other 'more natural' memory whose forward movement bears us on to action and to life.[5] Memory stored up in motor mechanism 'follows the direction of nature', while that stored in 'personal memory images', left to itself, would rather go the opposite way.[6] This turn backwards into the past, Bergson says, can demand a highly delicate effort of adjustment, 'something like the focusing of a camera'. But despite this conscious effort, recollection remains 'virtual': '. . . we simply prepare ourselves to receive it by adopting the appropriate attitude'.[7]

Bergson's descriptions of the effort to regain the past through recollection memory are, as we shall shortly see, strongly echoed in some of Proust's descriptions of the struggle to bring voluntary memory to bear on the deliverances of involuntary memory – to identify the source of the mysterious pleasure it gives. But Bergson's overriding emphasis on action means that for him there can be no bridging of the gap between past and present – no question of the past in its reality coming into the present.

In their 'pure' forms, Bergson's two kinds of memory are radically separated – the memory which 'recalls' through an image, and the memory which 'repeats' through movement. What can make it appear that the two forms of memory differ only in degree rather than in kind is that in their 'impure' forms they intermingle. 'Pure memory', 'memory image' and 'perception', though distinct, never really occur in separation. Perception is always 'impregnated with memory-images which complete it as they interpret it', and these in turn partake of the 'pure memory' which they begin to materialize and of the perceptions which embody them.[8] Pure memory seeks embodiment in an image. But even when the effort to find the image is successful, the approaching memory never really takes on the character of the present, the form of a perception.

Little by little it comes into view like a condensing cloud; from the virtual state it passes into the actual; and as its outline becomes more distinct and its surface takes on colour, it tends to imitate perception. But it remains attached to the past by its deepest roots, and if when once realized, it did not retain something of its original virtuality, if, being a present state, it were not also something which stands out distinct from the present, we should never know it for a memory.[9]

Despite the inseparability of the processes involved, there remains for Bergson a radical distinction between memory and perception, and between past and present. The past is not to be found in anything 'actual and already realized'. We might as well, he says, 'look for darkness beneath the light'.[10] And what *rapprochement* there is between past and present – between memory and perception – remains at the service of the needs of action. Only what can make itself useful can leave the state of 'pure memory' to come to coincide with a part of my present. For Bergson, memory actualized in an image differs profoundly from pure memory. The image is a present state. 'Memory, on the contrary, is powerless as long as it remains without utility, is pure from all admixture of sensation, is without attachment to the present, and is consequently unextended.'[11] Although Bergson does insist that the difference between past and present is not the difference between non-being and being, this is not because the past has the same actual existence as the present, but, as we have seen in Deleuze's elaboration of the point, because there is a non-psychological, 'virtual' coexistence of past and present – a coexistence which, unlike Augustine's distension of the soul, cannot be reduced to any form of psychological co-presence.

Bergson makes a number of claims about the relations between past and present which resonate in Proust's novel: that past and present, memory and perception are radically distinct but come into close relation; that the distinction between past and present is not aligned with the distinction between being and non-being; that past and present have a virtual coexistence. But none of these claims can be equated with the distinctive blending of past and present which Proust extracts from the experience of involuntary memory and has his narrator re-enact in the act of writing. It is of course possible that Proust's insistence that his own 'involuntary memory' was inconsistent with Bergson's philosophy rests on an inadequate understanding of

Bergson. But the blending of past and present which is supposed to ensue from Proustian involuntary memory cannot be readily mapped on to anything in Bergson's philosophy. It is true that there are a number of ways in which past and present come together for Bergson. But although the idea of a coming together of past and present is clearly in the background of the *Recherche*, none of the ways Bergson allows it to happen can provide a model for Proust's involuntary memory. It is not the prolongation of the past into the future in action. Nor is it the co-presence of memory and perception in 'impure' memory – a juxtaposition of two states which remain radically distinct. Nor is it the lodging of a memory in an image, allowing itself to be replaced by a present state with no essential attachment to the past.

Proust's 'involuntary' memory goes beyond the mere co-presence of memory and perception to assert a daring assimilation – a certain identity even – of memory and perception, of past and present. It is an identity which, as we shall see, poses something of the same paradox as Nietzsche's idea of eternal return. Proust's bringing together of past and present in involuntary memory goes beyond the qualified ways in which Bergson allows that memory can take on the character of a 'nascent perception'. In involuntary memory the past is restored in the fullness of its reality, while yet it is grasped in a present perception. Unlike Bergson's 'virtual' coexistence of past and present, Proust's involuntary memory brings the past into the present. But, unlike Augustine's treatment of time, it does not reduce the past to a form of presentness. Let us now turn to the novel to see how this is supposed to happen and what Proust takes to be its significance for the understanding of the relations between self-consciousness, time and narrative.

## INVOLUNTARY MEMORY

In the early sections of the novel the preservation of the past through involuntary memory is presented as a matter of chance – something we are powerless to bring about through any effort of will or intellect. The narrator refers to the 'Celtic belief' that the souls of the dead are held captive in some inanimate object – effectively lost to us until the day, which may not come at all, when we happen to pass by the tree or to obtain possession of the object which forms their prison, allowing them to 'overcome death and return to share our life'. We labour in vain to recapture our past. Here all efforts of intellect must prove futile.

> The past is hidden somewhere outside the realm, beyond the reach of intellect, in some material object which can give us a sensation of which as yet we have no inkling. And it depends on chance whether we come upon the object before we ourselves must die.
>
> (1, 47–8)

Intellect belongs with voluntary memory. Its pictures preserve nothing of the past itself. Regaining the past involves, as we shall see, a different kind of abstraction from the particularity of experience, a different kind of focus on what things have in common. The distance of involuntary memory from intellect is marked by the fact that the sensations which elicit it are characteristically not associated with sight – the sense traditionally regarded by philosophers as closest to intellect – but rather with the 'lower' senses – taste, smell or touch. In the taste of a morsel of cake moistened with tea, the hero feels his senses invaded with an exquisite pleasure – 'something isolated, detached, with no suggestion of its origin', but which clearly comes from the past. This pleasure in finding the past in the present – the full understanding of which is not revealed until the concluding sections of the novel – is associated with access to the truth of the self. The sensation has the effect of filling the hero with a 'precious essence' which is not so much in him as identical with him. He senses that this all-powerful joy infinitely transcends the taste of the tea and the cake, indeed that it cannot be of the same nature. The essence yielded by involuntary memory is already grasped as a truth which lies not outside but within himself. His seeking mind feels 'overtaken by itself'. The seeker is at the same time 'the dark region through which it must go seeking and where all its equipment will avail it nothing' – the region in which he must not only seek but create (I, 49).

In Proust's description of the release of the past in the taste of the *madeleine*, involuntary memory is already inchoately associated with the creativity of art. The mind is 'face to face with something which does not yet exist, to which it alone can give reality and substance, which it alone can bring to the light of day'. Activity and passivity come together in the effort to find the source of the mysterious pleasure. The narrator's description of the struggle to identify its source echoes Bergson's of the effort to recollect.

I place in position before my mind's eye the still recent taste of that first mouthful, and I feel something start within me, something that leaves its resting-place and attempts to rise, something that has been embedded like an anchor at a great depth; I do not know yet what it is, but I can feel it mounting slowly, I can measure the resistance, I can hear the echo of the great spaces traversed.

(I, 49)

Bergsonian 'recollection' – or Proustian 'voluntary' memory – can only try to identify the origin of a sensation which it has not itself provided. The desired explanation of the pleasure lies beyond anything that could be captured in the elusive visual images in which he initially seeks it. Visual memory tries unsuccessfully to follow the taste of the cake into his conscious mind. The magnetism of an identical moment travels 'to importune, to disturb', to raise up from the depths this old dead moment. Suddenly the memory reveals itself: the taste of the *madeleine* which his great-aunt Léonie used to give him, dipping it first in her fruit tisane. The dormant images had lost the 'power of expansion' which would have allowed them to resume their place in consciousness. But taste and smell, enduring in their fragility, carry with them the 'vast structure of recollection' (I, 50–51).

The hero does not yet know and must long postpone, the narrator tells us, the discovery of why this memory makes him so happy. But the previously unremembered details of life at Combray now spring into being, taking shape and solidity from his cup of tea (I, 51). The dead leaves in the tisane can retain something of the past when they may have been sprigs of real lime trees perfuming the evening air (I, 55). Just as the past can thus have a kind of presence in the dead flowers, so too, in a different way, the taste of the cake dipped in tea is supposed to bring back the past.

It is the past itself, the narrator insists, that is given in involuntary memory, in contrast to the mere pictures of the past that are delivered by voluntary memory. The distinctive pleasure found in involuntary memory is not a matter of describing a 'snapshot' of the past, any more than it can be found in describing something actually perceived. Such 'mental snapshots', the narrator reflects later in the novel, are as boring as an exhibition of photographs (III, 897–8). To understand the relations between involuntary memory and the real past, the hero must make a shift away from external reality towards what happens in his own consciousness. It is within himself that the past is to be found; and this allows Proust to insist that it is the past itself – not just a present image of it – which is given in these experiences. What is involved is not just a recurrence of something similar to the past but a restoration of past sensations, resuscitated by similar ones. Out of his reflections on involuntary memory comes the conviction that the real past is still within him. He experiences again the sensations of childhood. Although such moments will never be possible for him again, if he listens attentively he can catch the sound of his own crying as a young child. The echoes have in reality never ceased and are heard anew, now that life has grown quieter around him, like the convent bells which are drowned by street noise during the day but ring out through the silent evening air (I, 40). He can hear again the real peal of the garden gate bell that heralded the arrival of Swann to visit his family; and its reappearance from the past confirms for him the continuity of his own consciousness (III, 1105–6).

The reality of the past and its continuity with the present is assured by its being found in the self. The noise of water running in a pipe brings back, not a mere analogous sensation, or even an echo or replica of a past sensation, but the past sensation itself (III, 907). This internalization of the external, the spiritualization of material reality, also strikes Bergsonian echoes. But Proust's version of the collapse of dualism – if we were to take all this as expressing a philosophical position – is nearer to idealism. Where Bergson tries to undermine the opposition between realism and idealism in favour of a body image that can be accommodated on neither side of the division between mind and matter, Proust confidently affirms a kind of spiritualization of matter.

It is this aspect of Proust's thought which makes Sartre see in it a paradigm of the 'digestive' philosophy – the 'nutritional' assimilation of everything into consciousness – from which Husserl's notion of intentionality, with its stress on 'bursting out' of 'moist, gastric intimacy' into something beyond internal life, offered such a welcome release: '. . . if we love a woman it is because she is lovable. We are delivered from Proust.'[12] Sartre sees

Proust's writing as exuding an obnoxious 'genteel mist' of self-absorption. It is true that the novel does accentuate the internalization of the external. The inwardness of Proustian consciousness can suggest claustrophobia. But the philosophical implications of this inward turn are richer than the insipid subjective idealism evoked by Sartre. The recovery of the past delivers the self from obsession with the inwardness of present experience into a regaining of the real past. The artistic analogue of involuntary memory is not a dwelling on subjective impressions, but a transformation of the particularity of experience into something universal. Involuntary memory provides the model for the regaining of the real past through writing.

## THE 'MIRACLE OF ANALOGY': WRITING, SELF-CONSCIOUSNESS AND TIME

The youthful hero of the early sections of the novel is presented as longing to find a philosophical theme which will be the key to his future literary creativity. This, he thinks, is the meaning to be sought in the mysterious pleasures evoked in him by experiences of involuntary memory. Initially he thinks of this pleasure as deriving from some specific essence which intellect must uncover. But in truth, he later realizes, it is the experiences of involuntary memory themselves which hold the key to understanding the creative process. Strenuous intellectual activity is involved in transforming these experiences into art; and the process involves a contemplation of 'essences' which are, in a sense, 'outside time'. But the way in which Proustian essences are 'outside time' is very far from the timelessness of Platonic ideas. The mysterious pleasure of involuntary memory, the narrator comes to realize, does not in fact attach to the contemplation of an essence uncovered by intellect, but to the discovery of his own being in time.

The transformation of the external into the internal – the spiritualization of matter – becomes in the final volume the key to understanding both the recovery of the past and the process of artistic creation. But already in the opening sections of the novel the way is prepared for this understanding of art. Reading represents a stage in the young hero's progress towards this inward turn, allowing him to make of his thoughts a recess in which he can bury himself, remaining invisible even while he looks at what is going on outside. At this stage he sees the books he reads as external repositories of a philosophical richness and beauty which he can incorporate into himself.

The narrator, commenting from an external position of superior insight, can see the transformation of outer reality differently – not as a process of attaining to pre-existing truths, but rather as a transformation of particular events and characters into a kind of universal different from those grasped through intellectual reflection. The one essential element in the complicated structure of our emotions is a mediating mental image, and the ingenuity of the first novelist lay in understanding that the suppression of the irrelevant details accompanying it in real people would be a decided improvement. 'The novelist's happy discovery was to think of substituting for these opaque sections, impenetrable to the human soul, their equivalent in immaterial sections, things, that is, which one's soul can assimilate' (I, 91). The truths the hero is seeking are not to be found in any external reality to which he might break through. What he hears as he reads is not 'an echo from without', but the 'resonance of a vibration from within' (I, 93).

It is only in the narrator's final reflections on life and art that we see exactly how the themes of involuntary memory, time, self and writing come together. Here the narrator, having returned to Paris from a long absence in a sanatorium, attends a social gathering where he sees the passage of time made visible in the facial features and demeanour of his friends. The pleasure of involuntary memory, he now sees, arises from experiencing the past in the present – a kind of access to the eternal which yields also a pleasure in making contact with one's true self. Art allows us to 'travel back in the direction from which we have come to the depths where what has really existed lies unknown within us' (III, 932). Although the mystery is revealed only in these final passages, the way has been prepared in earlier episodes connecting involuntary memory with writing. Perhaps the most powerful and revealing illustrations of this idea of writing as a mode of access to the 'lost' past is the episode of the steeples described in the early 'Combray' section of the novel. The steeple at Combray has already been introduced as evoking the feeling of a 'unique essence', which keeps in thrall a whole section of the hero's inmost life – a 'tract of soil reclaimed from the waters of Lethe' (I, 72). As with the other experiences of the mysterious pleasure evoked by involuntary memory, the hero at this stage seeks to explain it as the expression of some external, elusive essence. He tries to recall the line of the roof, the colour of the stone, but impressions of this kind could not, he thinks, fulfil his hope of becoming an author, for they are associated with material objects devoid of intellectual significance. The mystery that lies hidden in a shape or a perfume eludes him. But the later episode, also involving steeples, brings him closer to the truth.

Riding on the box behind the coachman in a carriage, the young hero experiences at a bend in the road 'that special pleasure which is like no other' on catching sight of the twin steeples at Martinville, bathed in the setting sun and constantly changing their position with the movement of the carriage and the windings of the road. Then a third steeple, in fact separated from them by a hill and a valley, appears to be standing by their side. In noticing the shapes of their spires, their shifting lines, the sunny warmth of their surface, he feels that he is not penetrating to the core of his impressions, that something more lies behind that nobility, that luminosity – something which they seem at once to contain and to conceal. As he reflects on them, presently their outlines and their sunlit surfaces peel away, as though they had been 'a sort of rind'. The pleasure takes the form of words as a thought frames itself in his mind. He immediately writes a short description of the changing steeples (I, 196–8). By framing this youthful experiment in narration with reflections on involuntary memory and writing, Proust makes it illustrate the connections between involuntary memory, self-consciousness and time.

The desire to preserve, to salvage the transient from the destructive effects of time is central to the Proustian links between time and writing. Through writing some things are elected to survive in all their most ephemeral details – the scent of hawthorn, a sound of echoless footsteps on a gravel path, a bubble formed against the side of a water-plant, kept alive when the paths around them and the memory of those who trod them have vanished. Yet what in fact survives through being written about is not the thing itself in all its actual ephemeral details, but a transformation, a spiritualization of it – something which, as the narrator puts it in the concluding sections of the novel, becomes common property, a self-understanding which is detached from the particular things or happenings which prompted the desire to write.

It is this capacity for detachment from the particular which eludes Swann, whose love story is juxtaposed with the hero's childhood experiences. Swann's lack of understanding of the significance of involuntary memory mirrors that of his youthful friend. Swann too thinks of involuntary memory – in his case the pleasure in repeated hearings of the little phrase from the Vinteuil sonata – as giving access to a unique essence which lies outside himself, something which he tries to penetrate. The phrase, he thinks, belongs to a world of inexpressible delights – a world into which nothing else could initiate him, which he loves with a new and strange desire (I, 228). The phrase becomes an emblem of Swann's love for his mistress Odette and, as he sees it, a point of access to a truth, a reality that transcends the senses (I, 258). The 'little phrase' acts for him as a source of self-discovery – a means of access to the 'vast, unfathomed and forbidden night of our soul which we take to be an impenetrable void' (I, 380). The love of music becomes linked with the experience of love itself, speaking to him of another world, of another order, 'ideas veiled in shadow, unknown, impenetrable to the human mind, but none the less perfectly distinct from one another' (I, 379). But it is also internalized to his mind, and, thus transformed and spiritualized, it becomes a symbol of the hope for something that resists death. Perhaps they will be obliterated, if we return to nothingness. But so long as we are alive, we cannot bring ourselves to a state in which we shall not have known them. The destiny of the little phrase is linked to the reality of the soul itself.

> Perhaps it is not-being that is the true state, and all our dream of life is inexistent; but if so, we feel that these phrases of music, these conceptions which exist in relation to our dream, must be nothing either. We shall perish, but we have as hostages these divine captives who will follow and share our fate. And death in their company is somehow less bitter, less inglorious, perhaps even less probable.
>
> (I, 381)

Swann, we are given to understand, is right in seeing the phrase as a harbinger of truth. But he lacks the insight that will eventually come to the narrator, that the truth lies not outside but within himself. He glimpses the truth of the little phrase as something that transcends his own trivial loves and obsessions, but cannot follow it where it leads – away from his superficial self to bring him back to his true self. The phrase, though perhaps it symbolizes a 'call', is incapable of 'creating new powers and making Swann the writer that he was not' (III, 911).

Even in the midst of his obsession, Swann is well aware that his love for Odette does not correspond to anything independently real or valuable – that her qualities cannot warrant his valuing so highly the hours he spends with her. The little phrase has the power to alter the proportions of his soul, making it possible for him to enjoy a love which is not 'purely individual'. However he lacks the means to satisfy the thirst for an unknown delight which the phrase awakes in him. Those parts of his soul in which the little phrase obliterates all concern for material interest are left vacant, 'blank pages on which he was at liberty to inscribe the name of Odette' (I, 258–9).

Swann's response to the little phrase represents a false mode of the return to self – a mode which cannot find fulfilment in writing. The little phrase begins in him a process of detachment from the particular which can lead on to that transformation of life into art – the perception that life can be 'realized within the confines of a book' – which is also, for Proust, the discovery of life itself. But Swann, confusing the source of the delight the phrase gives him with the delights of love itself, cannot make that journey. It is this journey which the *Recherche* in its entirety narrates as the story of its hero's search for the connections between involuntary memory and writing. The revelation of the secret comes by chance. Having 'knocked at all the doors which lead nowhere', we stumble without knowing it on 'the only door through which one can enter' (III, 898). There is about the writer's eventual breakthrough into the beginning of his creative work the same element of chance that determines which of the multitude of episodes will be preserved through writing. The birth of the creative act itself, no less than the determination of the objects which it will salvage from the destructive effects of the past, is subject to chance.

Standing outside the Guermantes's house before the momentous matinée, the narrator feels again the sensation of standing on uneven paving stones previously experienced in Venice. The napkin on which he wipes his lips brings back the towel on which he dried his face in front of the window in the hotel he visited in his youth at Balbec, releasing from its folds 'the plumage of an ocean green and blue like the tail of a peacock' (III, 901). What he finds himself enjoying in these episodes is a whole instant of his life – something which a feeling of fatigue or sadness had perhaps prevented him from enjoying earlier, but which now, 'freed from what is necessarily imperfect in external perception, pure and disembodied', makes him 'swell with happiness' (III, 901). This is a joy which seems to make death a matter of indifference. The narrator now understands that the sensations awakened in him by the uneven paving stones, the stiffness of the napkin, the taste of the *madeleine*, have no connection with what he frequently tried to explicitly recall to himself of Venice, Balbec, Combray. He now experiences directly the reality of his life, as distinct from the images gained through voluntary memory which preserve nothing of it, just as the little phrase gives Swann back 'the days themselves just as they were when he had felt them in the past' (III, 902).

What is distinctive about the pleasures of involuntary memory, the narrator now knows, is that they involve the coming together of past and present, breaking the grip of time. The 'being within him' which had enjoyed these pleasures, he reflects, did so because they had in them something that was common to a day long past and the present, because they were in some way 'extra-temporal'. This being makes its appearance only when it is likely to find itself in the one and only medium in which it could exist – that is, 'outside time' (III, 904). Hence their connection with the loss of fear of death. That which enjoys these sensations which belong to both past and present, is outside time, unalarmed by the vicissitudes of the future.

The fear of death is interwoven throughout the novel with the fear of change to the self – a fear that is bound up with the demise of love. Love and death, the narrator reflects, resemble one another in that they make us probe deeper into the mystery of personality, in the fear that its reality may elude us (I, 336). Swann fears death itself no more than his recovery from his love, which would in fact amount to the death of all he now is. Like the young Augustine, he finds the prospect of losing his grief as unendurable as the loss which occasions it. But to the eventual diminution of his love there corresponds a simultaneous diminution of his desire to remain in love. 'For a man cannot change, that is to say become another person, while continuing to obey the dictates of the self which he has ceased to be' (I, 410). The fear of death, the narrator says in the final stages of the novel, has made him dread the end of each new love. He could not bear the idea that the 'I' who loved would one day cease to exist, since this in itself would be a kind of death. But by dint of repetition this fear has gradually been transformed into a calm confidence.

> So that if in those early days, as we have seen, the idea of death had cast a shadow over my loves, for a long time now the remembrance of love had helped me not to fear death. For I realized that dying was not something new, but that on the contrary since my childhood I had already died many times.
>
> (III, 1094)

Writing shares with the experience of involuntary memory this possibility of escape from time which can allay the fear of death. The 'miracle of an analogy' achieves through conscious effort a bringing together of different moments similar to that achieved through involuntary memory. Writing thus construed allows him to perform the task which had always defeated the efforts of his memory and intellect – to rediscover 'days that were long past, the Time that was Lost' (III, 904). It unifies past and present moments in a way that makes of them an identity – extracting from the past something universal which it can share with the present. 'A moment of the past, did I say? Was it not perhaps very much more: something that, common both to the past and to the present, is much more essential than either of them' (III, 905).

This coming together of past and present is also a coming together of perception and imagination – a 'marvellous expedient of nature' which causes a sensation to be mirrored at one and the same time in the past – so that his imagination is permitted to savour it – and in the present, which 'adds existence to it'. Reality has so often disappointed him in the course of his life, he reflects, because he can imagine only what is absent. But this law is annulled in involuntary memory, which makes it possible for imagination to work simultaneously with perception. This is what links involuntary memory with the creative process; for art, likewise, demands a coming together of perception and imagination. This 'subterfuge' allows the mind to imagine what is already present – 'to secure, to isolate, to immobilize – for a moment brief as a flash of lightning – what normally it never apprehends: a fragment of time in the pure state' (III, 905).

Turning away from world to self, spiritualizing things by transforming them into their internal non-material equivalents, is central to Proust's idea of art. Things, as soon as we have perceived them, are transformed into something immaterial – 'something of the same nature as all our preoccupations and sensations of that particular time, with which, indissolubly, they blend' (III, 920). It is this inner, immaterial equivalent of the external that is the proper concern of art. It is a defect of 'realism' as an artistic theory, the narrator suggests, that it severs all links of the present with the past and the future by ignoring this 'double' character which is a feature of all our impressions. Realism captures only the half which is 'sheathed' in the object, ignoring the other half prolonged in ourselves which we alone can know (III, 927). Experience teaches the narrator the impossibility of attaining in the real world to what lies deep within himself (III, 910). The objects to be regained lie within the self. But the effort to decipher and recover them is at the same time the process through which they become ours. 'From ourselves comes only that which we drag forth from the obscurity which lies within us, that which to others is unknown' (III, 914).

The discovery which art 'obliges us to make' is 'the discovery of our true life, of reality as we have felt it to be' (III, 915). Real life, at last laid bare and illuminated – the only life in consequence which can be said to be 'really lived' – is literature, although it is all the time immanent in ordinary human beings no less than in the artist (III, 931). Writing, the narrator says in the concluding sections, breaks habits, takes us into the depths of the self. Echoing Augustine, he sees the return of the past as an 'enlargement' of the mind, in which the past reforms and actualizes itself, momentarily giving him something whose value is eternal.

Art, like involuntary memory, is supposed to have access to the reality of past experience – to the essences of things, as distinct from 'the consideration of a past made arid by the intellect', or the anticipation of a future narrowed by utilitarian purposes. Here we see again the distance between Proust and Bergson. Bergson's 'intuition' is also of course supposed to transcend the narrowly utilitarian concerns of practical intellect. But the duration –the 'continuity of becoming' – which it captures remains directed towards the onward movement of time.

Art, like all activity, must of course be in a sense oriented to the future. But for the Proustian narrator, the focus is on the relations between past and present. The future is relevant to his art only in the threat its vicissitudes pose to the completion of his work.

In the creation of literature, as Proust conceives it, there is, then, a kind of detachment from the particular – a construction of a kind of universal different from that involved in the derivation of universal concepts out of particulars through intellectual abstraction. Involuntary memory embraces the incidental accompaniments of a sensation which are set aside by intellect – the things which logically have no connection with the sensation and so are irrelevant to the process of forming general concepts. Intellect can make nothing of such things for its own rational purposes. But in such things – the pink reflection of the evening on a flower-covered wall, the 'blue volutes of the morning sea', the simplest act or gesture remains immersed as within a sealed vessel (III, 902).

It is these recovered incidental accompaniments of a perception that release the past and with it the temporal reality of the self. A noise or scent, once heard or smelt, if it is heard or smelt again in the present, is both in the present and in the past. And with the liberation of the past, our true self is awakened and reanimated. A minute freed from the order of time re-creates in us, to feel it, a being 'freed from the order of time' – the mind which, being 'situated outside time', has no fear for the future, no fear of death. Writing reproduces this breaking of the grip of time achieved by involuntary memory. It brings together, as involuntary memory does, past and present, memory and perception, creating out of the particular experienced in the past something common to past and present – something 'more essential than both'.

## REPETITION AND THE REGAINING OF LOST TIME

For the hero of the *Recherche*, it is repetition – the experiencing again of what has been experienced before – that gives substance to consciousness. All the things in life that have once existed tend to recur; and its coming from the past is what gives depth and richness – reality even – to what he experiences. Reality takes shape in memory. If we breathe a new air, the sense of renewal comes precisely from having breathed it before: '. . . the true paradises are the paradises that we have lost' (III, 903). But what is restored through the recreation of the past in literature is never exactly what was lost. The particular things, persons, experiences which are 'preserved' in literature are for Proust transformed into an 'essence' which escapes time at the cost of no longer being exactly what it was, in all its ephemeral detail. There is in art, the narrator reflects at the end of the work, a certain inevitable infidelity. Involuntary memory gives a fragment of existence withdrawn from time. The narrator looks to writing as a way of giving permanence to these impressions, allowing him to savour them more fully by 'trying to get to know them more completely in the medium in which they existed, that is to say within himself, to try to make them translucid even to their very depths' (III, 911). But what he seeks is not so much to preserve the past moment itself, as rather to 'immobilize' the contemplation of essences. Art seeks to express the 'essence of the past a second time', and if it fails there is a lesson to be learnt from its impotence – that this essence is in part subjective and incommunicable. To the extent that it succeeds, it loses fidelity to the particularity of its origins. This unfaithfulness, however, is something for which the experience of love and loss has already prepared him. And it is also a painful but unavoidable reflection of the real nature of the unity of the self. It is akin to the processes by which we successively replace our loves, changing who we are, and to the process of dying. The things we have loved in their particularity are transformed to take on something of the character of ideas: '. . . it is not individuals who really exist and are, in consequence, capable of being expressed, but ideas' (III, 946).

The narrator's loves, to which he has clung so tenaciously, will in his book become so detached from any individual that different readers will apply them, even in detail, to what they have felt for other people. The forgotten words, which record the names on the tombs in the huge cemetery of past experience which constitutes a book, may first need to be transcribed into 'a language which is universal, but which for that very reason will at least be permanent' (III, 940–1). This language, he hopes, may make out of the 'truest essence' of those who are no more, a lasting acquisition for the minds of all mankind. Nothing has the power to survive, says the narrator, unless it can become general, and the mind's own past is dead to present consciousness (III, 941). But there is in this bleak truth a promise of happiness, too, for it shows that 'in every love the particular and the general lie side by side', and it teaches us to pass from one to the other by a 'species of gymnastics' which fortifies us against unhappiness by making us neglect its particular cause in order to gain a more profound understanding of its essence (III, 942). 'Ideas come to us as the successors to griefs, and griefs, at the moment when they change into ideas, lose some part of their power to injure our heart' (III, 944).

Throughout the novel memories are superimposed on one another – memories from different periods of the hero's life and also from other lives, especially Swann's, whose experiences are re-enacted in the narrator's – to form a single mass within which different layers can be discerned like the veining which points to differences of origin and age in rocks. This superimposition of memories gives self-consciousness what substance and unity it has.

> what we suppose to be our love or our jealousy is never a single, continuous and individual passion. It is composed of an infinity of successive loves, of different jealousies, each of which is ephemeral, although by their uninterrupted multiplicity they give us the impression of continuity, the illusion of unity.
>
> (I, 404)

There is in all this something of the same paradox we have seen in Nietzsche's idea of eternal return. How can an experience be both new and experienced before, both present and past? But in Proust's transformations of the particularity of experiences into the distinctive universality of art, and in his reflections on that process, we can perhaps see a way out of the paradox of the return of the same. For the paradoxes we encountered in Nietzsche in relation to eternal return are transcended in Proust's treatment of the consequences for time and self-consciousness of the creative transformations of experience into art. In literature, for Proust, the specific and the general stand in a different relationship from what we are familiar with in the relations between universal concepts and their instances. In the light of Proust, we can see in Nietzsche's eternal recurrence an image of the transformation of the particular into the 'concrete universal' of fictional narrative.

This is a different aspect of the transformation of life into art from what we have seen in Nehamas's interpretation of

Nietzsche, which stresses the connections between eternal return and the narrative unity of a life. That aspect of the relations between time, self and narrative we have seen also in the discussion of Augustine – the holding together of disparate things into a necessary unity which, in making its own temporal structure, also in a sense transcends time. But there is another aspect of eternal return which can be seen more clearly in the light of Proust's enactments of and reflections on the processes of literary creation – the grasping of past in present through involuntary memory; and this is also an incipient form of narrative.

The Proustian resolution of the dilemma of eternal return is through this kind of transformation of experience into art, of life into literature. The process, again, is fundamentally one of metaphor, the joining of two temporally disparate sensations – a bringing together, however, which is no mere decoration but a source of access to reality.

> An hour is not merely an hour, it is a vase full of scents and sounds and projects and climates, and what we call reality is a certain connection between these immediate sensations and the memories which envelop us simultaneously with them – a connexion that is suppressed in a simple cinematographic vision, which just because it professes to confine itself to the truth in fact departs widely from it – a unique connexion which the writer has to rediscover in order to link for ever in his phrase the two sets of phenomena which reality joins together.
>
> (III, 924)

The layering of different strata of time, the superimposing of past and present, is for Proust crucial to the expression of reality in writing.

> Truth – and life too – can be attained by us only when, by comparing a quality common to the two sensations, we succeed in extracting their common essence and in reuniting them to each other, liberated from the contingencies of time, within a metaphor.
>
> (III, 925)

The reality of a life lived in time is a perpetual weaving of fresh threads which link events and lives – threads that are crossed and rewound, double and redoubled to thicken the web, so that 'between any slightest point of our past and all the others a rich network of memories gives us an almost infinite variety of communicating paths to choose from' (III, 1086). To present the past just as it was when it was itself the present – as it might be captured in a successful act of 'voluntary' memory – would be, the narrator says, to 'suppress the mighty dimension of Time which is the dimension in which life is lived' (III, 1087). The 'three-dimensional psychology', through which might be told the story of a life, demands ways of showing how time disposes its different elements in different planes. Style for the writer, no less than colour for the painter, is 'a question not of technique but of vision' (III, 931). But vision, as Proust says in his essay on Flaubert, can also be a matter of 'style and technique'. And he makes use of the phenomenon of memory, in place of 'fact', to pass from one plane to another.[13]

To achieve the essential superimpositions of memory Proust draws on a range of narrative techniques. Genette has called attention, for example, to the ways in which his writing manifests narrative's capacity for temporal autonomy – to the ways in which he is able to liberate the forms of narrative temporality from their dramatic function, letting them play for their own sake. Even the narrator's philosophical reflections become subordinate to the demands of narrative. Passages which may appear superficially descriptive, for example, turn out to be, not so much descriptions of the object contemplated as narratives of the perceptual activity of the character contemplating – of his impressions, discoveries, shifts in distance and perspective, errors and corrections, enthusiasms or disappointments. Contemplation becomes a subject for narrative, just like any other activity. Description is absorbed into narration.[14]

Perhaps the most revealing aspect of Proust's technique for our purposes, however, is the manipulation of tenses which Genette calls his use of the 'iterative'.[15] Here, a single narrative sentence takes upon itself several events considered only in terms of their analogy. The text of 'Combray' narrates, in the French imperfect tense for repeated action, what used to happen regularly. The narrative of Swann's love for Odette is also carried on for the most part in this mode of custom and repetition; and the final scene in 'Time Regained' is treated almost continuously in this iterative mode. Each encounter with a drastically changed figure from the past takes on the role of symptom of the universal and relentless passage of time. The narrator's recognition of each in turn – predicating, as it does, contradictory things of a single subject, admitting that what was no longer exists and that what is here now is a person one did not know – takes him into a 'mystery almost as disturbing as that of death, of which it is, indeed, as it were the preface and the harbinger' (III, 982). Particular scenes are presented as symptomatic of a whole period of life. Things are expressed in the mode of repetition which could not be seriously regarded as recurring repeatedly in that manner. Françoise did not repeat that identical rambling speech, and even the well established rituals of French small-town life could not have accommodated the extent of repetition of behaviour and conversation which makes up the hero's memories of Sundays at Combray. A singular scene will be converted into a recurring one – treated as if it were to eternally return. Actions and events are presented as having a capacity for repetition and renewal which is quite contrary to their nature. The subtle use of the imperfect tense here accentuates the tendency of moments to come together, the precondition of voluntary memory. Keeping one's attention fixed on two moments at the same time allows them to be considered as merging. The alternation of iterative and singular gives a distinctive rhythm to the novel, accentuating the relations between the singular and the universal which are taken up and transformed in the process of artistic creation.

The use of narrative techniques is also central to Proust's presentation of self-consciousness. Writing, the narrator says in the concluding sections, 'breaks habits, takes us into the depths of the self'. But the novel is not written from any assumed depths of self-presence. The Proustian narrator exerts a strong control over the narration of the process by which the hero becomes the writer – over the gradual convergence of the 'I' of the hero and the 'I' of the narrator. Proust's use of 'free indirect speech', as Genette again has pointed out, allows the narrator to dominate the consciousness of the protagonist. The narrating voice, rather than being immersed within the consciousness of the character – speaking as he or she might speak in immediate monologue – retains an external perspective from which the truth can be revealed. The hero's self-deceptions, no less than Swann's, are exposed not through any explicit narratorial commentary, but simply by presenting the character's thoughts from an independent perspective. The narrator always retains the stronger position in relation to the character, even where, as throughout most of the novel, that character is the hero who shares an identity with the narrator. Here the use of the first person does not at all imply that the narrative is 'focalized' through the hero. It in fact gives the narrator more authority to speak in his own name than he would have in a third-person narrative. Nor does the constant presence of the narrator make the novel a subjective sequence of impressions. Here, as Genette puts it, there is no 'settling into the comfort of subjectivity', but perhaps exactly the opposite – a distancing from and off-centring of the self: the hero is 'neither completely himself nor completely someone else'.[16] The hero and the narrator cannot be completely identified either with each other or with Proust. The hero is constructed out of the same kind of process of detachment and transformation of the individual that produces other fictions. Although the theme of the novel is the internalization and spiritualization of things into the stuff of literature – equated with the discovery of the true self – this is in some ways not at all a return to the depths of the self but rather a transformation of the self too into something akin to a universal.

## VIRGINIA WOOLF: MOMENTS OF BEING

Concern with the inner contents of consciousness is a distinctive preoccupation of the modern novel, and recent narrative theory has enriched our appreciation of the diverse ways in which narrative techniques can engage with self-consciousness. Narrators position themselves in a variety of ways. Nor is it only the 'depths' of consciousness that exert a fascination in the modern novel. In her essay 'Modern Fiction', Virginia Woolf talks of an ideal of writing which captures the myriad impressions of an ordinary mind on an ordinary day, falling from all sides in an 'incessant shower of innumerable atoms', shaping themselves into the life of Monday or Tuesday. Life, she says there, is not 'a series of gig lamps symmetrically arranged', but a 'luminous halo, a semi-transparent envelope surrounding us from the beginning of consciousness to the end'. Is it not the task of the novelist, she asks, to convey this 'varying, unknown and uncircumscribed spirit, with as little mixture of the alien and external as possible?'[1]

Most of Virginia Woolf's fiction by no means conforms to the model of capturing the contents of an ordinary mind on an ordinary day. But much of it engages directly with the complexities of self-consciousness in its relations with time. She read Proust with admiration, commenting in her essay 'Phases of Fiction' on his capacity for a 'dual vision', embracing both the unconscious and what transcends consciousness.[2] In her diaries she remarks on his combination of the utmost sensibility with the utmost tenacity. 'He searches out those butterfly shades to the last grain. He is as tough as cat gut and as evanescent as a butterfly's bloom. And he will I suppose both influence me & make me out of temper with every sentence of my own.'[3] He induces in her, she says in a letter, an astonishing vibration and saturation and intensification of the desire to write.[4] And in another letter she describes reading Proust as a great adventure. He solidifies what has always escaped, making it into a 'beautiful and perfectly enduring substance', as if a miracle were being performed before her eyes. 'One has to put the book down and gasp. The pleasure becomes physical – like sun and wine and grapes and perfect serenity and intense vitality combined.' 'Well', she asks, ' – what remains to be written after that?'[5]

Woolf's own work, however, goes on to exploit, more than Proust's did, the range of narrative techniques that allow the novelist to engage with the complexities of consciousness in its relations to time. Where Proust's narrative for the most part moves between narrator and protagonist, her narratives move between a multiplicity of selves, and into a cosmic view from nowhere which both frames and disrupts individual consciousness.

Even within Proust's 'first-person' narrative, as we have seen, there is considerable complexity in the positioning of the self in relation to the contents of consciousness. But Woolf's novels display a richer use of narrative techniques to engage with the complexities and the predicaments of the self's identity and its relations with time. Ricoeur comments on the way she gives 'temporal depth' to the narrative through 'the entanglement of the narrated present with the remembered past'.[6] The effects are comparable to the temporal strata of what Proust describes as the 'psychology of time', but Woolf takes it further. For Proust, the layers are mainly within one consciousness – or at any rate within the unified consciousnesses of the hero and the narrator, with some overlaying from the story of Swann. And even Swann's story is reflected through the narrator's interpretations of the similarities between Swann and himself. Woolf's *Mrs Dalloway*, in contrast, presents temporal experience as belonging to no one character to the exclusion of the others. The experience of time is suggested to the reader as a whole network of consciousness – the reverberation of one solitary experience in another.[7]

The shifts in narratorial perspective that are such a striking feature of *Mrs Dalloway* are already present in *Jacob's Room*.[8] Here the narrator occupies a variety of positions, sometimes descending into the thoughts of a particular character, sometimes taking flight to the skies. The effects can be startling and they have their philosophical import, anticipating in some ways ideas of the dispersion of subjectivity, which become explicit in later theoretical writings. *Jacob's Room* has been seen as addressing the theme of the unknowability of the self. But although it is true that the question 'Who knows Jacob?' is explicitly raised, this is part of a broader concern with the question 'What is Jacob?' What is at stake is the very nature of the strange phenomenon of individual consciousness. What really changes at death, the novel asks, for a consciousness whose identity even in life is partly constituted through the perceptions, thoughts and emotional responses of others?

*Jacob's Room* is the story of the life of a young man who dies in war. Throughout the novel, Jacob seems to remain as elusive to himself as to other characters and to the reader. Although some situations are described from his perspective, we are not taken into any depths of inner character. The novel traces the growth of Jacob's individual consciousness. We see it emerge from formlessness as an outline against the background of 'the world of the elderly', and move on into the fixity of the 'obstinate irrepressible conviction which makes youth so intolerably disagreeable' – 'I am what I am, and intend to be it.' But this identity is unstable, shifting often between the individual and the general. The snatches we are given of Jacob's thoughts do not reveal individual character so much as typify young men of his time and class, marked out for death in war by the oppressive generalities of public speech.

Although the novel traces Jacob's childhood, young manhood and early death, it is in some ways, as commentators have pointed out, an 'anti-biography'.[9] It speaks to the inappropriate-ness of the biographical form – with its beginnings, middles and ends – to a young life that ends senselessly. There is no 'middle' in the story of Jacob's life. It is told as disconnected fragments, with no attempt to bring them into an idealized unity. There is no significant event towards which the different episodes lead. Certainly we are not permitted to think of his death as giving meaning to his life, or as having any meaning of its own. The narrative expresses a resistance to turning the deaths of young men into heroic stories, ironically intimating that the processes by which Jacob's individuality is absorbed into public identity, as he 'thickens' into manhood, are implicated in his death. But if the idea of a life as the formation of public identity through social roles and heroic death is mocked, so too is the idea of a life as an autonomously developing coherent personality. Jacob's story is told through fragments of thoughts and feelings – of other consciousnesses as much as his own.

The novel reverberates with the contrasts between female and male consciousness. Sometimes this contrast is conveyed through explicit narratorial reflection, telling us how sex affects perception. Sometimes it comes through in the tone of outraged irony, as in the description of battleships raging in the North Sea, of the nonchalance with which young men in the prime of life 'descend with composed faces into the depths of the sea; and there impassively (though with perfect mastery of machinery) suffocate uncomplainingly together', driven allegedly by an 'un-seizable force' (*Jacob's Room*, 151–2). But neither the consciousness of female 'gossip' nor that of 'men in clubs and Cabinets' can capture the elusive identity of Jacob.

The tenuousness of human presence in the indifferent im-mensity of cosmic time is another recurrent theme. The calling of Jacob's name on the beach in the opening sections has a poi-gnancy that resonates through the novel, evoking the transience of his presence, and its elusiveness even while he is alive. '"Ja-cob! Ja-cob!" . . . . The voice had an extraordinary sadness. Pure from all body, pure from all passion, going out into the world, solitary, unanswered, breaking against rocks – so it sounded' (*Jacob's Room*, 6–7). The sadness is echoed in Bonamy's call – 'Jacob! Jacob!' – as he sees the leaves rise and fall again from the window of Jacob's room after his death. The solidity of human presence alternates with its sudden disappearances, and the

voice of the narrator reinforces this theme through explicit reflections as well as through its own shifting presence and absence.
Life, it tells us, is 'but a procession of shadows', although we
embrace them so eagerly and see them depart with such anguish.
Yet we are surprised in the window corner by 'a sudden vision
that the young man in the chair is of all things in the world the
most real, the most solid, the best known to us', although the
moment after we know nothing of him. 'Such is the manner of
our seeing. Such the conditions of our love' (*Jacob's Room*, 69). It is
not as if the solidity of Jacob is undeniably there while he is alive
and mysteriously gone after his death. Death is not a sudden
transition from solidity to shadow; for these fluctuations go on
even while Jacob is alive. The elusiveness of Jacob's presence is
accentuated by the reader's realization that the whole story is
constructed backwards, as it were, from his death. There are no
sharp boundaries here between the presence of an individual
consciousness during life and its absence at death. Our lives are
insubstantial. It is not as if we lose at death a solidity we
assuredly have during life.

Virginia Woolf's novels grapple with issues of the continued
reality of the past – of the continued presence in life of the dead.
Death is not distanced from life in the way Victorian rites of
mourning were supposed to achieve. Her writing tries to give
expression to the fact – unacceptable to 'normality' – that the
dead do not stay tidily absent, and undergo no comforting
transformation into public symbols. Jacob does not cease to be
Jacob, and remains after his death, as before, unknowable in any
way that would allow him to be summed up, whether by female
gossip or by male public rhetoric. We are not permitted to think
of Jacob as transformed or solemnized. The point is not to deny
the reality of death. Jacob's room after his death has a sadness it
lacks when the same sentences are used to describe it when he
has only stepped out: 'Listless is the air in an empty room, just
swelling the curtain; the flowers in the jar shift. One fibre in the
wicker arm-chair creaks, though no one sits there' (*Jacob's Room*,
36–7). The point is not a minimizing of death but a refusal of a
certain way of thinking of the change – of the attempt embodied
in Victorian mourning rites to keep death at a reassuring distance from life, by providing a generalized social identity for the
dead. Jacob, epitomizing young men untimely dead in war, is to

be protected from such mourning, just as Percival's friends, later in *The Waves*, try to protect him from being 'covered with lilies'.

Sometimes the narrator's voice takes up a disembodied perspective. Sometimes it positions itself in the consciousness of a character. Sometimes it seems to hover between embodiment and disembodiment. In the description of Jacob in the quad at Cambridge we see him from outside, looking 'satisfied, indeed masterly', his expression changing as the sound of the clock conveys to him 'a sense of old buildings and time; and himself the inheritor; and then tomorrow; and friends; at the thought of whom, in sheer confidence and pleasure, it seemed, he yawned and stretched himself' (*Jacob's Room*, 42). This is not the description of an omniscient narrator. It is written from the perspective of an outside observer who must speculate about Jacob's state of mind on the basis of his facial expression. We are given no reason to think that the narrator is actually present in the scene, although the observations show signs of an ironic female perspective on the privileges of male Cambridge youth, and the ease with which their consciousness occupies time.

At another point in the narrative the shifts in perspective become even more complex. Jacob has already been described standing beneath a street light and is suddenly presented to us as if actually seen by one of the bystanders flitting about him. Then we are taken into Jacob's feelings on seeing his mistress with another man, as those feelings are displayed to an outside observation, although the detail and intensity of the description belies this external perspective. 'It was as if a stone were ground to dust; as if white sparks flew from a livid whetstone, which was his spine; as if the switchboard railway, having swooped to the depths, fell, fell, fell. This was in his face.' Then the observing position is disconcertingly embodied in a female form: 'Whether we know what was in his mind is another question. Granted ten years' seniority and a difference of sex, fear of him comes first.' Finally, when we may think the perspective is secured, however disconcertingly, in an embodied observer, we follow Jacob with the narrator into his empty room. 'He has turned to go. As for following him back to his room, no – that we won't do. Yet that, of course, is precisely what one does. He let himself in and shut the door' (*Jacob's Room*, 91–2).

A mercurial narratorial presence runs through the novel, taking up a variety of positions and varying degrees of embodiment, sometimes describing how things are in the absence of any observer, sometimes lodging in the perspective of a particular character. But there is continuity in the presence of the narrator throughout these shifts. Often the shifts focus our attention on the relations between consciousness and time, as in the description of the Cornish coast, seen from a boat by Jacob and his friend Bonamy. Here we move from the consciousness of a young man to a cosmic perspective that belongs to no mind in particular, reflecting on the sadness of the landscape.

> Yes, the chimneys and the coast-guard stations and the little bays with the waves breaking unseen by anyone make one remember the overpowering sorrow. And what can this sorrow be?

> It is brewed by the earth itself. It comes from the houses on the coast. We start transparent, and then the cloud thickens. All history backs our pane of glass. To escape is vain.
>
> (*Jacob's Room*, 46–7)

The break in the text – the white space, which Woolf uses so effectively throughout her novels – here separates the question from an answer which, when it comes, no longer has even the semblance of connection with the actual thoughts of the young men musing in the boat.

The shifts in narratorial perspective reinforce the contrasts between presence and absence. Mrs Pascoe, standing at the door of her cottage, shading her eyes and looking out to sea, (*Jacob's Room*, 51) has all the solidity that realist description could give. In the description of the crowds on a London omnibus, in contrast, shifts in perspective convey a sense of an equally astonishing transience. Here we see the striking effects of shifts of narratorial perspective, even in the course of a single description.

> The October sunlight rested upon all these men and women sitting immobile; and little Johnnie Sturgeon took the chance to swing down the staircase, carrying his large mysterious parcel, and so dodging a zig-zag course between the wheels he reached the pavement, started to whistle a tune and was soon out of sight – for ever.
>
> (*Jacob's Room*, 62)

It is from the passengers' perspective that he disappears for ever. But from their perspective, as strangers in an omnibus, he is presumably not 'little Johnnie Sturgeon'.

Sometimes the narrator takes on a voice that seems to break out of the novel to give us a glimpse of the circumstances of its production – of the author's languor after illness, for example (*Jacob's Room*, 114–15). At the other extreme the narrator seems at times to merge into the onward movement of time, independent of human consciousness – into the flight of boughs in a gale, the squirming of the corn, the swelling and subsiding of air in the street (*Jacob's Room*, 117). The position of the narrator in this novel, as more dramatically in *Orlando*, makes it possible to transcend time, making it indeterminate even what century we are in, as we watch an old man who has been crossing the bridge 'these six hundred years' (*Jacob's Room*, 110).

The juxtaposition of cosmic and human time is a recurring element in Woolf's novels. In *Jacob's Room* the time of the moors, resisting questions of what and why, coexists with the church clock striking twelve. The time of clocks is juxtaposed with the time of 'the wild horse within us' and the juxtaposition of different narrative positions reinforces the sense of the flight of time which 'hurries us so tragically along'. The narrator's voice can shift between individual consciousnesses and from individuality to a cosmic perspective. It can also bring them together into unity, shifting between tenses and perspectives – from the English sky to the salt gale blowing through Betty Flanders's window making her sigh 'like one who realizes, but would fain ward off a little longer – oh a little longer – the oppression of eternity' (*Jacob's Room*, 156).

The cosmic perspective, as well as giving a poignancy to mundane human affairs, can also convey a gentle irony which makes of them something richer, nobler. The sunlight striking upon sporting-glasses on a summer's day, having 'long since vanquished chaos' and 'dried the melancholy medieval mists', now lights up the 'armoury of weapons' for the conduct of daily life (*Jacob's Room*, 159). This mixture of cosmic terror and domestic ordinariness lends force to the hush of Jacob's unspoken death as the sound of the guns heard in the Greek islands – the nocturnal women beating great carpets – is imagined as mingling into Betty Flanders's sleepy concern for her hens (*Jacob's Room*, 171–2).

Ricoeur has discussed Woolf's exploitation in *Mrs Dalloway* of the resources of fiction to communicate the 'subtle variations between the time of consciousness and chronological time'.[10] In that novel Woolf addresses more directly the contrasts between 'mortal' and 'monumental' time – the weaving together of the world of action and the world of introspection, of the time of the clocks and the time of inner consciousness. The doctor, Sir William Bradshaw, epitomizes the 'sense of proportion' which sets an entire professional and social life within the 'monumental time' of public events – the counterweight to the living times experienced by Clarissa, reminiscing as she prepares for her party, and the disintegrating consciousness of Septimus, the young man recently returned from war, as he descends into madness and suicide. *Mrs Dalloway*, Ricoeur suggests, explores and brings to language the divorce between world views and their irreconcilable perspectives on time – a divorce that undermines public time. Here again the narrator is given the ability to move from one consciousness to another. The characters meet in the same places – London streets, a public park – and perceive the same sounds, are present at the same incidents. But in addition to this organized time of public events in which organized selves – if they can manage it – go about their affairs, we are shown a time of consciousness. Woolf captures for us the passing of internal time, 'pulled back by memory and thrust ahead by expectation', as Ricoeur describes it, in a way reminiscent of Augustine's 'distension of the soul'. The interweaving of different consciousnesses of time allows the death of one character to be seen reverberating in other consciousnesses. Clarissa, without herself dying, takes on, in her reflections on Septimus's suicide, something of the perception of death as the background against which life becomes visible, giving to her instinctive love for life a tone of defiance and resolution. 'He made her feel the beauty; made her feel the fun.'[11] The force of a death makes Clarissa herself more clearly visible, more solidly present: 'For there she was.'

It is in *The Waves*, however, that we see the full maturity of Woolf's engagement with issues of self-consciousness and time.[12] Here she uses techniques of multiple perspective to explore the ways in which consciousnesses collectively constitute a common world of objects, and the coexistence of that shared reality with the isolation of individual consciousnesses.

The form of this novel is a multiple-voiced narrative. Six consciousnesses in turn tell the story of the interconnections of their lives from childhood to middle age – interconnections with one another and with a seventh character, Percival, whose death is a central shattering event in their single and shared consciousnesses. Their narrations are interspersed with descriptions – from no particular point of view – of the sun's passage over the sky in the course of a day, as waves break on a beach. Even where the narrating voice speaks from the position of an individual mind, there is no question of expressing a 'stream of consciousness'. What is 'said' is not in the form of any speech or inner monologue which might have been formulated by the characters.

These consciousnesses gradually come to individual identity out of disconnected fragments. Self-identity is experienced as having no sharp borders, as adulterated by the 'additions' made by friends. Friendship adds parts to the self, but also strangely contracts it into a single being (*The Waves*, 60). For Louis the fluidity of the self extends back to times long before his own existence. For Rhoda the implosion of other identities is experienced as casting her like a cork on a rough sea. 'Like a ribbon of weed I am flung far every time the door opens. I am the foam that sweeps up and fills the uttermost rims of the rocks with whiteness; I am also a girl, here in this room' (*The Waves*, 72). The experience of fragmentation is a recurring theme throughout *The Waves*. Louis attempts to 'fix the moment in one effort of supreme endeavour', to piece together, to integrate his shattered mind: 'This shall endure.' Rhoda fears that 'nothing persists'. For her consciousness, 'one moment does not lead to another'. She does not know how to 'run minute to minute and hour to hour, solving them by some natural force until they make the whole and indivisible mass that others call life' (*The Waves*, 88). For her there is no substance in which repeated moments are embedded (*The Waves*, 150). The unity of consciousness is associated by Bernard with the sound of the knocking together of railway tracks in a siding, the 'happy concatenation of one event following another in our lives. Knock, knock, knock. Must, must, must' (*The Waves*, 158). He himself experiences the lack of merging of moments after Percival's death – a reluctance to accept the return of the 'sequence of things', one thing leading to another in the usual order.

The soliloquies go on against the background of the organized time of clocks – school time, experienced as oppressive in its regimentation – and also against a background of cosmic time epitomized in the ominous 'sullen thud of the waves', which Louis hears as a chained beast stamping on the beach. The sea functions throughout the novel as symbol of life underlying, but eventually also overcoming, the differentiation of individual consciousnesses. Rhoda throws violets into the surging sea as her offering to Percival. For her the sea is origin and continuing connection. 'With intermittent shocks, sudden as the springs of a tiger, life emerges heaving its dark crest from the sea. It is to this we are attached: it is to this we are bound, as bodies to wild horses' (*The Waves*, 43–4). The individuality of consciousnesses is experienced as thin sheets separating us from the infinite depths. The petals Rhoda floats in a bowl as a child prefigure the rolling of the waves which shoulder her under at death – 'everything falling in a tremendous shower, dissolving me'.

The waves represent death, though also, as we shall see, ongoing life. For Neville, their ominous thud mingles with the recurring metaphor of the great beast stamping on the beach; and that image mingles in turn with the stamping of the horse that throws Percival in India. The dissolution of Percival's individual consciousness is experienced by his friends as an abrupt halt in the flow of their own – as the end of their own past and the anticipation of their own loss of differentiated consciousness. '"He is dead!", said Neville. "He fell. his horse tripped. He was thrown. The sails of the world have swung round and caught me on the head. All is over. The lights of the world have gone out"' (*The Waves*, 101). It is not just Percival's life that is past, not just his world that is over. '"Barns and summer days in the country, rooms where we sat – all now lie in the unreal world which is gone. My past is cut from me."'

It is not only Percival who goes through the experience of the blow on the head that ends consciousness in a shower of flashing trees and white rails. Neville has himself been 'hit on the head by the sails of the world'. He experiences this death as the loss of both past and future. The past, in which Percival belonged, is no longer a real past. The world in which things continue to happen – in which they come running to Percival's body – is now an unreal world, a world forever changed by Percival's death. In this afterlife, time no longer operates in the same way. The grieving are deprived of both past and future. The past lies in the world which is gone, and the future vanishes too, leaving consciousness stranded in a disconnected present. Words are lacking, Bernard reflects, for pain, and for the images of death, beneath all of which appears something important yet remote, to be 'just held in solitude'. The death leaves Bernard with the feeling of being 'admitted behind the scenes: like one shown how the effects are produced' (*The Waves*, 180). His identity merges with that of Percival: 'I said "Give him (myself) another moment's respite", as I went downstairs. "Now in this drawing-room he is going to suffer. There is no escape"' (*The Waves*, 178).

The connecting thread in these stark and often startling ruminations on time and death is the fragility of individual consciousness, which is linked with the theme of writing. The narrative gives centrality to the consciousness of Bernard, the writer. His capacity to transcend the limits of his own consciousness gives him a privileged position amid the shifts of perspective. By the end of the novel, in fact, we are left wondering whether the apparently separate monologues have not all been the product of his imaginative construction. Bernard has the liberty to 'sink down, deep, into what passes, this omnipresent general life' (*The Waves*, 76). The surface of his mind 'slips along like a pale-grey stream reflecting what passes'. Beneath individual consciousness there are 'profound depths' to be explored – 'to hear vague, ancestral sounds of boughs creaking, of mammoths; to indulge impossible desires to embrace the whole world with the arms of understanding – impossible to those who act'. And the fluctuating identity of the writer mirrors the truth of identity itself – constantly forming, disintegrating, re-forming.

Bernard's orientation to the complexities and predicaments of individual consciousness is just one among others, and it has limitations which the others lack. As a writer, he 'traverses the sunless territory of non-identity'. But he is unable to be sure what is his own self without the illumination of other people's eyes. 'I am not one person, I am many people', he reflects in the extended one-sided dialogue that makes the remarkable final section of the novel. 'Am I all of them? Am I one and distinct? I do not know' (*The Waves*, 195). For Susan, at the other end of the spectrum, the mediating mode of dependence is the 'bestial and beautiful passion of maternity', with its selective affection, its elimination of all that is not one's own – a selectivity which achieves, though with costs of its own, a solidity of identity, and a stake in the onward movement of time, which eludes the consciousness of the writer.

*The Waves* ends on an ambiguous note. The waves eclipse human time, but also merge with it. Individual consciousness is overcome in the ceaseless breaking of the waves; but in flinging itself at the waves it seems to attain in its very dispersion also a kind of victory.

> Against you I will fling myself, unvanquished and unyielding. O Death!

> *The waves broke on the shore.*

Life passes through its embodiments in individual consciousness, and its passage is experienced both as the relentless force of inhuman time and as the return of human interest and hope. Consciousness merges with the breaking of the waves, the pounding on the shore. Writing becomes a way of resisting the destructive effects of cosmic time by joining forces with it. Human and cosmic time join together in the making of new differentiations.

> Fight! Fight!, I repeated. It is the effort and the struggle, it is the perpetual warfare, it is the shattering and piecing together – this is the daily battle, defeat or victory, the absorbing pursuit. The trees, scattered, put on order; the thick green of the leaves thinned itself to a dancing light, I netted them under with a sudden phrase. I retrieved them from formlessness with words.

> (*The Waves*, 182)

For Virginia Woolf, writing is a way of going 'active and positive' to death – a way of resisting its power, capturing 'moments of being' and fixing them in words. Writing is a struggle of life against death. As far as any individual consciousness is concerned, death must prevail. But writing has affinities with the continuing power of life to bring form out of formlessness, to construct individuality. This gives another twist to the theme of the fragmentation of consciousness which runs through her works. Through writing she tries to make complete those fragments of being which stand out from the rest of experience. In 'A Sketch of the Past', she talks of these exceptional moments which 'come to the surface unexpectedly', often in an experience of shock which renders her passive in the face of reality.[13] With maturity she comes to see these experiences as revelations of some order, tokens of some real thing behind appearances which she makes real by putting it into words, making it whole, putting the severed parts together. The world takes on the form of a work of art in which we participate: 'we are the words; we are the music; we are the thing itself' (A Sketch of the Past, 84).

Writing has the power to rid us of the grip of the past of the obsessiveness of grief. But whereas for Proust writing regains the past by transforming particulars into 'ideas', for Woolf writing makes it possible to regain the past – paradoxically, by letting it go. Writing To the Lighthouse, she says in 'A Sketch of the Past', freed her of her obsession with her dead mother. She did for herself, she supposes, what psychoanalysts do for their patients, expressing some long and deeply felt emotion and, in expressing it, explaining it and laying it to rest, although it remains obscure to her what is the meaning of this explanation. Writing has the power to overcome both the loss of the past and the fragmentation of the self. By bringing the 'severed parts' together, we are able to internalize the past in a way that allows us to move on into the future. In the interlude 'Time Passes' in To the Lighthouse, this theme of the overcoming of fragmentation takes on a cosmic dimension. Wholeness is glimpsed, 'single, distinct', in the wave falling, the boat rocking. But this wholeness is not intact, waiting to be grasped by the writer. It is evoked by imagination, assembling outwardly the 'scattered parts of the vision within'.

Can Proust and Virginia Woolf be said to articulate a distinctively modern way in which the self experiences being in time as a problem? If so, how does it differ from Augustine's 'problem' of the self? Are they posing different problems of selfhood? Or is it rather that they are refusing a certain kind of resolution of the old problems? For Augustine the problem of the self's fragmentation was to be resolved through discovering the truth of the self. For these modern novelists, in contrast, the 'problem' lies rather in the very truth of selfhood. Fragmentation comes to be seen not as a distortion based on failure to grasp the true nature of the self, but as the truth of what it is to be a self; and if narrative offers a resolution it must take a different form. For Augustine the problem of the self's relations with time was to be resolved through holding together the fragments of self-consciousness. By telling a coherent story, with a beginning, a middle and an end, centred on the discovery of the true nature of the self, he tries to give life the structured unity of autobiography – a form which approximates to God's 'eternal now'. We have seen the echoes of this version of the idea of overcoming fragmentation mocked in *Jacob's Room*. Woolf offers a different kind of resolution of the problem of fragmentation. It is partly an idea of writing as therapy. By writing about a deeply felt emotion she brings together fragments of being, making them whole and thus leaving them behind without a tormenting sense of loss. But there is also in her work a strong sense of the act of writing as itself, through the bringing of form out of formlessness, a way of participating in the differentiation of individuality from formlessness – a blow on behalf of the feeble power of life against death, which draws its strength from the very acknowledgement of transience and fragility.

Writing, for Virginia Woolf, takes on the poignant but wonderful power of life which she describes in her remarkable essay 'Death of a Moth'. In a struggle which seems at once so marvellous and so pathetic, the moth crosses and re-crosses the window pane. It is, we are told, as if a thin but pure fibre of the enormous energy of the world has been thrust into his frail and diminutive body – 'as if someone had taken a tiny bead of pure life and decking it as lightly as possible with down and feathers had set it dancing and zig-zagging to show us the real nature of life' – life as it cannot be seen when it is so 'garnished and cumbered' that it has to move with the greatest circumspection and dignity. The moth struggles against the irresistible power of death, and when it comes death seems as strange as life had seemed strange a few minutes before. As he lies most decently and uncomplainingly composed, 'O yes', he seems to say, 'death is stronger than I am.'[14]

# Conclusion: philosophy and literature

If the truth of our being in time is indeed fragmentation and discontinuity, what becomes of the ideal of truth itself? Should we see philosophy's traditional aspiration to truth as dependent on an ideal of stable selfhood, the illusoriness of which is now apparent? If it depends on a picture of unified knowing subject confronting more or less stable object, can it survive the deconstructive dismantling of that idea? As we have seen, the idea that unified selfhood is fictitious is not new to philosophical thought, although it is now associated especially with the work of Derrida. Some formulations of the upshot of Derrida's thought, taking his views perhaps to be more novel than they in fact are, suggest that we should adjust to living in a 'post-philosophical' intellectual age – that to see through the illusions of 'self-presence' is also to see through the illusions of philosophy. One of the concerns of this book has been to show that philosophical awareness of the tenuousness of the idea of a unified knowing subject confronting stable objects did not have to await our own times. Some critiques of philosophy inspired by Derrida seem to suggest that the whole of western philosophy has been premised on an unquestioned assumption of an untroubled translucent presence of mind to object. But philosophers have been long aware of the fragility of the unified subject, and have provided their own critiques of various versions of that idea. Contemporary critiques such as Derrida's, however, have a different mood from older ones in the philosophical tradition. Derrida refuses to see the complexities of being in time as problems that admit of resolution, rejecting the nostalgic yearning for lost unity, and identifying positively with the movement of differentiation rather than its determinate outcomes. Derrida refuses to look to anything external to stabilize the inherent movement and transience of consciousness which more traditional philosophy – with some notable exceptions such as Hume – tried to anchor in God or eternity, in the metaphysical status of substance, in unknowable things in themselves or idealized alternative forms of consciousness which might apprehend in some other way the reality we experience as temporal.

Although scepticism about the unified self still seems capable of shocking academic philosophers, it is by no means new to twentieth-century literature. The issue of truth in a reality experienced as fragmentation and unified only through multiple perspectives runs through Virginia Woolf's work. She makes it explicit in the short piece 'Monday or Tuesday'[1] where the refrain '– and truth?' recurs amidst a flurry of impressions, some imagined from a human perspective, some from that of a heron passing under the sky – impressions of movement over shifting landscapes, of movement in crowded streets, of rest in the closeness of firelight. The writer's consciousness merges with cries in the street, with the strokes of the clock, the striking of wheels, the light shedding gold scales, the swarming of children – laboriously distilling a few words, 'for ever desiring truth'. The paradox of this succinct piece is that in articulating the desire for truth in the midst of fragmentation of impressions, writing also satisfies that desire. 'Monday or Tuesday' enacts in a page the truth of being in time.

Writing can find truth by making it. As we have seen especially in relation to Proust, discovery and invention can come together. It may seem that philosophy's aspiration to truth is radically different – and much less easily reconciled with the repudiation of the unity of the knowing subject. But is it? Some of the recurring metaphors we have seen in philosophical writing suggest that it is through reflection on the unity of action and of the spoken word that we can best understand what it is to be a self in time. They also perhaps suggest a way of understanding the philosophical aspiration to truth in the midst of fragmentation. We have seen in several philosophies the idea that the unity of consciousness is not the unity of substance enduring through time but rather the unity that we find in action or speech. This points us in the direction of alternative ways of thinking of truth and knowledge to that of a stable subject confronting a stable

object. Even Descartes – that well established target of deconstructive criticism – was, as we have seen, well aware of the
crucial difference between being in time in the manner of a rock
standing in a flowing stream and the tenuous active stretching
out of consciousness which makes for unity of thought. Kant too,
despite his talk of the possibility of an intuitive consciousness
providing its own objects behind the scenes of human sensibility, was also clearly aware that consciousness can grasp itself
as unified only to the extent that it actively produces unity in
thought. The idea that the unity of consciousness is the unity of
action has coexisted with ideas of 'self-presence' more commonly
associated with traditional philosophy. Here, too, discovery and
invention can come together: unity is not discovered but made.

What exactly does this coming together of invention and
discovery amount to? And what does it show us about philosophical truth and its contrasts with literature? Does it imply that
each self is many unities – that we are as diverse as the acts we
perform, as the speeches we utter? Such a 'unity' seems hardly
less disconnected than the fragments it is supposed to bring
together. But this is to take too literally what is in fact an
operation of philosophical metaphor – metaphors of the unfolding of action, speech and narrative. It is also – though this is for
our purposes less relevant – to leave out of account the crucial role
played in individual self-consciousness by the awareness of our
bodies as centres of activity and passivity, of force and resistance.
We are in time not as disembodied consciousness but as awareness of living bodies, which set limits to what we can be and do
and perhaps even to what we can coherently imagine – an
intractable though reassuring substratum to the stories we tell of
our lives. However, such bodily awareness cannot of itself resolve
the issues of unity of consciousness we have seen addressed by
philosophers.

To think of myself as unified is to enact a unity – to tell a story.
That story can have many sub-plots and it can be told from a
variety of perspectives. The truth of consciousness may be fragmentation. But out of the fragments the writer can construct a
unity; and each of us, on the model we are now considering, does
something akin to what the writer does. If there are no stories,
asks Bernard in *The Waves*, what end can there be, or what
beginning? Our stories may not have conventional beginnings,
middles and ends. They may be more like the multiple-

perspective narratives of modern novels – respecting the fragments while making of them a satisfying unity. Narrative forms can respond to contingent features of consciousness at a particular period while remaining continuous with a much older phenomenon – mind responding to the experience of fragmentation by creating unities.

If both philosophy and literature can be seen as bringing together discovery and invention, how do they differ? A fruitful way of considering the issue is to come at it through an examination of philosophical metaphor. The idea of 'metaphorical truth' underlies Ricoeur's treatment in *Time and Narrative* of the way in which fictional narrative engages with the reality of human action and experience. The idea is developed more fully in Ricoeur's earlier book *The Rule of Metaphor*. Metaphor, he argues, rather than being an ornament of thought, engages with reality in ways that elude literal meaning; and narrative, likewise, responds to *aporias* of time which elude philosophical resolution. Ricoeur develops this way of thinking of metaphor and of narrative out of Aristotle's discussion of mimesis in the *Poetics*.[2] Tragedy, Aristotle suggests, captures the truth of 'what might have happened'. Where history merely tells us what did happen, the poet describes 'a kind of thing that might be'. The difference makes poetry 'something more philosophical and of graver import than history'. The statements of poetry are of the nature of universals, whereas those of history are singular. Out of this Aristotelian view of the figurative, Ricoeur develops a theory of fiction's transformation of particular experiences and emotional states into a kind of universal.

Proust, as we saw, has his narrator present this artistic transformation as a kind of infidelity to the original particular in the service of making something universal. Ricoeur's version of the artistic transformation of particular into universal stresses, in contrast, that this process is also a mode of engagement with the particularity of experience. Our ordinary pre-reflective understanding of human action involves, he suggests, incipient narratives, stories through which we make sense of our lives. The 'employment' of fictional narrative is not a falsifying imposition of meaning but a 'configuration' through which we come to understand and 'refigure' those pre-reflective figurations. By being seen in the light of artistically created poetic universals, ordinary experience is understood and transformed.

Ricoeur's account of the coming together of discovery and invention in fictional narrative draws on his earlier discussion of Aristotle's treatment of the relations between metaphor and truth in *The Rule of Metaphor*. For Aristotle, poetry can be 'philosophical' and serious although, despite the graveness of its import, it remains ancillary to philosophy. But it is also true that for Aristotle philosophical activity is closer to literature than it had been for Plato – and closer than it would come to be seen in later philosophy. At the centre of the Aristotelian drawing together of the philosophical and the literary is the philosopher's use of metaphor. The greatest thing by far in philosophical discourse, he says in the *Poetics*, is to be 'master of metaphor'. It is the one thing that cannot be learned from others, and a sign of genius, since a good metaphor implies an intuitive perception of the similarity in dissimilars – a capacity to perceive the broader difference and consequently substitute one term for another.

For Aristotle, metaphor is a central activity of the intellectual life – a means to the forming of new meanings, as distinct from the rehearsal of old truths. It has its natural origin in a trait which is essential to, and distinctive of, human nature – the pleasurable capacity to learn through imitating. Metaphor and mimesis have a common base in the basic human delight in learning through imitation, 'gathering the meaning of things' in the assimilation of one sphere to another. In the *Rhetoric* he talks of the instructive value of metaphor in terms of the pleasure of understanding that comes of surprise.[3] To get hold of ideas is agreeable, and those words are most agreeable that enable us to get hold of new ideas. Strange words simply puzzle us and ordinary words convey only what we know already. It is from metaphor that we can get hold of something fresh. Metaphor involves a pleasurable movement of the mind, and in understanding this movement it is hard to keep the metaphorical and the literal separate.

Ideas of activity and movement are essential in Aristotle's account of metaphor. The nature of metaphor is articulated through metaphors drawn from movement; and good philosophical metaphors bring about a movement of the mind – an expansion in the possibilities for thought, a shaking of preconceptions. This mental movement and expansion is perhaps itself inexpressible without metaphor. For it is not simply using one name in place of another but – and how else could one say it? – a movement into new intellectual space. Metaphor involves a lively intellectual activity – not merely a capacity to perceive similarities, but an active transporting of meaning from one sphere to another. Activity figures at a number of levels in Aristotle's treatment of metaphor. It is there as part of the content of good metaphors – animating the inanimate. But it is also involved in the very idea of metaphor which Aristotle conceptualizes through metaphors drawn from movement – metaphors of transference or transportation. Metaphor consists in a carrying of meaning from one sphere to another. Its definition involves movement, and this movement in itself is an instantiation of metaphor.

There is another way, too, in which ideas of movement and activity figure in the Aristotelian treatment of metaphor. Living metaphor, he says in the *Rhetoric*, puts something before the eyes by representing things as in a state of activity (1411b24–5).[4] When the poet animates inanimate things, his verse represents things as active, moving and living. What Aristotle means by representing things as in a state of activity does not speak for itself. Clearly it is connected with Aristotle's rejection of the remoteness of Platonic Forms in favour of a contemplative vision of things in their actuality and particularity. In *The Rule of Metaphor*, Ricoeur glosses Aristotle's idea of representing things in a state of activity in terms of seeing the world as a grand gesture – seeing things in the manner of a work of art. It is a theme we have seen in Proust's and Virginia Woolf's reflections on the relations between life and literature, in Nietzsche, and earlier in Plotinus's and Augustine's ideas of the world as taking on the form of speech, the unity of action, the structure of narrative.

The Aristotelian treatment of metaphor elaborated by Ricoeur yields a *rapprochement* between philosophy and literature. Rather than being aligned with discovery and invention respectively, both involve the operations of metaphor and an interaction between discovery and invention. But this need not at all mean that the distinction between philosophy and literature collapses, or that there is nothing that differentiates philosophical from poetic metaphor. What then can be said of their differences? There is a way of thinking of philosophy's relations with metaphor, evoked by Derrida's critique of philosophical metaphor in 'White Mythology',[5] which would align philosophical thought itself with 'discovery', reserving for 'invention' the task of the communication of philosophical thought through metaphor. The model which Derrida attacks there rests on a way of taking Aristotle's description of the philosopher as 'master of metaphor', according to which the philosopher adopts a speaking position above and beyond the figurative – a position of control from which he can communicate philosophical thought through the medium of metaphor. What is distinctive about philosophical thought is then seen as this metaphor-free position from which 'mastery' can be exerted. Metaphor is seen as belonging not with philosophical truth, but with its expression. What the philosopher says through metaphor can always in principle be said, even if less elegantly, without it. Against this elaboration of Aristotle's reference to the philosopher as master of metaphor, Derrida argues that philosophy cannot succeed in getting outside the chain of metaphorical signifiers to attain a standpoint from which metaphor might be controlled. His argument emphasizes the presence of inactive 'dead' metaphors in philosophical texts. It is impossible, he thinks, to dominate philosophical metaphors from outside. Metaphor is less in the philosophical text than the philosophical text is within metaphor.

Aristotle, on Derrida's interpretation, subordinates metaphor to an ideal of univocity – saying one thing; the philosopher speaks *through* metaphor. It is a way of thinking of philosophical metaphor which is, he thinks, caught up in a metaphor of the spiritualization of matter which is constitutive of philosophy. At the heart of philosophy, he argues, is the spiritualizing of sensation – a process which is simultaneously 'erased' in such a way that there is no ultimate distinction to be drawn between the philosophical and the literal. Philosophy, rather than mastering metaphor from a speaking position independent of it, is born out of metaphor, although it systematically suppresses that origin.

There is, however, another way of taking Aristotle's talk of the philosopher as 'master of metaphor'. Rather than seeing the philosopher as exerting control over metaphor from a position of pure thought, we might see him or her simply as a particularly adept performer of those uses of metaphor which are conceptually innovative – as a maestro rather than a circus ringmaster. This is an aspect of philosophical metaphor which Ricoeur stresses in his response to Derrida in *The Rule of Metaphor*.[6] In relation to philosophical thought, 'dead' metaphor – the extended use of words of ordinary language – is of less importance and interest than the cases where philosophers deliberately have recourse to living metaphor to bring to light new aspects of reality by means of semantic innovation. This active mode of metaphor can be applied to the rejuvenation of dead metaphors as well as to other semantic innovation. Concepts can be actively articulated in metaphors which are themselves dead (293). To think of metaphor in this way, as a conscious act, is at odds with Derrida's implicit denial of any ultimate distinction between the metaphorical and the literal. Philosophical metaphor, unlike the poetic variety, which may be inactive and barely distinguished from the literal, is an active extension of meaning. But Ricoeur's emphasis on the philosopher's 'active' use of metaphor points us in the direction of what may be a fruitful way of thinking of philosophical truth − as a form of metaphorical truth. Good philosophical metaphors are inventive in a way that increases our understanding of reality. Rather than being fanciful impositions of meaning, they articulate what is 'possible' in the sense used by Aristotle in the *Poetics*; they allow us to articulate what *might* be.

How then, finally, should we see the differences between the coming together of invention and discovery in philosophy and in literature? I have suggested that whereas fiction engages with reality through the construction of a 'concrete' universal, the inventive aspect of philosophy can be illustrated through its use of metaphors to 'shift' thought, opening up possibilities for thinking differently. Not all metaphors that occur in philosophical writing are, in this strong sense, inventive. Some of the metaphors used by philosophers discussed in this book can be seen as facilitating the expression of a thought, rather than as constitutive of it. Kant's metaphor of the ship of reason sailing recklessly out of sight of experience could be readily expressed, though perhaps less elegantly, without metaphor; and indeed it is, in some of the more tortuous sentences of the *Critique of Pure Reason*. The metaphors of the spoken word, of the unity of action, of mental 'stretchings out', seem in contrast to belong to the philosophical thought itself rather than to the means of its expression. These uses of philosophical metaphor, as we have seen, can involve radical shifts in the conceptualization of time's relations with consciousness. It is in such conceptual transformations that we see philosophy's version of the coming together of discovery and invention. Where fiction transforms particular experience into something akin to universals, through which particulars can be understood, creative philosophy transforms the relations between universal concepts. This does not mean that philosophy should appropriate to itself all conceptually innovative 'active' uses of metaphor. Nor can all philosophical conceptual innovation be equated with metaphor. But it is in the understanding and creative transformation of concepts that philosophy shows both its affinities with and its differences from fiction.

There is in philosophical writing no clear analogue of fiction's concern with 'character'. Fictional narrative engages directly with action and experience through the creation of character. Modern fiction may – indeed, Virginia Woolf has argued that it must – create character in a radically different way from older forms of fictional narrative. But character still figures, even if in a transformed way, in the novelists's mode of engagement with the human world. In her essay 'Mr Bennett and Mrs Brown',[7] Virginia Woolf expresses dissatisfaction with the received narrative forms of the Edwardian novel. Here she sketches her ideal of capturing the elusive glimpses of character we are given under the conditions of fragmentation and disconnection of consciousness associated with the modern social world – illustrated through her desire to capture the 'eternal' essence of an old lady sitting in the corner of a train carriage. The essay responds to a remark of Arnold Bennett's – that it is only if characters are real that the novel has any chance of surviving. But, Woolf asks, what is reality, and who judges it? The essay presents the writer's attempt to capture the 'surprising apparition' of Mrs Brown as symptomatic of the strange and interesting experiences that make up daily life – the scraps of talk that fill us with amazement, the complexity of feelings and thoughts, the collisions and disappearances in astonishing disorder of thousands of ideas and emotions. The fascination of this 'old lady of infinite capacity and infinite variety' derives from her identity with 'the spirit we live by, life itself', to capture which we must be prepared to tolerate 'the spasmodic, the obscure, the fragmentary, the failure' (87).

Fiction transforms particulars in order to understand them better; and the creation of character is central to that exercise, even in the new forms it takes in response to the predicament that arises when the tools of one generation are found useless by the next. Ricoeur's elaborations of Aristotle have shown the affinities between that process and the formation of philosophy's abstract universals. But philosophical universals are not in that way directed to the understanding of particulars. 'Poetic' universals,

despite their inevitable 'infidelity' to their origins, are sufficiently like the concrete particularities of ordinary experience for
us to move readily between the two. Philosophy does not take
human action, experience and emotion as its object in the direct
way that literature does; and there is in it no analogue of
characters. Its direct focus is rather on concepts – on universals
themselves, in all their fascinating shifts and concatenations –
and in the philosopher's transformation of those concepts, discovery and invention can come together.

To become clearer about the contrasts between the philosophical and the literary can make us more sensitive to the ways in
which they complement one another. Good philosophical writing often creates 'fictions' through which we can better
understand both general concepts and ourselves. We have seen
in this book some 'fictions' of the self as knower – fictions
perhaps far removed from the 'characters' of literary creation, but
just as harmless and instructive, even if less diverting. And we
have seen a succession of creative realignments of concepts,
which yield that pleasure which Aristotle regarded as so basic to
human life – the pleasure of finding a new way of looking at
things, and especially at ourselves.

It is not only through metaphor that philosophy can bring
about enriching movements of thought. We have seen in the
philosophical writing discussed in this book a succession of
shifts in perspective – changes in the angle of intellectual vision,
as it were, on the relations between time and consciousness.
Aristotle looks outward to the physical world to define time as
having 'something to do with movement'. Plotinus, in reaction,
insists that if we would understand time we must look not at the
physical world but within, and outward from ourselves only to
the eternity which time mimics. Augustine pushes the insight to
a more extreme version of the internalization of time in the
stretching out of consciousness. And Kant tries to reconcile the
inward and the outward focus: time is the form of inner sense,
but if consciousness is to be anything more than a mere rhapsody
of perceptions it must be directed outward to a world of objective
physical change. Mind shifts and turns its gaze in response to the
philosophers' manipulations of focus. And philosophers too tell
stories. Something thus, says Plotinus, the story of time must go.
But there is, of course, no final necessity in how the story must be
told. It is retold again and again, with subtle shifts and changes

showing us ever new possibilities for thinking ourselves and our being in time.

Since philosophy does not focus as directly as literature on the particularities of human experience, it is characteristically more distanced than literature from the emotional aspects of time. But there are often deep emotional resonances in good philosophical writing – resonances which can be masked by readings which ignore its literary dimensions. Ricoeur talks in his discussion of metaphor of a 'heuristic' function of mood in poetic metaphor – something which can go unnoticed when representation becomes the sole route to knowledge and the model of every relationship between subject and object. Holderlin's 'joyous undulation of the waves' is neither an objective reality in the positivist sense nor a mood in the emotivist sense. It makes for participation in things, for a lack of distinction between interior and exterior.[8] Taking emotion seriously can of itself unsettle the sharp distinctions between knowing subject and objective world which are so often associated with the history of western philosophy. And the literary dimensions of philosophical texts can give us access to ways in which even those philosophies regarded as epitomizing the 'metaphysics of presence' contain within them, not just a 'secret narrative' of unacknowledged and subversive 'dead' metaphor, but their own mode of responding through active metaphor and the construction of 'fictions' to the predicaments posed by our experience of time.

Rather than seeing philosophy, as Ricoeur suggests in *Time and Narrative*, as offering inconclusive 'theories' of time, while fictional narrative offers a 'poetic resolution', we might fruitfully regard both philosophy and literature as offering different kinds of 'fiction' through which we may come to a deeper understanding of what is problematic and troubling in the human experience of time. To rediscover the literary dimensions of philosophical writing can also reinforce in contemporary readers something of which traditional philosophers were well aware – that good philosophy is inherently pleasurable. The mind's movement to a greater state of activity is, in Spinoza's definition, the essence of delight. This is perhaps the greatest commonality between literature and philosophy – their capacity to respond to even the most painful of subjects, the most hopeless of passions, with that movement of spirit which is the continuation of life and of joy.

# Afterword

But how it curtails the future: how it reduces one's vision to one's own life . . . as if one had been living in another body, which is removed & all that living is ended. As usual, the remedy is to enter other lives, I suppose; & the old friction of the brain.

Virginia Woolf, *Diary*, 6 August 1937

This is not a book about grief. But the theme of grief runs through much of the philosophical and literary reflection which it addresses. And grief has motivated much of my own reflection on these issues of time and consciousness. The book is dedicated to my daughter Rachel, who was killed in a car crash on 12 July 1987, aged 22 years. I would like what is pleasurable in it to be my tribute to her delight in the movement of thought and of life; to her laughter; to her intent gaze; to the quiet strength of her presence. 'For there she was.'

# Bibliographical essay

The theme of the disappearance of the 'knowing subject' has taken many forms in contemporary discussion. In some versions, it has more to do with the rejection of continuities in the history of thought than with issues of individual self-consciousness. Michel Foucault, especially, has linked it with the role of the concept of 'man' in the emergence of the human sciences – the peculiar object of knowledge within which the conditions of knowledge itself are supposed to become visible, only to disappear again. His early books, *The Order of Things: An Archaeology of the Human Sciences* (1966), (London: Tavistock, 1970) – especially Chapters 1 and 9 – and *The Archaeology of Knowledge* (1969), translated by A. M. Sheridan Smith (London: Tavistock, 1972), are useful background reading for this aspect of the connection between ideas of narrative and ideas of the knowing subject. Ann Game's *Undoing the Social: Towards a Deconstructive Sociology* (Buckingham: Open University Press, 1991) has a useful chapter on Foucault, Freud, Bergson and Irigaray on 'the subject' (Part Two, Chapter 3). However, the aspects of the disappearing subject which are most relevant to this book are those associated with the work of Jacques Derrida. See especially his 'Différance', in *Margins of Philosophy* (1972), translated by Alan Bass (New York: University of Chicago Press; Brighton: Harvester, 1982), 1–27, which brings questions of meaning into explicit connection with issues of time and self-consciousness. For a useful discussion of these aspects of Derrida's work, centred on the idea of 'reflection', see Rodolphe Gasché's *The Tain of the Mirror: Derrida and the Philosophy of Reflection* (Cambridge, Mass.: Harvard University Press, 1986), especially Part One, 13–105. David Wood's *The Deconstruction of*

*Time* (Atlantic Highlands, N.J.: Humanities Press, International, 1988) includes an interesting chapter on 'Derrida's Deconstruction of Time and its Limitations'. *Acts of Literature* (London: Routledge, 1992), edited by Derek Attridge, is a selection of Derrida's writings related to literature, with a bibliography of his works engaging either with literary works or with questions of literature.

Although Heidegger's *Being and Time* (1927), translated by John Macquarrie and Edward Robinson (Oxford: Blackwell, 1962), receives little explicit discussion in this book, it is an unavoidable 'presence' for all subsequent discussion of the connections between time and consciousness. Readers interested in relating the issues discussed in this book more directly to Heidegger's philosophy should read especially the sections in his introduction to *Being and Time* discussing the 'destruction' of the 'History of Ontology' (#6, 41–49), the discussion of 'being-towards-death' in Division Two, Part 1 (#46–52, 279–304), and the concluding sections on 'within-time-ness' and the 'ordinary conception of time' (#78–82, 456–486).

Because this book is not primarily concerned with the 'phenomenology' of time, it also omits to discuss that other landmark of twentieth-century philosophy of time, Husserl's *Phenomenology of Internal Time Consciousness* (1928), edited by Martin Heidegger, translated by James S. Churchill (Bloomington: Indiana University Press, 1964). Readers who – like many professional philosophers – find Husserl's treatment of time heavy going, may find the discussion of it in Maurice Merleau-Ponty's *Phenomenology of Perception* (1945), translated by Colin Smith (London: Routledge, 1962), 410–33, more accessible.

For discussions of time-consciousness in relation to modernity see especially David Frisby's excellent *Fragments of Modernity: Theories of Modernity in the Work of Simmel, Kracauer and Benjamin* (Cambridge: Polity Press, 1985). Walter Benjamin discusses Baudelaire's treatment of time-consciousness in relation to Bergson and Proust in 'Some Motifs in Baudelaire' in his *Charles Baudelaire: A Lyric Poet in the Era of High Capitalism*, translated by H. Zohn (London: New Left Books, 1973). Jürgen Habermas's *Philosophical Discourse of Modernity* (1985), translated by Frederick Lawrence (Cambridge Mass.: MIT Press, 1987), includes an interesting chapter on 'Modernity's Consciousness of Time and its Need for Self-Reassurance'. Charles

Taylor's *Sources of the Self: The Making of Modern Identity* (Cambridge: Harvard University Press, 1989) discusses the origins of modern subjectivity. There is now a vast literature on the theory of narrative. The most important work for philosophical aspects of narrative in relation to time is undoubtedly Paul Ricoeur's *Time and Narrative* (1983), translated by Kathleen McLaughlin and David Pellauer, 3 vols. (Chicago and London: University of Chicago Press, 1984–5). See also the collection edited by David Wood, *On Paul Ricoeur: Narrative and Interpretation* (London: Routledge, 1992). Wayne Booth's *The Rhetoric of Fiction* (Chicago: University of Chicago Press, 1961; 2nd edn. 1983) is invaluable for its treatment of narrative in relation to issues of realism, objectivity and point of view and contains an extensive bibliography. Gérard Genette's *Narrative Discourse: An Essay in Method* (1972), translated by Jane Lewin (Ithaca: Cornell University Press, 1988), offers a structuralist analysis of narrative techniques, illustrated with extensive reference to Proust's *Remembrance of Things Past*. His *Narrative Discourse Revisited* (1983), translated by Jane Lewin (Ithaca: Cornell University Press, 1983), responds to critical discussion of *Narrative Discourse*. Other works on theory of narrative include Mieke Bal, *Narratology* (1977), translated by Christine van Boheemen (Toronto: University of Toronto Press, 1985); Seymour Chatwin, *Story and Discourse: Narrative Structure in Fiction and Film* (Ithaca: Cornell University Press, 1978); Dorrit Cohn, *Transparent Minds: Narrative Modes for Presenting Consciousness in Fiction* (Princeton: Princeton University Press, 1978); Arthur C. Danto, *Narration and Knowledge* (New York: Columbia University Press, 1985); Susan Sniader Lanser, *The Narrative Act: Point of View in Prose Fiction* (Princeton: Princeton University Press, 1981); Wallace Martin, *Recent Theories of Narrative* (Ithaca; Cornell University Press, 1986); Roy Pascal, *The Dual Voice: Free Indirect Speech and Its Function in the Nineteenth-Century European Novel* (Manchester: Manchester University Press, 1977); Gerald Prince, *Narratology: the Form and Functioning of Narrative* (Berlin/New York: Mouton, 1982); Robert Scholes and Robert Kellogg, *The Nature of Narrative* (London/New York: Oxford University Press, 1966); Franz K. Stanzel, *Theory of Narrative* (1979), translated by Charlotte Goedsche (Cambridge: Cambridge University Press, 1984). A special issue of the journal *Critical Inquiry* was devoted to narrative in 1980 (7) and republished as a book edited by W. J. T. Mitchell, *On Narrative* (Chicago; University of Chicago Press, 1980).

For background to Augustine's *Confessions*, including his relations to Plotinus, see Peter Brown's excellent *Augustine of Hippo: a Biography* (London: Faber & Faber, 1969). See also Christopher Kirwan's *Augustine* (London: Routledge, 1991). The relevance of the autobiographical form to Augustine's treatment of self-consciousness is discussed by W. C. Spengemann in *The Forms of Autobiography: Episodes in the History of a Literary Genre* (New Haven: Yale University Press, 1980); by John Freccero in 'Autobiography and Narrative', in *Reconstructing Individualism: Autonomy, Individuality and the Self in Western Thought*, edited by Thomas C. Heller, Morton Sosna and David Wellbery, (Stanford: Stanford University Press, 1986); and by Genevieve Lloyd in 'The Self as Fiction: Philosophy and Autobiography', *Philosophy and Literature*, 10 (1986), 168–185.

John F. Callahan's *Four Views of Time* (Cambridge, Mass.: Harvard University Press, 1948) provides a useful overview of the concept of time in Plato, Aristotle, Plotinus and Augustine. Richard Sorabji's *Time, Creation and the Continuum: Theories in Antiquity and the Early Middle Ages* (Ithaca: Cornell University Press, 1983) is a very useful survey of ancient theories of time, with an extensive bibliography. For the context of Plato's description of time as the moving image of eternity, see Francis M. Cornford's *Plato's Cosmology* (London: Routledge, 1937), a translation of and commentary on the *Timaeus*. On Aristotle's treatment of time, see Julia Annas, 'Aristotle, Number and Time', *Philosophical Quarterly* (1975), 97–113; Fred D. Miller, Jr., 'Aristotle on the reality of time', *Archiv für Geschichte der Philosophie* 56 (1974), 132–55; G. E. L. Owen, 'Aristotle on Time', in *Motion and Time, Space and Matter*, edited by P. Machamer and R. Turnbull, (Columbus: Ohio State University Press, 1976), 3–27; reprinted in *Logic, Science and Dialectic: Collected Papers in Greek Philosophy by G. E. L. Owen*, edited by Martha Nussbaum, (Ithaca: Cornell University Press, 1986), 295–314. On time and eternity in Plotinus and Augustine, see Jean Guitton, *Le temps et l'éternité chez Plotin et Saint Augustin* (Paris: Vrin, 1933); Etienne Gilson, 'Notes sur l'être et le temps chez Saint Augustin', *Recherches Augustiniennes* 2 (1962), 204–23; Hugh Lacey 'Empiricism and Augustine's Problems About Time', *Review of Metaphysics* 22 (1968); and J. L.

Morrison, 'Augustine's Two Theories of Time', *New Scolasticism* (1971), 600–10.

Étienne Gilson discusses Descartes's relations with Augustine in his *Etudes sur le role de la pensée médiévale dans la formation du système cartésien* (Paris: Vrin, 1930), especially the chapter on 'Le Cogito et la Tradition Augustinienne'. The chapter on 'Spinoza interprèté de Descartes' is also relevant. Gilson also discusses Augustine's version of the *Cogito* in his *Introduction a l'étude de Saint Augustin* (Paris: Vrin, 1930). See also Geneviève Rodis-Lewis, 'Augustinisme et Cartésianisme à Port Royal' in *Descartes et le Cartésianisme Hollandais*, edited by E. J. Dijksterhius (Paris: PUF, 1950), 131–82; and her 'Augustinisme et Cartésianisme', *Augustinius Magister* 2 (1954), 1087–1104.

Susan Bordo's *The Flight to Objectivity: Essays on Cartesianism and Culture* (Albany: State University of New York Press, 1987) discusses the significance of themes of discontinuity in Descartes's treatment of consciousness. Martial Guéroult discusses Descartes's views on the discontinuity of time in *Descartes' Philosophy Interpreted According to the Order of Reasons*, vol. 1, *The Soul and God* (1968), translated by Roger Ariew, Chapter VI, Section II (193–202) (Minneapolis: University of Minnesota Press, 1984). See also Jean-Marie Beyssade, *La philosophie première de Descartes: le temps et le cohérence de la métaphysique* (Paris: Flammarion, 1979).

Most philosophical discussions of Hume on self-consciousness focus more on themes of personal identity than on the issues of unity of consciousness addressed in this book. The most useful commentary on this aspect of Hume is in Chapter VI of Barry Stroud's *Hume* (London: Routledge, 1977). See also Terence Penelhum, *Hume* (London: Macmillan, 1975); Robert J. Fogelin, *Hume's Scepticism in the Treatise of Human Nature* (London/Boston: Routledge, 1985), Chapter 8; Julius Weinberg, *Ockham, Descartes and Hume: Self-Knowledge, Substance and Causality* (Madison: University of Wisconsin Press, 1977); and Annette Baier, *A Progress of Sentiments* (Cambridge, Mass.: Harvard University Press, 1992).

Gilles Deleuze's *Kant's Critical Philosophy: The Doctrine of the Faculties* (1983), translated by Hugh Tomlinson and Barbara Habberjam (Minneapolis: University of Minnesota Press, 1984) is an excellent short introduction to the central themes of Kantian thought, locating the concept of synthesis in the context of all three

Critiques. Readers sufficiently challenged by the complexities of the transcendental deduction of the categories may like to tackle H. J. Vleeschauwer's monumental commentary *La Déduction transcendentale dans l'oeuvre de Kant* (Paris/La Haye: Anvers, 1934–7). Those less entranced by the topic will find a lucid and interesting discussion of Kant's treatment of time and self-consciousness in P. F. Strawson's *The Bounds of Sense* (London: Methuen, 1966), Part II, Sections I and II and Part III, Section II, 47–117 and 163–74. Other useful commentaries are Henry Allison, *Kant's Transcendental Idealism* (New Haven: Yale University Press, 1983); E. Bencivenga, *Kant's Copernican Revolution* (New York: Oxford University Press, 1987); Moltke Gram, *The Transcendental Turn: the Foundation of Kant's Idealism* (Gainesville: University Press of Florida, 1984); Arthur Melnick, *Space, Time and Thought in Kant* (Dordrecht/Boston: Kluwer Academic Publishers, 1989).

Gilles Deleuze's short *Le Bergsonisme* (1966), translated by Hugh Tomlinson and Barbara Habberjam as *Bergsonism* (New York: Zone Books, 1988) offers a useful and interesting discussion of Bergson on time. The Zone Book edition of *Matter and Memory* (1896), translated by N. M. Paul and W. S. Palmer (New York: Zone Books, 1991) includes a bibliography of works on Bergson. Also of interest are Milič Čapek, 'Stream of Consciousness and "Durée Réelle"', *Philosophy and Phenomenological Research* 20 (1950), 331–53; and his *Bergson and Modern Physics: A Reinterpretation and Re-evaluation* (Dordrecht: Reidel, 1971); Shiv Kumar, *Bergson and the Stream of Consciousness Novel* (London: Blackie, 1962); A. E. Pilkington, *Bergson and His Influence: a Reassessment* (Cambridge: Cambridge University Press, 1976). See also A. R. Lacey's *Bergson* (London: Routledge, 1989).

The best starting point for further reading on Nietzsche's doctrine of eternal return is Chapter 5 of Alexander Nehamas's *Nietzsche: Life as Literature* (Cambridge: Harvard University Press, 1985). A useful short bibliography is included in the notes. Georg Simmel's *Schopenhauer and Nietzsche* (1907), translated by Helmut Loiskandl, Deina Weinstein and Michael Weinstein (London: Routledge; and Boston: University of Massachusetts Press, 1986) raises some interesting and important criticisms of the idea. Heidegger offers a close and interesting reading of the various versions of the doctrine in the second volume of his four-volume commentary, *Nietzsche* (1961), edited by David Farrell Krell (New York: HarperCollins, 1984), and returns to it in relation to issues of nihilism and the 'will to power' in Parts Two and Three of the third volume, translated by Joan Stambaugh, David Farrell Krell and Frank A. Capuzzi (New York: Harper-Collins, 1991). There is a useful discussion of the doctrine in the context of *Thus Spake Zarathustra* in Kathleen Higgins's *Nietzsche's Zarathustra* (Philadelphia: Temple University Press, 1987). Joan Stambaugh has an excellent discussion of the doctrine in its historical context in *Nietzsche's Thought of Eternal Return* (Washington: University Press of America, 1988). See also David Allison, *The New Nietzsche* (New York: Dell, 1977); Arthur C. Danto, *Nietzsche as Philosopher* (New York: Macmillan, 1965); James Gutman, 'The Tremendous Moment', *Journal of Philosophy* 51, 1954; R. Hester, *Eternal Recurrence* (La Salle, Ill.: Open Court, 1932); Karl Lowith, 'Nietzsche's Doctrine of Eternal Return', *Journal of the History of Ideas* 6 (1945); Bernd Magnus, 'Nietzsche's Eternalistic Countermyth', *Review of Metaphysics* 26 (1973), 604–16; Robert B. Pippin, 'Irony and Affirmation in Nietzsche's *Thus Spake Zarathustra*' in *Nietzsche's New Seas: Explorations in Philosophy, Aesthetics and Politics*, edited by Michael A. Gillespie and Tracy B. Strong, (Chicago and London: University of Chicago Press, 1988), pp. 45–71; M. C. Sterling, 'Recent Discussions of Eternal Recurrence', *Nietzsche-Studien* VI (1977); and Magnus's response, 'Eternal Recurrence', *Nietzsche-Studien* IX (1980), 362–77; Ivan Soll, 'Reflections on Recurrence', in *Nietzsche: A Collection of Critical Essays*, edited by Robert Solomon, (Garden City, N.Y.: Doubleday, 1973), 322–42.

George Painter's famous two-volume biography of Proust (Harmondsworth: Penguin, 1977) offers a fascinating account of the transformation of the particularities of Proust's life into literature. On the relations between Bergson and Proust, there is a useful essay by Floris Delattre, 'Bergson et Proust: accords et dissonances', in *Les Études Bergsoniennes*, vol. 1 (Paris: PUF, 1968), 13–127. See also Joyce Megay's *Bergson et Proust: Essai de mise en point de la question de l'influence de Bergson sur Proust* (Paris: Vrin, 1976); and David Gross, 'Bergson, Proust and the Revaluation of Memory', *International Philosophical Quarterly* 25 (1985), 369–80. Gilles Deleuze's *Proust and Signs* (1964), translated by Richard Howard (London: Allen Lane, 1973) discusses the relations between Proust's treatment of time and memory and his treatment of language. Georges Poulet's *Studies in Human Time* 1 (1949), translated by Elliott Coleman (Baltimore: Johns Hopkins,

1956) contains a chapter on Proust. His *Proustian Space* (1963), translated by Elliott Coleman (Baltimore: Johns Hopkins, 1977) includes an excellent discussion of the connections between time and self-consciousness. Paul de Man's essay 'The Literary Self as Origin: The Work of Georges Poulet', in his collection *Blindness and Insight: Essays in the Rhetoric of Contemporary Criticism* (2nd edn. revised; Minneapolis: University of Minnesota Press, 1983), 79–101, contains a discussion of Poulet's work on Proust. See also Germaine Brée, *Marcel Proust and Deliverance from Time* (1950), translated by C. J. Richards and A. D. Truitt (London: Chatto and Windus, 1956); Vincent Descombes, *Proust: Philosophie du Roman* (Paris: Minuit, 1987); Elizabeth R. Jackson, *Evolution de la mémoire involuntaire dans l'oeuvre de Marcel Proust* (Paris: Nizet, 1966); Margaret Mien, *Proust's Challenge to Time* (Manchester: Manchester University Press, 1962); Roger Shattuck, *Proust's Binoculars: A Study of Memory, Time and Recognition in A La Recherche du Temps Perdu* (London: Chatto and Windus, 1963). Chapter Five of Richard Rorty's *Contingency, Irony and Solidarity* (Cambridge: Cambridge University Press, 1989) explores the idea of self-creation in Proust, Nietzsche and Heidegger.

Lyndal Gordon's biography *Virginia Woolf: A Writer's Life* (Oxford: Oxford University Press, 1986) is an excellent introduction to Woolf's life and work, and offers interesting insights into the role in her writing of her experiences of death. John Mepham's *Virginia Woolf: A Literary Life* (London: Macmillan, 1991) is also invaluable for the aspects of Woolf's work addressed in this book. See also his excellent paper 'Mourning and Modernism' in *Virginia Woolf: New Critical Essays*, edited by Patricia Clements and Isobel Grundy, (U.K. Vision Press; U.S.A., Barnes and Noble, 1983), 137–56; ànd his 'Figures of Desire: Narration and Fiction in *To the Lighthouse*', in *The Modern English Novel: The Reader, The Writer and the Work*, edited by Gabriel P. Josipovici, (London: Open Books, 1976). Mark Spilka's *Virginia Woolf's Quarrel with Grieving* (Nebraska: University of Nebraska Press, 1980) is also useful background for the themes of death and grief in Woolf's novels.

On the relations between philosophy and literature see especially Jonathan Rée's *Philosophical Tales* (London: Methuen, 1987); Bernard Harrison's *Inconvenient Fictions: Literature and the Limits of Theory* (London: Macmillan, 1991); and Martha C. Nussbaum's *Love's Knowledge: Essays on Philosophy and Literature*

(Oxford: Oxford University Press, 1990). The journal *Philosophy and Literature*, edited by Denis Dutton and distributed by Johns Hopkins University Press, has been published since 1976. A special issue of *The Monist* was devoted to Philosophy and Literary Theory in January 1986 (69) edited by Richard Rorty. On philosophical metaphor, Jacques Derrida's 'White Mythology' in *Margins of Philosophy* and Paul Ricoeur's *The Rule of Metaphor: Multi-disciplinary studies of the creation of meaning in language* (London: Routledge, 1986) are essential reading. See also Derrida's essay, 'The *Retrait* of Metaphor', translated by F. Gasdner and others, *Enclitic* 2 (Fall 1978), 5–33. A special issue of *Critical Inquiry* 7 (1980) was devoted to metaphor and also published as a book, *On Metaphor*, edited by Sheldon Sacks (Chicago: University of Chicago Press, 1980). Aspects of metaphor discussed in this book are also discussed in Genevieve Lloyd, 'Texts, Metaphors and the Pretentions of Philosophy', in *The Monist* (69), 1968. There is a useful discussion of Derrida's views on metaphor in the concluding section of Rodolphe Gasché's *The Tain of the Mirror: Derrida and the Philosophy of Reflection*, (Cambridge, Mass.: Harvard University Press, 1986) 293–318. Terence Hawkes's *Metaphor* (London: Methuen, 1972) offers a concise overview of treatments of metaphor from Aristotle to the twentieth century, with a useful bibliography. More generally, on questions of truth and fiction, Kendall Walton's 'Fearing Fictions', *Journal of Philosophy* 75 (1978), 5–27; and his book *Mimesis as Make Believe: On the Foundations of the Representational Arts* (Cambridge, Mass.: Harvard University Press, 1990) are of interest. *Chronotypes: The Construction of Time*, edited by John Bender and David Wellbery (Stanford: Stanford University Press, 1991) is a useful interdisciplinary collection of essays by philosophers, historians, literary critics and anthropologists.

Of particular interest, for its illumination of aspects of time in the novel, is the work of Mikhail Bakhtin. See especially 'The *Bildungsroman* and Its Significance in the History of Realism (Toward a Historical Typology of the Novel)' in his *Speech Genres and Other Late Essays*, edited by Caryl Emerson and Michael Holquist, translated by Vernon W. McGee (Austin: University of Texas Press, 1992) 10–59, and 'Forms of Time and the Chronotope in the Novel' in his *The Dialogic Imagination*, edited by Michael Holquist, translated by Caryl Emerson and Michael Holquist (Austin: University of Texas Press, 1990), 84–258.

# Notes

## Introduction

1 Kant, *Critique of Pure Reason*, translated by Norman Kemp Smith (London: Macmillan, 1956), A362, 341.

2 Umberto Eco, 'The Crisis of the Crisis of Reason', in *Travels in Hyperreality*, translated by William Weaver (London: Picador, 1987), 127.

3 See especially Jacques Derrida, 'Différance', in his *Margins of Philosophy*, translated by Alan Bass (New York: University of Chicago Press, 1982), 1–27.

4 Martin Heidegger, *Being and Time*, translated by John Macquarrie and Edward Robinson (Oxford: Blackwell, 1962), 39.

5 Heidegger, op. cit., 48.

6 Derrida, op. cit., 11.

7 Derrida, op. cit., 21–2.

8 Charles Baudelaire, 'The Painter of Modern Life', in *The Painter of Modern Life and Other Essays*, translated and edited by Jonathan Mayne (London: Phaidon, 1964).

9 Georg Simmel, 'The Metropolis and Mental Life' in *The Sociology of Georg Simmel*, edited by Kurt H. Wolff (New York: Free Press, 1964).

10 Georg Simmel, 'Rodin', in *Philosophische Kultur* (Leipzig: Kroner, 1911), quoted in David Frisby, *Fragments of Modernity*, (Cambridge: Polity Press, 1988), 46.

11 For an interesting discussion of this theme in Simmel, Kracauer and Benjamin, see Frisby, *Fragments of Modernity*.

12 Paul Ricoeur, *Time and Narrative*, translated by Kathleen McLaughlin and David Pellauer, 3 vols. (Chicago and London: University of Chicago Press, 1985).

## 1 Augustine and the 'problem' of time

1 Quotations and page references are from R. S. Pine-Coffin's translation of Augustine's *Confessions* (Harmondsworth: Penguin, 1962).

2 Quotations are from Aristotle's *Physics*, translated by W. D. Ross, in *The Works of Aristotle*, edited by Richard McKeon, vol. 11 (Oxford: Clarendon Press, 1930), Book IV, chs 10–14, 289–300.

3 Quotations and page references are as in Plotinus's *Enneads*, translated by Stephen McKenna, 3rd edn revised (London: Faber & Faber, 1962).

4 Paul Ricoeur, *Time and Narrative*, 3 vols, translated by Kathleen McLaughlin and David Pellauer (Chicago: University of Chicago Press, 1984), vol. 3, 19.

5 Ibid., vol. I, 26.

## 2 The self: unity and fragmentation

### Descartes: the unity of thinking substance

1 Etienne Gilson, *Etudes sur le role de la pensée médiévale dans la formation du système cartésien* (Paris: Vrin, 1930), Chapter Two, 'Le Cogito et la tradition Augustinienne', 191–201.

2 Descartes, reply to Fourth Set of Objections, in *The Philosophical Writings of Descartes*, translated by John Cottingham, Robert Stoothoff and Dugald Murdoch (Cambridge: Cambridge University Press, 1984), vol. II, 154.

3 Pascal, 'De l'esprit géométrique', *Ecrits sur la Grâce et autres textes*, edited by André Clair (Paris: Flammarion, 1985), 93.

4 Gilson, op. cit., 195–6.

5 Descartes, *Meditations*, in Cottingham *et al.*, op. cit., vol. II, p. 18.

6 Gilson, op. cit., 300.

7 Susan Bordo, *The Flight to Objectivity* (Albany: SUNY Press, 1987), 23 ff.

8 Gassendi, Fifth Set of Objections, in Cottingham *et al.*, op. cit., vol. II, 209.

9 Descartes, reply to Fifth Set of Objections, in Cottingham *et al.*, op. cit., vol. II, 254–5.

10 Descartes, reply to Fifth Set of Objections, in Cottingham *et al.*, op. cit., vol. II, 255.

11 *Principles*, Part One, section 21, in Cottingham *et al.*, op. cit., vol. I, 200.

12 Arnauld, Fourth Set of Objections, in Cottingham *et al.*, op. cit., vol. II, 148.

13 *Principles*, Part One, section 55, in Cottingham *et al.*, op. cit., vol. I, 211.

14 Spinoza, *Descartes's Principles of Philosophy, Appendix containing the Metaphysical Thoughts*, Part Two, Chapter One, in *The Collected Works of Spinoza*, translated and edited by Edwin Curley (Princeton: Princeton University Press, 1985), p 318.

15 Spinoza, *Ethics*, Part Two, Def. 5, and Part One, Def. 8; in Curley, op. cit., 447 and 409.

16 Descartes, *Principles*, Part One, section 51, in Cottingham *et al.*, op. cit., vol. I, 210.

17 Descartes, *Principles*, Part One, section 20, in Cottingham *et al.*, op. cit., vol. I, 200.

18 Descartes, Second Set of Replies, in Cottingham *et al.*, op. cit., vol. II, 100.
19 Descartes, Sixth Set of Replies, in Cottingham *et al.*, op. cit., vol. II, 289.
20 Hobbes, Third Set of Objections, in Cottingham *et al.*, op. cit., vol. II, 137.
21 Descartes, Third Set of Replies, in Cottingham *et al.*, op. cit., vol. II, 137.
22 Descartes, *Rules for the Direction of the Mind*, Rule Three, in Cottingham *et al.*, op. cit., vol. I, 15.
23 Descartes, *Rules for the Direction of the Mind*, Rule Eleven, in Cottingham *et al.*, vol. I, 38.

## Hume's Labyrinth and the Painting of Modern Life

1 David Hume, *A Treatise of Human Nature*, edited by L. A. Selby-Bigge (Oxford: Oxford University Press, 1960), Book I, Part IV, section VI, 252.
2 Selby-Bigge, op. cit., 253.
3 Selby-Bigge, op. cit., 633–6.
4 Barry Stroud, *Hume* (London: Routledge, 1977), Chapter VI.
5 Hume, *Treatise*, Book I, Part II, section VI. Selby-Bigge, op. cit., 67–8.
6 Selby-Bigge, op. cit., Book I, Part IV, section V, 240–4.
7 Selby-Bigge, op. cit., 242–3.
8 The section is included as an addition to the 1777 version of the *Inquiry*. Quotations and page references are from the edition edited by Charles W. Hendel (New York: Bobbs-Merrill, 1955), 33–9.
9 Hume, *Inquiry*, op. cit., 35.
10 *Treatise*, Book II, Part I, section II, Selby-Bigge, op. cit., 277–9.
11 Hume, 'Of Essay Writing', in *Essays, Moral, Political and Literary* (Oxford: Oxford University Press, 1963), 568–72.
12 Georg Simmel, 'The Metropolis and Mental Life', in *The Sociology of Georg Simmel*, edited by K. H. Wolff (New York: Free Press, 1964), 413.
13 Charles Baudelaire, 'The Painter of Modern Life', in *The Painter of Modern Life and Other Essays*, translated and edited by J. Mayne (London: Phaidon, 1964).

## Kant: the unity of apperception

1 Quotations and page references are from Immanuel Kant's *Critique of Pure Reason*, translated by Norman Kemp Smith (London: Macmillan, 1956), abbreviated in this section as K.S. Passages from the first and second edition versions of the *Critique* are indicated as 'A' and 'B' respectively.
2 Paul Ricoeur, *Time and Narrative*, translated by Kathleen McLaughlin and David Pellauer (Chicago: University of Chicago Press, 1984), 3 vols; vol. 3, 58.
3 David Wood, *The Deconstruction of Time* (Atlantic Highlands: Humanities Press, 1988), 270–1.

4 Kant, *The Critique of Judgement*, translated by J. C. Meredith (Oxford: Clarendon Press, 1982), 18–20.
5 Ricoeur, *Time and Narrative*, vol. I, 66.

## 3 The past: loss or eternal return?

### Bergson: Time and Loss

1 Henri Bergson, *Matter and Memory*, translated by Nancy M. Paul and W. Scott Palmer (London: George Allen, 1913).
2 Henri Bergson, *Creative Evolution*, translated by Arthur Mitchell (London: Macmillan, 1913), 202.
3 *Matter and Memory*, 213.
4 *Creative Evolution*, 336.
5 *Matter and Memory*, 281.
6 op. cit., 289.
7 op. cit., 293.
8 *Creative Evolution*, 213.
9 *Matter and Memory*, 273.
10 op. cit., 248.
11 *Creative Evolution*, 322–3.
12 op. cit., 326.
13 op. cit., 96.
14 op. cit., 212.
15 op. cit., 220–2.
16 *Matter and Memory*, 185–6.
17 op. cit., 194.
18 op. cit., 87.
19 op. cit., 197.
20 op. cit., 219.
21 op. cit., 229.
22 op. cit., 319–20.
23 *Creative Evolution*, 310.
24 op. cit., 311.
25 op. cit., 41–2.
26 op. cit., 48.
27 op. cit., 48–9.
28 op. cit., 31.
29 Gilles Deleuze, *Le Bergsonisme* (1966), translated by Hugh Tomlinson and Barbara Habberjam as *Bergsonism* (New York: Zone Books, 1988).
30 op. cit., 55.
31 op. cit., 63.
32 op. cit., 58–9.
33 op. cit., 60.

## Nietzsche: 'Ill Will Towards Time'

1 *Untimely Meditations*, translated by R. J. Hollingdale (Cambridge: Cambridge University Press, 1983), III, I.

2 Georg Simmel, *Schopenhauer and Nietzsche*, translated by Helmut Loiskandl, Deina Weinstein and Michael Weinstein (London: Routledge, 1986), 171.

3 Simmel, op. cit., 172–3.

4 Nietzsche, *The Gay Science*, translated by Walter Kaufmann in (New York: Vintage Press, 1974), Book IV, 341.

5 Nietzsche, *Thus Spake Zarathustra*, translated by R. J. Hollingdale (London: Penguin, 1961), Part Three, Section Two, 176–80.

6 Nietzsche, op. cit., 179.

7 Nietzsche, op. cit., Book III, Section 13, 232–8.

8 Nietzsche, op. cit., 234.

9 Nietzsche, op. cit., 237–8.

10 Martin Heidegger, *Nietzsche*, translated by David F. Krell (New York, Harper and Row, 1984), vol. II, 37–62.

11 Heidegger, op. cit., 56.

12 Heidegger, op. cit., 57.

13 Heidegger, op. cit., 99.

14 Nietzsche, *The Will to Power*, translated by Walter Kaufmann and R. J. Hollingdale (New York: Random House, 1967), section 617.

15 Nietzsche, op. cit., section 617.

16 *Thus Spake Zarathustra*, Book IV, section 19, sub-section 9, op. cit., 331.

17 Nietzsche, *Human, All Too Human*, translated by R. J. Hollingdale (Cambridge: Cambridge University Press, 1986), vol. I, section 4, 96.

18 Joan Stambaugh, *Nietzsche's Thought of Eternal Return* (Washington: University Press of America, 1988), 125.

19 Alexander Nehamas, *Nietzsche: Life as Literature* (Cambridge: Harvard University Press, 1985), 160–1.

20 Nehamas, op. cit., 168.

21 Nehamas, op. cit., 167–8.

## 4 Life and literature

### Proust: 'life realized within the confines of a book'

1 Quotations and page references are from Marcel Proust, *Remembrance of Things Past*, translated by C. K. Scott Moncrieff, T. Kilmartin and A. Mayor, 3 vols. (Harmondsworth: Penguin, 1983).

2 Paul Ricoeur, *Time and Narrative*, translated by Kathleen McLaughlin and David Pellauer (Chicago: University of Chicago Press), vol. 2, 143.

3 Ricoeur, op. cit., 148.

4 Quoted by Floris Delattre, 'Bergson et Proust: Accords et Dissonances' in *Les Etudes Bergsoniennes*, vol. I (Paris: PUF, 1968), 78. Proust's article appeared in *Le Temps* on 12 November 1913.

5 Henri Bergson, *Matter and Memory*, translated by Nancy M. Paul and W. Scott Palmer (London: Macmillan, 1913), 94.
6 Bergson, op. cit., 102.
7 Bergson, op. cit., 171.
8 Bergson, op. cit., 170.
9 Bergson, op. cit., 171.
10 Bergson, op. cit., 173.
11 Bergson, op. cit., 180–1.
12 Jean-Paul Sartre, 'Intentionality: A Fundamental Idea of Husserl's Phenomenology', *Journal of the British Society for Phenomenology* 1, 1970, 4–5.
13 Proust, 'About Flaubert's Style', in *Marcel Proust, A Selection from His Writings*, translated by G. Hopkins (London: Allan Wingate, 1948), 159.
14 Gérard Genette, *Narrative Discourse: An Essay in Method*, translated by Jane E. Lewin (Ithaca: Cornell University Press, 1980), 102.
15 Genette, op. cit., 113–27.
16 Genette, op. cit., 249.

## Virginia Woolf: moments of being

1 Virginia Woolf, 'Modern Fiction', in *The Common Reader* (London: Hogarth Press, 1957), 189.
2 Virginia Woolf, 'Phases of Fiction', in *Collected Essays*, edited by Leonard Woolf (London: Chatto and Windus, 1966–7), II, 85.
3 *The Diary of Virginia Woolf*, edited by Angelica Bell, vol. 3, 1925–30 (New York and London: Harvest and Harcourt Brace Jovanovich, 1980), 7.
4 *The Letters of Virginia Woolf*, edited by Nigel Nicholson, vol. 2, 'The Question of Things Happening', letter of May 6, 1922 (London: Chatto and Windus, 1980), 525.
5 op cit., letter of October 3, 1922, 565–6.
6 Paul Ricoeur, *Time and Narrative*, translated by Kathleen McLaughlin and David Pellaeur (Chicago: University of Chicago, 1985), 104.
7 Ricoeur, op. cit., 112.
8 Quotations are from Virginia Woolf, *Jacob's Room* (London: Triad/Panther, 1976).
9 See especially John Mepham's perceptive discussion of this aspect of *Jacob's Room* in *Virginia Woolf: A Literary Life* (London: Macmillan, 1991), 76–84.
10 Paul Ricoeur, *Time and Narrative*, vol. 3, 101–12.
11 Ricoeur, op. cit., 111.
12 Quotations are from Virginia Woolf, *The Waves* (London: Granada, 1977).
13 Quotations are from Virginia Woolf, 'A Sketch of the Past', in *Moments of Being: Unpublished Autobiographical Writings*, edited by Jeanne Schulkind (London: Triad/Granada, 1978).
14 Virginia Woolf, 'The Death of the Moth', in *The Death of the Moth and Other Essays* (London: Hogarth Press, 1981), 9–11.

## Conclusion: philosophy and literature

1 Virginia Woolf, 'Monday or Tuesday', in *The Complete Shorter Fiction of Virginia Woolf*, edited by Susan Dick (London: Hogarth Press, 1985), 131.

2 Quotations are from Aristotle, *Poetics*, translated by Ingram Bywater in *The Basic Works of Aristotle*, edited by Richard McKeon (New York: Random House, 1941), 1455–87.

3 Aristotle, *The Art of Rhetoric*, translated by Hugh Lawson-Tancred (London: Penguin, 1991), Part Three, 3.10 (1410b), 235. The point is discussed by Paul Ricoeur in *The Rule of Metaphor*, translated by Robert Czerny (London: Routledge, 1986) 33.

4 Aristotle, *Rhetoric*, Part Three, 3.11 (1411b24–5), op. cit., 238–9.

5 Derrida, 'White Mythology' in *Margins of Philosophy*, translated by Alan Bass (New York: University of Chicago Press, 1982).

6 Ricoeur, *The Rule of Metaphor*, Study 8, section 3, 280–95.

7 Virginia Woolf, 'Mr Bennett and Mrs Brown' in *A Woman's Essays* (London: Penguin, 1992), 69–87.

8 Ricoeur, op. cit., 246.

# Index

Printed in the United Kingdom
by Lightning Source UK Ltd.
117037UKS00001B/28